whips off his sunglasses.
pair of sunglasses.

(co...)
As you know, ...
Striker, dur...
have enough on ...out
remembering those days when- well, when
things weren't so good.

McCROSKY
Well, right now things aren't so good.
And while we're talking there are 138
lives waiting on us for a decision.

KRAMER
Let me tell you something, Steve.
Striker was a top-notch squadron
leader--a long time ago...

A spear slams into the wall behind Kramer.

KRAMER (cont'd)
...but my feeling is that when
when the going gets rough upstairs
tonight, Ted Striker's gonna fold up.

McCROSKEY
Look, Rex - I want you to get on
the horn and talk this guy down!
you're going to have to let him
get the feel of this airplane on
the way; you'll have to talk him
onto the approach; and so help me,
you'll have to talk him right down
to the ground!

A watermelon falls from TOP OF FRAME, splattering
on the table.

KRAMER
Very well then. Put Striker on
the speaker.

McCROSKEY
OK, you can use the RADIO over there.
Looks like I picked the wrong week to
quit drinking.

He pulls a flask from the drawer and takes a swig.

183A   INT. ~~CHICAGO~~ DISPATCH - NITE

Kramer at dispatch radio. He picks up mike.

142

.O.S.)

EY (V.O.)
aine, where

oveur. Over.

143

He's
going down.

279   EXT. AIRPLANE - NIGHT

It knocks the radio tower off a building and
John Hancock Building.

Surely You Can't Be Serious

THE TRUE STORY OF

Surely You Can't Be Serious

THE TRUE STORY OF

David Zucker Jim Abrahams
Jerry Zucker

Interviews by Will Harris

ST. MARTIN'S PRESS
NEW YORK

First published in the United States by St. Martin's Press, an imprint of St. Martin's Publishing Group

www.stmartins.com

Production by Stonesong
Interior design by studio2pt0, llc

The Library of Congress Cataloging-in-Publication Data is available upon request.

ISBN 978-1-250-28931-5 (hardcover)
ISBN 978-1-250-28932-2 (ebook)

Our books may be purchased in bulk for promotional, educational, or business use. Please contact your local bookseller or the Macmillan Corporate and Premium Sales Department at 1-800-221-7945, extension 5442, or by email at MacmillanSpecialMarkets@macmillan.com.

First Edition: 2023

10 9 8 7 6 5 4 3 2 1

to everyone who said yes

CONTENTS

INTRODUCTION

Never assume that just because it's someone's job, they know how to do it. If you have a better idea, put down your laundry and do something about it.

MRS. ZUBATSKY'S LAW

From Jerry Zucker's Commencement speech at The University of Wisconsin Madison, Wisconsin, 2003

One day, when I was a kid, our house caught fire. A large section of the wood-shingle roof was burning as the fire trucks pulled up. The firemen ran into the backyard with a large hose and began assembling their metal ladders and positioning them against the house.

Mrs. Zubatsky was our next-door neighbor, and at the time she was standing on her upstairs porch taking in the laundry. She watched anxiously as the firemen struggled with their ladders. Suddenly she leaned over the balcony and shouted down to the professional firefighters, "Forget the ladders! Just point the hose at the fire!" The firemen, to their credit, responded immediately. They dropped their ladders, pointed the hose at the fire, and extinguished the blaze in about forty seconds.

There are two morals in this story: One, never assume that just because it's someone's job, they know how to do it. And two, don't let yourself be intimidated by professionals and their uniforms.

Growing up in Wisconsin, my brother, David, and I and our friend Jim Abrahams never knew anyone in the movie business. We never even knew anyone who knew anyone in the movie business. That world had previously held a mystique that made it seem unattainable to us. But, like Mrs. Zubatsky, when we found ourselves sitting on our porch watching someone else do it, we all turned to each other and said, "Hey, we can do this!" And like Mrs. Zubatsky, we seized the moment.

If you have a better idea, if your plan makes more sense, if you have a vision, then put down your laundry and scream a little bit. Throw your hat into the ring, and never let professionals or their uniforms prevent you from telling anyone where to point their hose.

THE PREMIERE

I can honestly say that I wouldn't be in the business today without ZAZ. Not a chance. *Airplane!* just knocked my socks off. It's arguably the funniest movie of all time. I don't ever remember laughing like that. But after that, I saw the three of them on *Late Night with David Letterman*, and I remember watching them and hearing their story, that they're from Wisconsin and how they got into comedy, and I remember thinking, Oh! They're just like me! I was expecting something different, like some slick Hollywood guys who were just unbelievably clever. But they were just like the guys I hung out with! And yet they'd gone and done this thing. And that was the first time I got it in my head, "Hey, maybe I can do this!" And that's the God's honest truth. I don't think I ever would've attempted it without those guys having paved the way.

PETER FARRELLY

David: By the summer of 1980 we'd been working on *Airplane!* for the better part of five years. Finally, in early July, it was finished and ready for release. The night arrived. The premiere was on the lot at Paramount Studios. Three Midwestern boys' Hollywood fantasy come true.

Jim: The lights went down. The movie started. In those days films were projected from reels. *Airplane!* was on five reels. Up in the booth, the projectionist put up the reels: one, two, three . . . five? The guy skipped reel four.

Jerry: Clearly a disaster, but I remember we had three completely different reactions to it.

Jim: I was really nervous before the premiere, so I went to a bar around the corner from Paramount with some friends and had a couple Bloody Marys to calm my nerves. When reel five came up instead of reel four, I remember thinking, *Wow! This is great! We thought we had a pacing problem, but this is moving along really nicely.*

David: I was mortified at first: oh shit, what's happening!? But then I immediately rationalized. Hollywood premieres usually don't get a great reaction anyway, since everyone's rooting for you to fail. So my first thought was, *Oh, good, now we'll have an excuse for why this thing flopped.*

Jerry: I just bolted up to the projection booth and screamed at the guy, "Take it off! It's the wrong reel!" And the guy's telling me, "No, no, it says here . . ." I shouted, "No! You're showing the wrong reel! I'm the director! It's out of order!" There had been a recent George C. Scott film, *Hard Core*, where he had to watch his daughter in a porn movie, and he's screaming, "TAKE IT OFF! TAKE IT OFF!" So, I found myself screaming just like George C. Scott, "TAKE IT OFF! TAKE IT OFF!" Finally, I screamed loud enough that the guy must've realized that either I'm the director, or his life is in danger, trapped in the booth with a homicidal maniac. So he stops the projector, looks at the reel, and says, "Oh, yeah."

Jim: So they stopped the movie, turned the lights on in the audience, put the right reel up, and started the movie again. Thank God for Bloody Marys!

David: I remember the beginning of the wrong reel started with the shit hitting the fan.

Jerry: Talk about life imitating art. So then when they played it in the correct order, the shit hit the fan again! Afterward people were coming up to us and saying, "You know, it's great, but I don't think you should have the shit hitting the fan twice . . ."

CHAPTER 1

"GET ME REX KRAMER!"

They created an entirely new thing that no one had seen! And now, to have gone from a fan to someone who works in comedy, it's more that I kind of watch it in awe, that it can sustain that many jokes, where everything is a bit, and it works.

BILL HADER

Jerry: The seeds for our kind of humor were planted when we were kids. Growing up in the 1960s in Milwaukee, we consumed a steady diet of hard-hitting dramas like, *The Untouchables*, *Sea Hunt*, *Dragnet*, and *Mission Impossible*. Shows where the characters just took themselves so seriously, and we'd blurt out ridiculous lines for them to say. Later, we'd dub old movies, and then in *Airplane!* we actually got those same tough-guy actors to say the lines we always wished they would have said. There was a part of us that couldn't believe that they would really do that.

BILL HADER

Robert Stack, the way he delivers his lines . . . I mean, the hardest I laugh now when I watch the movie is his kind of spinout at the end of the movie, where he's talking about, "Municipal bonds, Ted!" "Do you know what it's like to fall in the mud and get kicked in the head with an iron boot? Of course you don't, no one does. That never happens."

"Christmas, Ted. What does it mean to you?"

Jim: And the most serious and humorless was Robert Stack. He was the one guy who we knew we wanted in *Airplane!* from the get-go, from when we first started writing the script. He was sort of our key to it all.

David: I remember us saying, "We will camp out on his lawn until he signs!" We were not going to accept "no." In fact, with the first 1975 incarnation of the *Airplane!* script—amateurs that we were—we called Stack's agent and said, "We've got this script, *Airplane!*, and we want Robert Stack for the lead, and could he read the script?" And the agent says, "Is this a 'go' picture?" And we said, "What's a 'go' picture?" There's a pause, and the guy says, "Come back when you have the money."

> **ROBERT STACK (Rex Kramer)**
> They came after me for about two and a half years, and I kept saying, "Fellas, you sound like Judy Garland and Mickey Rooney, 'Let's put on a show in a garage.'" I said to my wife, "No one's got any money, all three are gonna direct it." And my wife said, "I think it's funny." I said, "I think it's funny, too, but c'mon already, it's their first picture, and well . . ." I finally said I would do it, under great trepidation, of course. They offered me a piece, and I didn't take it. Well, it turned out to make a hundred million dollars, and that just goes to show how terribly clever I am.

Jerry: When we finally did sign him and I told my sister in Hartford, Connecticut, her reaction was, "Oh my God! I can't believe you get to tell Elliot Ness what to do!"

David: But when we actually met him, instead of the stern, humorless Ness, we get this jovial, smiling guy, constantly telling jokes and funny stories. I started calling him Bob. In addition to that, he asked us if we could write more jokes into the script for him! And we did.

> **ROBERT HAYS (Ted Striker)**
> I worked with Bob Stack on a TV series that he had done before *Airplane!* called *Most Wanted.* My folks came to the *Airplane!* set to visit one day, and I introduced them to Bob, and he—being the incredibly gracious guy that he was—said, "You know, Bob was a guest star on my show when I was doing *Most Wanted,* and now I just look at this like I'm a guest star on his show!" And I thought, God, how cool was it that he just said that?! He was exceptional. I just loved that guy.

David: Starting with *Kentucky Fried Movie*, we named all our characters after our high school friends. Rex Kramer was in Jerry's class; I dated his sister, Randy, which is the name of Lorna Patterson's stewardess character. Steve McCroskey was my best friend from grade school. In our *KFM* parody "Fistful of Yen," we named the evil villain after our Shorewood High principal, Dr. Klahn. In fact, as I remember, not much more liked than the evil Mr. Han of Bruce Lee's *Enter the Dragon*. Jim's best friends, Prussing and Macias, were two of the guys in the tower. The list went on.

Dr. Klahn, Steve McCroskey, Rex Kramer, Pete Prussing, Ed Macias

David: For Lloyd Bridges's role, we first approached Jack Webb from *Dragnet*. He came in for a meeting, but he turned down the role.

Jim: Probably because we let him read the script.

Jerry: Always a mistake.

BEAU BRIDGES

Airplane! really kind of reinvented my dad's career. We were so happy to see it happen, my brother and I and our family, because we always felt he had a real funny bone in there. Rarely did he get a chance to show his comic chops. *Airplane!* really started it for him in that arena. It was wonderful, because he did have a great sense of humor, and it finally came to light with that wonderful movie. I just loved it.

David: There may have been a few other actors we went to who were more well-known at the time. People like Efrem Zimbalist Jr. from *The FBI*. And Lloyd Bridges. We all used to watch him on *Sea Hunt*, and we loved how serious he was on that show. We thought he'd be perfect for McCroskey.

Jim: He played Mike Nelson, a Navy diver. Big hit, but very low budget. Lots of underwater scenes. He told us they'd get letters from the audience complaining that they recognized the same fish.

> **ROBERT HAYS**
> In the beginning, Lloyd was kind of just trying to figure the whole thing out. I remember one day, Lloyd Bridges and Bob Stack were rehearsing a scene in the control room. I remember Lloyd being kind of a little frustrated and confused, and saying, "What the hell's going on here?" Because it was so stupid! It was so crazy, and he didn't quite get it.

Jim: I do believe that when *Airplane!* is really clicking, it elevates stupidity to an art form. I mean, we were writing dad jokes before they became an official category.

David: So finally Stack jumps in and says, "Look, there's a spear going into the wall behind me and a watermelon falling on the desk in front of you. No one's listening to us! Just keep talkin', Lloyd!" Stack got that they were cardboard characters in the foreground, and the jokes were going on behind them. It's the concept of what we came to call "floocher" dialogue, a word we made up to mean "filler."

Jerry: It's what we imagined the word for "filler" would have been in Yiddish.

"Where the hell is Kramer?"

David: It's either delivered while something else was going on in the background or it was for the characters to keep talking to cover a laugh and therefore appearing not to acknowledge a joke.

ADAM MCKAY

When I was at *Saturday Night Live*, we utilized the Zucker-Abrahams-Zucker formula anytime we had older, high-status White dudes on the show hosting, and especially when they weren't really actors, like when Rudy Giuliani or Steve Forbes hosted. Basically, any older, high-status white dudes were the easiest to write comedy for, because they just could fall a lot further, and it was so fun to hear them say crazy, crazy things. The higher the status of the person you're playing with, the more fun it is to have them say crazy things. And those guys cracked that code, there's no question.

Jim: In Lloyd's defense—and we ran into a similar problem later with Val Kilmer in *Top Secret!*—if you're a trained actor, then you look for who your character is, what he's feeling, and how he would react. Why was he into smoking, drinking, amphetamines, and sniffing glue? But all we wanted him to do was say the lines. A lot of Lloyd's confusion came from the fact that he was looking for his character and there was none. So it took a while for him to adjust.

Jerry: In our minds, the character he was playing was Lloyd Bridges. We would never tell actors to play it straight. We always told them to act like they had no idea they were in a comedy. I really believe that's the magic of *Airplane!*, but it requires a lot of discipline.

BILL HADER

I would watch these old movies and TV shows, and my dad was really helpful, because he'd say, "Oh, Peter Graves from *Mission: Impossible*. And Lloyd Bridges was in *Sea Hunt*, and Leslie Nielsen was in *Forbidden Planet*." But to do a movie like that—where I think at the time Jimmie Walker was the biggest name, and he's in it for five seconds and doesn't even have a line—I mean, that's pretty insane.

BEAU BRIDGES

My dad was a real conscientious actor. He really worked everything to death. He wanted it to be as perfect as it could be. That was really true about any job he took on. He was a real taskmaster. He gave his all.

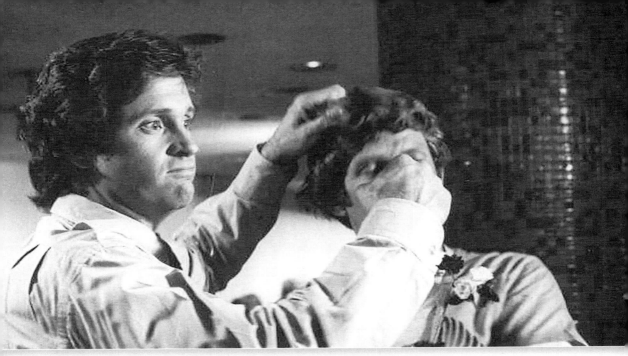

"Hello, we'd like you to have this. . . ."

ADAM MCKAY

People think that, with comedy, you've got to play it broad. But you always play it straight, and you let the broadness come out of playing it real. You never directly go to the broadness. If you do, it all breaks apart. And that's another thing that was groundbreaking about that movie: the deadpan nature of it. And using old-school film stars and having them deliver those lines in deadpan—nobody did that.

"They're coming right at us!"

My father was such a
purist as far as putting bad stuff
in his body so, to see him sniffing glue
and all of that stuff, and all his lines...
We just got a tremendous
kick out of that!
—JEFF BRIDGES

Jerry: I think it's hard for actors to be in a comedy and not *act* funny in the middle of all the craziness. It doesn't feel right, so it requires a leap of faith. But as time went on, they all gave in to it. They were like, "Okay, whatever. Bring on the dancing penguins."

MOLLY SHANNON

When Lloyd bridges says, "Looks like I picked the wrong week to quit smoking." Then the next scene . . . drinking. Then . . . amphetamines and then it progresses to the most absurd and funniest line in the movie "Looks like I picked the wrong week to quit sniffing glue." That's one of my favorite series of scenes.

Jerry: I couldn't believe how long he could stay upside-down—like five minutes at a time. I was getting a headache just watching him.

BEAU BRIDGES

Jeff and I really howled when they hung him upside down and he said, "Looks like I picked the wrong week to quit sniffing glue," because our father was such a straight arrow. So when we first talked to him after seeing the movie we said, "Dad, how could you do that? How could you accept that role when you know there are so many young people who look up to you and see you as a champion of morality and good habits? And here you are sniffing glue! We can't believe it!" He was freaked out. He said, "You're kidding! I didn't mean it!" "Tell it to all those poor kids!"

JEFF BRIDGES

Years later, when we were doing a movie called *Blown Away*, there was a big part for somebody to play my uncle, and I said to the producer, "Gee, you know, I know a wonderful actor who could play my uncle. He looks a bit like me. His name is Lloyd Bridges. Have you heard of the guy?" He laughed, and he said, "Well, your dad is . . . he's a terrific actor, but he's really thought of as more of a comedian!" And I said, "What the . . . ? What are you talking about?" And he said, "Well, you know, *Airplane!* and all the different movies that kind of spun out of that film." I said, "Are you gonna make him come in and read for this part?!" And they said, "Do you think he would?" So he came in, and he got the part. But he was such a versatile actor, and *Airplane!* was a wonderful film to show his comedic side.

Howard Koch, David, Lloyd Bridges, Jerry, Jim, Robert Stack

Jim: I worked with Lloyd on several movies after *Airplane!* The movies worked. We got to be friends. Our families got to know each other. Then, after we had finished the script for one more movie I called him up to tell him about a part we had written for him. "Hi Lloyd," I said. "This is Jim Abrahams." "Yeah?" Not the warm guy I knew. "Just wanted you to know we finished a new script and we have a great part for you." "Uh-huh?" Very suspicious. "Right. It's a spoof of *The Godfather*, and you are like Don Corleone." He kept being incredibly skeptical and I kept pitching away. Finally he said, "Wait a minute. Who is this?" "Jim Abrahams." "Ohhh. I thought you said you were Jim Nabors." I got to tell that story at Lloyd's memorial service. Everyone laughed.

David: Plenty of actors turned us down for *Airplane!* But who we got ended up being just right. And those guys who said no, it's not that they were strangers to humor. Both Charlton Heston and Jack Webb had done comedy sketches with Johnny Carson on *The Tonight Show*. So it wasn't that they didn't want to do comedy; it was just that they didn't understand what we were doing. But then again, neither did Peter Graves! We got a flat no. I think it may have appeared to him that his character was a pedophile.

Scene from *Zero Hour!*	Scene from *Airplane!*
CAPTAIN (TO JOEY) Come on, move up here, you can see better. [takes out a toy DC-4] Joey, here's something we give our special visitors. Would you like to have it? JOEY Thank you. Thanks a lot! CAPTAIN Have you ever been in a cockpit before? JOEY No, sir! I've never been up in a plane before! FIRST OFFICER How do you like it?	OVEUR Joey, here's something we give our special visitors. Would you like to have it? Joey a small toy airplane and puts his ar im. JOEY Thank you. Thanks a lot! OVEUR Have you ever been in a cockpit before? JOEY No, sir. I've never been up in a plane before. OVEUR Have you ever seen a grown man naked?

PETER GRAVES

I thought, Gee, this is dangerous. I can't do this. And I told my agent no, and he said, "Okay." And I got a call ten minutes later from Howard Koch, the "godfather" of Hollywood, and he said, "Why don't you come in and meet these young guys? 'Cause you might get something from 'em."

Jerry: Peter came in to meet us at Howard Koch's office. We were just ourselves, so probably not terribly impressive, but at least we weren't the drugged-out Hollywood weirdos he had expected.

David: Or enough to make him forget we wrote his character as a pedophile.

> **PETER GRAVES**
>
> I went in and said, "You should have Harvey Korman do it, he would be perfect." But they said, "We want somebody of your stature and dignity," and so forth, who plays it absolutely straight. They had Bob Stack doing the same thing, and Lloyd Bridges and many others. And then I started thinking about it, and I said, "Ooh, this could be funny, but, now wait a minute, this is old iron pants from *Mission: Impossible* and *Fury* and all that stuff. Are audiences gonna buy this from me?" And I couldn't believe it. So I crossed my fingers, said, "Okay," and did all that stuff. I went for it. They say you're supposed to stretch as an actor, so let's go stretch it.

David: With Peter, we had to be very specific in our directions. In the cockpit scene with the little boy, that was tricky. We had to get it just right, or else the gag wouldn't work at all. So we had to dial in his actions by the numbers: look left, look down, grab the wheel, look away, say the line, put your arm around the kid—there was no leeway. To pull that off, it had to be exactly crafted. But he did whatever we asked.

Can you find Kareem in this picture?

Jim: More than any other joke in *Airplane!* there was absolutely zero room for margin of error with Captain Oveur. If the actor had been a comedian it would have been tasteless. If Peter had winked or played it any other way, it would have been a turnoff. If his fishing expedition dialogue with Joey had been any less preposterous, it could have been repulsive. But Turkish prisons and movies about gladiators . . . I still laugh.

TREY PARKER

The jokes that my friends and I kept doing—and keep in mind that I was ten years old!—were things like, "Joey, have you ever seen a grown man naked?" and "Joey, do you like gladiator movies?" And at ten years old, I don't think I even quite got what they were even about.

MATT STONE

"Joey, have you ever been in a Turkish prison?" It was, like, "A Turkish prison?! What the fuck is that supposed to mean?!"

TREY PARKER

I knew it was funny, but I didn't know why

David: None of these guys were natural comedians. The comedy was all in the dialogue and in the deadpan delivery. That's what we realized all those years ago, watching all those heavy TV dramas and imagining these guys saying funny or ridiculous things. I don't think we ever outgrew that.

Jerry: And we never will. In a few years, the three of us will still be doing that in some nursing home.

DAVID LETTERMAN

My son and I, when we're driving in the city, he will say to me, "Just move over a lane," and I'll say, "I'll move over, but quit calling me Elaine." And I've heard other people ask, "Have you ever seen a grown man naked?" "Do you like gladiator movies?" It just goes on and on and on and on. Film comedy became different after that movie.

CHAPTER 2

KENTUCKY FRIED THEATER

When you make a list of the best movies of all time, you're always going to put *Airplane!* on it. And if movies like that aren't being made right now, it's because people aren't smart enough or funny enough to make them. If someone made a movie as funny as *Airplane!* right now, it would make a billion dollars.

JUDD APATOW

David: Back in college, at the University of Wisconsin, Madison, I knew what I wanted to do. It was to make funny movies and make people laugh. And I knew it was possible; I had gotten a short taste of it during my junior year when I made my first short film. It was an assignment for my Introduction to Radio, Television and Film class, taught by a professor named Richard Sherman.

Jerry: David recruited me for the lead role. Complete nepotism. I played this guy who takes psychedelic drugs (something David and I never actually did). Everything looks dreamy and trippy at first, but then I have to go to the bathroom, and for the rest of the ten minutes, I'm running around campus, desperately looking for a place to pee. When my character was finally able to relieve himself, it gave him more pleasure than the LSD. So in a sense, maybe we had made an early anti-drug movie. David was brave enough to actually show it in class.

Jerry in *The Best Things in Life are Free*

David: So I showed it in my study section. The other films were all very esoteric studies of light and shadow, weird camera angles, deep meaning, shown through the prism of . . . whatever . . . and then it's my turn, and Jerry comes onscreen, and he's being chased by a guy with no pants on as he's climbing to pee off the the the top of a statue of Abraham Lincoln. They all laughed, maybe despite themselves. When the lights came on, I remember I'm at the back of the room with the projector and a Sony tape recorder, and everyone's just looking back at me. The teaching assistant just shook his head and said, "You gotta enter that in a film festival."

Jerry: The next week, David called me and said his T.A. had shown it to the professor, who wanted us to show it to the entire lecture class!

David: So there we were a week later, in this enormous lecture hall. The movie played on a large screen, in front of six hundred students. Whatever laughs it got in the quiz section were magnified a thousand times. When the lights came on and the applause died down, the professor said, "If you think I'm gonna follow that, you're crazy. Class dismissed."

Jerry: We were hooked!

Cameo: David as "Cecil B." trying to look like a real director.

David: That was our first movie audience. That's what I wanted to do. But in the fall of 1970, after I'd graduated, I found myself back in Milwaukee, living at home and having no idea how I was gonna make funny movies. Dad came to the rescue, offering me a job as a construction expediter on his office-building project. It was an okay job, and I learned a lot about carpentry and drywall, which would come in handy later, but I think Dad

"Just try to relax and enjoy the movie."

realized how frustrated I was. So one day he comes up to me and says, "I talked to my friend Bill Kesselman, who owns a couple of videotape recorders and a camera he's not using. He's offering to lend them to you."

Jerry: David thought, *What could I do with videotape? I want to make film!*

David: Dad suggested, "Maybe you could make industrial videos for local factories." Needless to say, this did not get me excited.

Jim: At the time I was a private investigator for a law firm in Milwaukee, DeVries, Vlasak, and Schallert. Basically, I sneaked around and tried to catch people who were filing false claims of being injured in accidents. My job was to get pictures of them playing tennis or shingling their roofs or just get dirt on them from their neighbors. At first I was reluctant, but usually I'd knock on someone's door and say, "I'd like to talk about your neighbor across the street." Invariably, they'd say, "Oh, come on in. Can I get you a cup of coffee?" And then they'd start to dump on the neighbor. My hours were my own, plus it came with a car. A Ford Fairlane 500! My office was in one of Mr. Zucker's buildings on Mayfair Road, and one day I ran into David walking outside.

Jerry: We'd see Jim occasionally over the years when we were still in high school. The Abrahams family and the Zucker family would get together for dinner, and afterward the three of us would end up in the rec room, playing ping-pong and making each other laugh. We bonded over our shared sense of humor.

David: So, out on the sidewalk in front of Jim's office, Jim and I were chatting, and we asked each other, "What are you doing?" I told him about my short film and how I wanted to submit it to festivals. Maybe even make more. Jim said he had an idea for a short film.

Jim: Oh right. I had forgotten. I had just started running long distances, and as I ran, I was so taken by how awkward even the most elegant dogs looked while they were relieving themselves. The idea was a slow-motion montage of dogs peeing and pooping, set to Beethoven's "Moonlight Sonata." I still think it has blockbuster potential.

Jerry: Definitely. Today it could go on one of the "streaming" channels.

David: The next week, I drove to Chicago to visit a girl who I was dating, and her roommate suggested we go see this show called *Void Where Prohibited by Law*, which had been *The Groove Tube* when it had started a couple of years before in New York. I had no idea what it was, but we went anyway to a loft on Broadway Street in New Town. We paid a couple of dollars and went upstairs to one of the rooms where a packed audience sat on a giant waterbed. At one end was a Coke machine, and at the other was a twenty-five-inch black and white television monitor which played a seventy-minute show of video sketches.

David: They were original sketches and mostly scatological. But I was laughing hard. I don't recall my date finding it all that funny, and looking back on it, she was probably right. I probably wouldn't find it at all funny today, but for me this was an epiphany! They were using the same type of video equipment that Dad had mentioned. *Wait a minute*, I thought, *we could do this!* We didn't need to get a job from somebody else. We could make videos, get a place like this loft, and charge admission! The next morning, instead of driving back to Milwaukee, I drove straight to Madison and pounded on Jerry's door.

Jerry: David was ranting incoherently. Little bits of foam were dripping from the corners of his mouth. I wasn't sure if I should let him into my apartment. He said, "We have to get the video machine from Mr. Kesselman! And we have to call Jim!"

David: When I talked to Jim I also asked him what Dick Chudnow was doing. Dick had been kind of a legend at Shorewood High School, a naturally funny guy who'd get a smile at just the mention of his name.

NIGHT SCENE
Good entertainment off the beaten track

● TV LIKE YOU'LL NEVER SEE AT HOME: "Void Where Prohibited by Law," a Chicago-produced sequel to Groove Tube, is playing in the Video Lounge of Rush Up, 907 N. Rush St., and at Richard Klein's Broadway Broadcasting Company, 2827 N. Broadway. Catch it at the BBC from the giant water bed or in one of three other rooms with closed circuit telecasts and free potato chips and ice cream bars. But you'd better be—or THINK—younger than 30 or you'll be all shook up over the irreverence of it all. Some funny skits but stuffed shirts and suits-and-ties night owls should stay away. Admission at both galleries is $3 on Friday and Saturday; $2.50 other nights.

CHICAGO TRIBUNE 1/8/71   *Larry Townsend*
ENTERTAINMENT EDITOR

Jim: I first met Dick when I transferred to Shorewood High School in my junior year. He was this really popular, really funny guy, and for some reason he looked me up. We got to be good friends. He was very sweet and hysterically funny. One time, in class, he gave a report on battleships from the 1500s. All he brought with him was a picture of a battleship with five hundred sails on it. He held it up on the podium in front of him. All you could see was this picture of the battleship, and he just read the name of each sail. "The left forward jib mast hub. The right forward jib mast hub." And it went on like that for fifteen minutes, and that was the report!

Jim

Dick Chudnow

Jerry: Did everybody get what he was doing? Were they laughing?

Jim: It was hysterical. But Mr. Swan, the history teacher, was clueless. That's part of what made it so funny. He was like Leslie Nielsen.

David: In the drama club musicals, Dick would get the funniest role, or would get to play some ordinary character and *make* it funny. For the school talent show, he put together a rock band and sang Elvis songs. The auditorium got so loud, I mean, I never heard it get to that decibel level again.

Jim: In college, we'd entertain ourselves by doing pranks in the library.

DICK CHUDNOW
Co-Founder of Kentucky Fried Theater, creator of Comedy Sportz

There were three or four floors to the library, and we'd start on the bottom floor. I'd sit down and study or look like I was studying. And then Jim would walk in using a cane with one foot bandaged. I'd get up, kick out the cane, he'd fall down groaning, books splayed all over the floor, and I'd kick his books away and yell, "Why don't you watch where you're going, you lousy cripple?" Then while Jim crawled on the floor gathering his books, I'd walk out. We kept doing that on each floor until we got to the fourth floor. And this huge sumo wrestler—I don't know what he was—grabbed me and spun me around and said, "You don't do that to people!" And we got kicked out of the fourth floor, and went down to the first floor and did it all over again!

Jerry: And people knew it was all an act?

Jim: Eventually. I think. I mostly remember thinking this was such a creative way to avoid doing homework. I mean it was finals. And we were doing bits in the library.

DICK CHUDNOW

Jim was my partner. We used to go into bathrooms, and it was a contest: one of us would go into the stall with a whoopie cushion, close the door, and just fart away like crazy, and the other one had to be at the sink. The contest was to see who could keep from laughing the longest. The one at the sink would have to ask, "Jim, are you okay? You all right?" And the other would respond in a tortured voice, " Yeah, I am . . ." Grunt. Whoopie cushion. Flush. Groan. Just to see people react. It was hysterical. I was able to not laugh. Jim was helpless.

David: Too bad there's no video of that. Or of the elevator bit.

Jim: The three of us would go into a crowded elevator, and we'd ask David, "So what did the doctor say?" He'd reply, "Ah, it's contagious." The people in the elevator shifted

---

First ever meeting: pay no attention to the joints in the ashtray.

uncomfortably. David continued, "Yeah, I have to be quarantined. I can't be within ten feet of anyone," pausing to cough, not even covering his mouth. "The worst part of it is the genital rash." And he'd grab the guy's sleeve next to him and start sneezing into it. I had to keep my nose plastered to the elevator door so no one could see me laughing.

David: That was Jim's problem. He could never keep a straight face. So he would do pranks where he wouldn't have to be there at all. Like when Jerry and I made the mistake of telling Jim that we were going to visit our mutual friend Kenny Hurwitz.

Jerry: Oh, right. And he immediately said, "Kenny told me you were coming and he's cooking a really great dinner for you."

David: So we went to Ken's apartment, had a nice afternoon, but after a while we realized that Ken wasn't making dinner. It got uncomfortable. We were waiting for dinner and Ken was waiting for us to leave. He finally had to tell us we had to go. He had other plans for the evening.

Jerry: That was Jim's favorite thing. To light a fuse and be miles away when the bomb went off.

DICK CHUDNOW

I was in Milwaukee, driving down the street, and Jim pulls up next to me and rolls down his window. And I rolled down mine. He says, "Hey! Do you want to meet with David and Jerry Zucker? They're thinking of doing something along the lines of *Groove Tube*."

David: We all met in Milwaukee over Easter break. Jerry was home from college. Jim and Dick arrived together.

Jerry: So it was the four of us, sitting there with this enormous Sony videotape machine with half-inch reel-to-reel tape. The camera was huge. It had a really long zoom lens attached with a thick cord. The video was black and white and not anywhere near the quality of any cell phone today. But to us it was a technological marvel.

David: But the quality didn't matter as much as the content we were creating. We finally had the means to shoot funny videos and to start experimenting. We used to record clips from TV and put our own soundtrack on them.

Jim: One bit began with a tight shot of fingers playing a guitar. We hear, overdubbed, "In-A-Gadda-Da-Vida," for its time, the equivalent of a heavy metal song. As the shot widens out, you see this nerdy-looking country and western band. They looked like they just stepped off *The Lawrence Welk Show*.

David: We did another bit, a spoof on those kitchen gadget ads called Veg-o Slice-o. The guy on the video is trying to slice vegetables, and nothing actually gets cut. But more vegetables keep getting thrown in, followed by all sorts of other objects.

Jerry: And then there was the Wonder Thimble. It was just a regular metal thimble. It was a purposely chauvinist ad saying, "Now you can darn his shirts better and have them ready when he gets home!" And then at the end of the ad, the housewife, played by our mother, proudly displays the thimble, which, of course, is on her middle finger.

David: And Miracle Cup.

Jim: That was a spoof of an infomercial about this regular little glass teacup that was perfect for storing anything. So we panned along a line of Miracle Cups, holding tea, nuts, a grapefruit, cigarettes, and a cucumber lying on top of two of them.

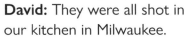

David: They were all shot in our kitchen in Milwaukee.

Jim: There were also some movie spoofs. *Love Story* had just come out, so we did a parody. The woman is dying in a hospital bed and asks her

boyfriend, who's visiting, how he's doing, and he says, "Well, I've got this kink in the back of my neck." She's dying and he's whining about a sore neck.

David: When we'd shoot outdoors, we'd have to run three extension cords to plug in the big reel-to-reel deck, and we'd mount that huge camera on a tripod. But, we do owe a debt of gratitude to Dad's friend, Mr. Kesselman.

Mr. Kesselman's video tape recorder

Jerry: We were endlessly grateful. Many years later, we were at Universal Studios taping a promotional video created by *South Park*'s Trey Parker and Matt Stone called *Your Studio and You*. There were a lot of actors and directors, including Steven Spielberg.

David: The taping coincided with the Kesselmans being honored at a Milwaukee charity event, and we were asked to send in a congratulations video. We were doing our part the same day Steven Spielberg was doing his, so we asked him to do a ten-second bit with us.

Jerry: As a result, we have this wonderful video of us thanking the Kesselmans, then Spielberg barges in and says, "Hey, what are you guys doing?" And we say, "Oh, we're just thanking Bill and Fanny Kesselman, because if it hadn't been for them, we never would've gotten started in show business." And Spielberg says, "Really? Bill and Fanny Kesselman?! They gave me *my* start in the business too!"

Spielberg: thanking Bill and Fanny

"He'll be a menace to himself and everything else in the air... yes, birds too."

David: You can imagine the reaction of the audience in Milwaukee. And, of course, the audience in Milwaukee was thinking, *Wow, Jerry and David must just hang out with these people all the time!*

Jerry: We didn't.

David: No, we did not.

DICK CHUDNOW

The four of us bonded relatively easily, creatively speaking. We all had ideas, some that had been stored up, some that came out of just talking. You know, there were four of us, so some decisions were hard to make. I remember at one point we would play a record and pass a ball around, and whoever ended up with the ball at the end of the music could make the decision. We played off each other very well. It was a lot of fun writing together. It was four really funny guys.

Jerry: We started compiling bits and showing them to anyone we could find to watch. The more people laughed, the more we started to talk excitedly about figuring out a way to make this into some sort of a show.

David: The main thing was, since it was video, we could try a lot of things, see them, erase them, and shoot them again. In 1971, this was revolutionary technology, replacing 8mm film.

Jerry: Editing was a bit clumsy, and the sound wasn't great, but good enough to make the joke. It was fast and it was cheap, and that immediacy, the instant gratification, made it perfect. It was playful and pure creative fun. That was really the beginning of everything we did together.

Jim: I love that you used the word "playful," because that's exactly what it was. We just got together and played. There was no intent other than having a good time.

David: Well, as far as my attitude at the time, the goal was to have a theater like the one I saw in Chicago. We wanted to string together an hour of material. It was later that we combined it with the live stuff.

Jim: So at the get-go, we weren't just getting together to mess around?

David: Well, in my mind, we were never just getting together to mess around.

Jerry: I don't think I ever even thought about it. I just knew that I loved it.

Jim: That's my recollection, too. I think Miracle Cup and stuff like that was before we ever thought about a theater.

David: I was working in construction, and I wanted to make movies! When I saw that video show in Chicago, it became instantly clear to me that we could do a video theater.

> **DICK CHUDNOW**
> I had an improv group in Madison and had been doing improv classes, so I suggested that instead of doing just video bits, we should do a live show, with live bits, video bits, and improv.

Jim: Yes, the live part of it—which really became the largest part—was motivated by Dick and his live performing skill.

Jerry: Chris Keene, Lisa Davis, and Bill West—at the time, students—were all in Dick's improv group, and they subsequently became part of Kentucky Fried Theater.

David: It took us a couple of months to assemble enough material for a show. Dick found a building near campus where we could rent the vacant second floor. We built a whole theater, complete with a stage, control room, and fifty chairs, which we bought for a dollar apiece from a Milwaukee rental company.

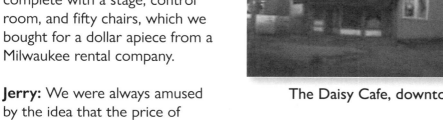

The Daisy Cafe, downtown Madison

Jerry: We were always amused by the idea that the price of admission was more than we had paid for the chairs.

Jim: David and I still had jobs in Milwaukee, so we drove up to Madison on weekends.

David: Two weeks before we were set to open, we still had no name for the theater, and there was an ad deadline the next day for the Madison paper. So the four of us started tossing out dozens of names, all ending in "theater."

DICK CHUDNOW

We were in a Big Boy restaurant where they also served Kentucky Fried Chicken, and we were going, "Should we call it this? Should we call it that?" And this sign, "Colonel Sanders' Kentucky Fried Chicken," popped into my view, and I said, "How about Kernel Sanders's Kentucky Fried Theater?" And that was it. Everybody went, "Yeah! Yeah, that's it!"

Jerry: We were so excited to put it all in front of an audience, but three days before opening night, the building inspector closed us down. Apparently, the owner had never applied for a city permit to have a theater there.

David: This after three weeks of building a complete stage and control room! Jim and I had been driving up on weekends to work on it. We couldn't believe it.

Jim: So then we rented a room at the Wisconsin Student Union and opened the first-ever Kentucky Fried Theater show.

Early KFT Troupe: outside Daisy Cafe. Top row: Jerry, Dick, David, Jim.
Bottom row: Chris Keene, Bill West, Sally Siggins.

David: In our blind optimism, we had advertised two shows, an eight p.m. and a ten p.m. For a full-length show, that would have been a tight turnaround, but at this stage, we weren't planning out every detail.

Jerry: Details were never our strong suit.

Jim: There had been a newspaper article in the Milwaukee paper the week before, and they listed our home addresses! I think that was so the audience would know where to retaliate.

Jerry: And we gave them a really good reason. Opening night didn't exactly go as planned.

David: It was a disaster. I had invited a friend from my college days who had a great, infectious laugh. He was famous for it. I told Jim and Jerry, "He'll get the audience going, this is a slam dunk!" But the guy arrived high on acid and was talking to himself out loud. During the performance, he was lying on his back screaming, "OH MY GOD! OH MY GOD!" He had to be carried out of the room.

Jim: Lots of things went wrong. At one point the videotape machine broke, and I have this picture in my mind of Jerry on all fours, leaning out from behind the video machine, and telling the audience, "We're having some . . . technical difficulties." In show business terms, it was a fucking disaster.

First-ever KFT poster

DICK CHUDNOW

I'd been a performer, and I know you don't just walk away from an audience. But they were talking about giving the money back and everything! So Lisa and I went back on stage and did improvisations.

Jerry: It was billed as a ninety-minute show, but we ran out of material after about twenty minutes.

David: Only because we had never rehearsed it!

Jim: We were panicked and made a quick decision. We would call an intermission.

Jerry: After twenty minutes!

David: While the audience waited, Jim, Jerry, and I huddled backstage and debated how much money we should refund! But Dick and Lisa had other ideas.

Jerry: Yeah, Dick and Lisa saved the day. They were great at improv. They asked the audience for suggestions, and then just rolled with it. Dick was fearless. He had such confidence in front of an audience—in his ability to make people laugh. David, Jim, and I weren't born with that gene. We were writers, and much too insecure to perform live unless we knew we had something funny to say. We needed a script.

Friday, May 7, 1971   MILWAUKEE SENTINEL

Mixed Bag of Theater Planned by 4 at UW

Theater Embodying satire, improvisation, underground films and television films will be presented at 8 p.m. Saturday at the University of Wisconsin Union South by four young men calling themselves Kernel Sanders Kentucky Fried Theater.

The Madison show will include a 20 minute film entitled "Mission Impossible," a satire of the television show of the same name, said David Zucker, 23, of 4395 N. Wildwood Ave., Shorewood.

He and his brother, Jerome, 21, a UW junior, and Richard Chudnow, 26, of 4332 N. Sheffield Ave., Shorewood, and Jim Abrahams, 26, of 1732 N. Prospect Ave., also plan to offer a home version of the show.

The delivery service, Zucker said, would begin sometime next week. The customer would call the theater and for a small fee — about $5 — two performers would go to the home and perform for about 10 minutes.

"Do you know anything about planes?"

David: But that night, despite all of Dick's efforts, we took it as a complete failure. It was a definite low point. We had no idea what we were going to do. Forget movies or TV. At that point, our only concern was figuring out a way to find a theater locally and enough material to last through a performance.

CHAPTER 3

BOB AND JULIE

Probably the single greatest work of art to my mind
in the last thirty years—and it's a film I've seen about
five times—and that's *Airplane!*

GORE VIDAL

Jim: When people talk about the casting of *Airplane!*, of course, Leslie Nielson, Robert Stack, Peter Graves, and Lloyd Bridges usually come to mind. But it's the romantic leads that hold it all together.

Jerry: And those turned out to be the hardest to cast. In the end, no one even came close to Robert Hays and Julie Hagerty.

David: Shelley Long, later the star of *Cheers*, read for the part, and was very good. Also, Sigourney Weaver came in, dressed in a 1940s stewardess costume complete with full makeup and a forties hairstyle. Right off the bat she told us that she refused to do the "sit on your face and wriggle" line.

Jim: And we were, like, "Um . . . okay . . . good to know."

David: Amazingly she managed to recover from losing the *Airplane!* role and went on to have a decent career.

Jerry: And then this woman walked in—I think they said she'd maybe done some theater and a small part in a film, and that she was a model. I don't think we thought one thing or the other about her résumé, but when she started reading, she was better than anything we had ever hoped for. She played it exactly the way our humor should be played, believing every word she was saying. Julie was hysterical without ever thinking she was funny. She was brilliant! As soon as she left, we all cheered. It was a huge moment for us.

Jim: It was a thunderbolt.

David: Julie was reading the same lines that we had lived with for years and heard a thousand times, but this time we were laughing.

"It's a damn good thing you don't know how much he hates your guts."

JULIE HAGERTY (Elaine Dickinson)
I was doing my first play at my brother's theater, one that Norman René had directed called *Mutual Benefit Life*, and Gretchen Rennell from Paramount saw it and invited me to come and audition. I'd always wanted to act. So I went in to audition—it was at the Gulf and Western building—and the guys . . . I didn't know it was the guys at that time, but we were all four in the elevator together when I was going up for my audition. Which was sort of funny: I didn't know who they were, they didn't know who I was, but then we all got off at the same place. There were many girls in the waiting room, and then I went in to audition, and they were very nice.

Jim: An actress named Linda Darnell played Julie's role in *Zero Hour!* so I think we were looking for more of a heavy melodramatic type. You can have whatever you want in mind, but when an actor like Julie comes in and is just perfect for the role, you just know it's right. She was so endearing, so sweet, and so sincere. It made it funnier. We all instantly liked her.

ROBERT HAYS

People ask, "What was she like?" And I say that there's one scene which describes what she's like more than anything else to me, but it's not in the film. The scene is, but what happened isn't. We were filming right behind the cockpit, we were standing there, and it was a two shot, with both of us standing in profile, talking to each other. They said, "Action!" We started to film, and as we went along, she flubbed a line, and they said, "Cut!" And she said, with that little voice of hers, "I'm sorry." "No, no, no, Julie, that's okay, don't worry about it. Script! Have you got her line for her?" And she said, "I'm sorry." "Don't worry about it! That's okay!" And so they went over the line, and she said, "Yeah, yeah, I've got it. I'm just . . . I'm so sorry." "No, don't worry about it, Julie!" So, we start again, and I blew my line on purpose, and they said, "Cut!" And she said, "I'm sorry!" "No, no, no, Julie, that wasn't you. That was Bob." And she said, "Oh." And then she said, "I'm sorry." It was so cute!

Everybody loved Julie!

ROBERT HAYS

I remember one time when some guy came to the set to take her to lunch—it was, like, a lunch date—Jerry and David and Jim and I, the four of us, stood there at the big soundstage door that was open, and we said, "All right, now, you have her back at such and such a time." We were like dads with shotguns. "Now you be nice, and you take care of her, and you have her back on time."

JULIE HAGERTY

After *Airplane!* came out, I was doing a TV news interview, and I was so shy, and I had two interviewers. And one would ask me a question, and I'd look at them—I was sitting in the middle of the two anchors, so I'd look at the one— and by the time I calculated the answer in my head, the other person would ask me another question. So I thought about that question, and then the other person asked me a question. It was like Bingo. But I never got a chance to answer anything. And finally the woman said, "Well, how many auditioned for the role?" And I just went, "I DON'T KNOW!" I was so excited that I'd said something at all. But later I found out that it was seventy-five. Getting the role—it changed my life. *Airplane!*, I think it changed all our lives. It was pretty exciting.

SHELLEY LONG

I have to admit, I was surprised that I didn't get the role. But, you know, the way Julie did the blowing up of the autopilot, she was so wonderfully innocent that you kind of think, She doesn't know what the hell she's doing! Which was a great way to play it.

JULIE HAGERTY

To be honest, to me, I was just blowing up Otto the autopilot; he was a balloon, and that's as far as it went with me. So whatever anybody else wants to think, they can. But he needed to be blown up, and I blew him up. So that was the end of the saga for me. But I think the crew had a lot of fun making his head bob up and down.

JOYCE BULIFANT (Mrs. Davis)

That's the whole thing about comedic acting: the minute you start thinking, Oh, this is so funny, I'm gonna be so funny, it isn't funny. You have to play the truth in comedy.

David: Because she was so sweet, we of course saw that as an opportunity to tease her. Fortunately, she had a good sense of humor about it.

Jerry: We loved to make fun of pretentious people, and Julie was the least pretentious person any of us had ever met.

David: It was a great advantage for us to have Julie, because she didn't have to act it. She wasn't acting her way to being funny. That's really her. She really is that person. She was Elaine. And a big part of it was her voice. It was so sweet and innocent. You could see the little girl inside her. I could recognize that voice anywhere. When she calls me up, I instantly know it's her.

GREGORY ITZIN (Religious Zealot #1)

I had gone to college with the Zucker brothers. They were a crazy bunch. I did *Guys and Dolls* with Jerry back at college. Once they were out in L.A., I got a call to read for *Airplane!* I auditioned for the Robert Hays part but got the part of the first religious zealot. And then the Zuckers and Jim Abrahams went on to do other movies, and they didn't use me. But, you know, I was the first on-camera speaker in *Airplane!* When Julie Hagerty comes in the door, I offer her a flower and ask, "Would you like to make a donation?" I missed being punched out like some of the other religious guys, but I was the first person to speak on camera. So, there's that.

Jerry: We didn't find Bob until much later. We'd read a lot of guys by then and we were starting to worry. It was getting late, and we still hadn't found anybody we thought was even close.

Jim: We had any actor who we knew from high school or college come in to read for a part.

David: We had such a hard time casting the role of Ted Striker that the studio started throwing out names like Bruce Jenner. He came in three times. I think there was someone pushing it; I'm not sure who.

Jerry: He came in to meet, and we said, "Okay, fine, anyone who wins the Olympic decathlon is

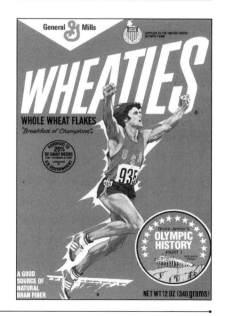

automatically allowed to read." But he wanted to work on it first, so he came over to my apartment to run lines. He was very nice, but he kept saying, "What do you think Mr. Koch is looking for?" He was very focused on pleasing the producer. It was all about "Mr. Koch!" I think he thought I was some kind of acting coach.

Jim: I remember Bruce was really tenacious. The first two times he auditioned for Striker, but then the third time he came in, he read for Elaine. I thought, *This guy really wants to be an actor!* I had no idea there might be deeper feelings involved.

David: We had seen David Letterman at the Comedy Store and were big fans, so we asked him to come in to read for *Airplane!*

> **DAVID LETTERMAN**
> They were really nice to consider me for a film, because I can see where people would think, "Oh, we have a thing where we're opening an Alpha Beta (supermarket); can you come out and talk to the bag boys?" That made sense. But a movie? And the guy who produced it was Howard Koch, who had a legitimate movie career and big-time credits. He was somebody that even I was aware of, and so I thought, Geez, he's not gonna want anything to do with me!

Jerry: He wasn't an actor, but he was funny. And he looked great onscreen—like, leading-man good looks. But the thing about David is, he's just really uncomfortable with the whole idea of acting. I think it all seems too phony to him, like he's bullshitting. It just wasn't him.

> **DAVID LETTERMAN**
> I liked those guys, and when I saw the movie, it was just delightful, and I was delighted to see it knowing that I didn't have to look at myself. Because that would've ruined it. If not the whole movie, it certainly would've ruined it for me.

Jerry: I think we really hoped Letterman could be an actor, so we screen-tested him.

> **DAVID LETTERMAN**
> I get out there, and they had set up a cockpit for the aircraft with chairs. I had a chair, and there was another chair where the copilot would be. We did the scene once, and then they came in and gave me some notes, and then we did it maybe two more times. And I kept saying all along, "I can't act, I can't act, I can't act," and then one of them came to me after the audition and said, "You're right: you *can't* act!" It was all so good-natured that I just laughed my way back to the car. I never felt any sense of disappointment, because from the very beginning I told them, "I can't act." And then I was right, and we all ended up parting as friends. So it was a good time.

Jerry: Letterman's agent was on the set, and I came up to the guy, trying to be optimistic, and said, "Well, I think we can make an actor out of him." And the agent said, "Fat chance!" I remember calling Letterman to tell him he didn't get the part. He thanked me profusely.

Jim: I have never seen anyone so elated to be told he didn't get the role.

DAVID LETTERMAN

I had done enough attempting to act to know that in my life it was a third rail: just don't even touch it. I can remember that I had an agent or a manager who thought the idea was that any stand-up comedian wanted to have their own half-hour sitcom, because the mold was set with Freddie Prinze: he's nineteen years old, and he's now Chico, and the other guy, Jack Albertson, was The Man. So she assumed that was the template for everyone. And for a while I played along and would have to go out and read for these sitcoms, and I can remember one day driving somewhere—you know, anyplace is a thousand miles away in L.A.—and I get there, and it's a room full of guys. It's just all guys. And the sitcom is *Makin' It*, and they're casting the John Travolta character. What I have to do is pretend that I'm in front of a bathroom mirror, blow-drying my hair to go out on a Saturday night, and while I'm looking in the mirror, blow-drying my hair, I also have to dance. I said to the person, "Oh, you know, I think I left my car running!" I left and I just never went back.

Jerry: After the film came out, we were on his show, *Late Night with David Letterman*, and blindsided him with his *Airplane!* screen test.

David: Whether or not he was actually blindsided, or if his staff prepared him in advance for the clip, he was a good sport about it, and looked appropriately embarrassed, playing it to big laughs. Now *that* was acting!

ZAZ with David Letterman, 1982

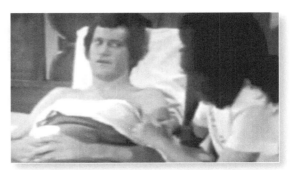

Letterman screen test: "Fat chance."

Jim: But in any case, during that preproduction period we were feeling a bit worried with no one to play the lead role and less than six weeks to the start of shooting.

David: We were only around three weeks away when Tom Parry, our development executive, came into our office with big news.

TOM PARRY (Development Executive)
The Paramount executive building is on the south side of the main quadrangle, with kind of a grassy area, and catty-corner is the directors' building. Howard Koch had taken over Robert Evans's suite on the first floor. So I went over and knocked on the door, no answer. I opened the door, and the guys were playing Nerfball and making jokes. And they took one look at me and said, "Oh, my God! What's happened, Tom?" I walked in, closed the door, and said, "Okay, um, promise me that, after I tell you this, you will give me twenty-four hours." "Oh, my God! What is it? What's wrong?!" I said, "The studio has decided that Barry Manilow is going to be the star of *Airplane!*" And their jaws dropped . . . and then they broke into gales of laughter. And they said, "You got us! You got us! That's the funniest thing we've ever heard! You got us!" The thing is, the guys used to do things like toilet-paper my car, and it was like they thought I was getting back at them. And I said, "No, no, no! It's real!" "No, Tom, it's all right, you got us, you don't have to keep playing it up!"

David: At that point the door opened, and Howard Koch, our executive producer, walked in and said, "I suppose you heard the news?" We said, "Barry Manilow?" He nodded, and Tom said, "Guys, let me take this one."

TOM PARRY
So I go back to my office, shut the door, get on the phone with Manilow's development guy. He said he was sent a whole bunch of scripts that Paramount's actually going to be making, and he read *Airplane!* and thought it was very funny. And I thought to myself, *Shit, the one person in town who actually understands how good this movie is!* So I said, "Well, do you know anything about the three guys who are making the picture?" He said, "Oh, there are three of them?" I said, "Yeah, they're gonna all be co-directing it. This is only the first studio picture they've ever worked on; they've never directed actors before. But, I mean, if you're okay with that, I think it's very brave of Barry to do something like that!" There's this long silence on the other end of the phone, and then he said, "Oh, I didn't realize that. Let me get back to you."

David: We didn't know how much longer we could dodge these studio suggestions. As we neared the start of production, we were getting into a scary territory, where we thought maybe we'd have to compromise. But a young woman named Beth Voyku came to our rescue.

> **ROBERT HAYS**
>
> My agent was Arnie Soloway, and there was a gal who'd just come to his agency—a new agent, Beth Voyku—and she'd worked with Howard Koch on some stuff. This was when the boys had apparently already been back east to New York and all over the place looking for someone to play Ted Striker, and they didn't find anybody. So she called him up and said, "Howard, I've got your Ted Striker!" And he said, "Bring him over!"

Jerry: Bob was on a half-hour ABC sitcom called *Angie* at the time. I remember Howard bringing in Bob's photo. He plunked it down and said, "Hey, what do you think about this guy?" I mean, Howard didn't know him, and I don't think he'd ever seen *Angie*, but at that point we had stopped asking questions. We just said, "Sure, he looks nice. Bring him in."

David: So he came in to read, and he was great. We all looked at each other, kind of like we had when Julie read in New York, and we knew we had our Striker.

> **ROBERT HAYS**
>
> So then they came over to the set of *Angie*, where we were filming the show. And they were behind the set, and there wasn't much room between the wall and the set, but they said, "Well, that's it: you're the one. We chose you! Congratulations!" And they left. But Jim told me later that, on the way out, he said, "You know, we ought to take a look at this show he's doing, so we can see what it is we've got." So they watched an episode of *Angie*, which is a totally different animal, and they looked at each other and said, "Oh, my God! What have we done?"

Jim: Bob was perfect. Movie-star handsome, cinematic, with a real gift for doing comedy—without being comedic.

David: At the time, we were so focused on our own particular brand of humor, and it was a narrow definition. I think we were such "purists" and because of that . . .

Jerry: . . . seeing Bob in the *Angie* sitcom was a little jarring to us. Watching him in this setup, joke, laugh-track rhythm gave us a brief scare. But by this time we had gotten used to brief scares and it was gone by the next morning.

Jim: Since the leads were a major decision, and in this case, unknowns, the studio wanted us to screen test at least four couples. Bob and Julie were our leading candidates, so we had them test together.

Jerry: Bob and Julie had great chemistry right off the bat; they liked each other, they loved doing comedy, they were both

"You're too low, Ted! You're too low!"

very selfless actors, and thrilled that they might actually be starring in a movie.

ROBERT HAYS

Julie and I really tried to flesh out the love story aspect of it and not lose it in the jokes. We felt it was really important to have that serious part of the film work. One day, after lunch, the boys came running up to us having just come from dailies. They said, "You know, this is a really cool love story!" Julie and I looked at each other, then looked back at them and said, "Well, yeah, it is. Too. Kinda."

JULIE HAGERTY

I didn't have a lot of experience when I did *Airplane!* But I just don't look at a part and say, "Oh, this is really funny!" I look at it and say, "Well, this is the situation, and I have to listen to what's happening and then respond to the situation." It can be Ibsen or *Airplane!* But in *Airplane!* there were other circumstances beyond the love story. If you're going to sell Tupperware in the jungle, you've got to do it from the heart, or nobody's going to buy it

David: Besides great chemistry, I think they kind of bonded through all the punishment they had to endure. Like the *From Here to Eternity* scene—an easy scene to write, but . . .

JOHN FRAZIER (Special Effects)
When we did that beach scene, we had a big dunk tank behind them, and it was full of fish, seaweed, and anything else we could find to put in it. That was pretty funny.

JULIE HAGERTY
Bob said they were going to pour I don't know how many tons of water on us, and when we were lying there, he said, "Close your eyes, and hold on to me!" He saw what was coming, and I didn't! And all of a sudden, those thousands of gallons of water swept over us . . . and he held on to me! It was so sweet. And he could see the catfish in my hair, but I didn't see it until I saw the movie!

ROBERT HAYS
It was ten thousand gallons of water! It was one of those containers where you could put the sides up, and when they opened it, it all came out. The water hit us so hard, it pushed our eyelids open, so the sand got all in our eyes. It was really, really harsh.

David: As writers, it's one thing to imagine these scenes happening in our minds. But often, we're not really thinking about the people who actually have to perform them. We also often forget how many people it takes behind the scenes to make those gags work.

JOHN FRAZIER
A couple of weeks prior to shooting the beach scene, I had to procure the escape slide for the plane. I knew a friend of mine who dealt in used military and aircraft equipment, so I called him and said, "I'm looking for an escape slide for a plane." He said, "Well, the only one I have is for a 747." So we went and picked it up and brought it to the shop. One day we're just kind of milling around, and somebody says, "Hey, let's try that slide and see how big the thing really gets!" Well, when we popped that valve and that thing came undone, it was like the size of the stage! I mean, everybody was running from this thing. It was huge! So I said, "Hey, you know what? Why don't we take this thing to the beach when we go down there, and we'll all go out and have lunch on this big old surf raft?" So while they're doing the beach scene, one of the other guys is blowing up the raft. It was supposed to be half a day at the beach and half a day at the studio. Well, we all got on the raft, and we got it out into the water, out on the ocean, everybody's on this thing and having lunch on it until

it's time for us to wrap up and return to the studio, and we can't get back in! It was too big! The waves would just roll underneath it. We tried everything to get the raft back to the shore, and I think they finally had to call the Coast Guard. Meanwhile, our producer Jon Davison is on the shore because he wouldn't go out on the water because he's the one who's supposed to keep people in line. So he's yelling, "John Frazier, I'm gonna kill you!" I think everybody who could swim jumped off, and the ones who couldn't swim had to stay on until they hauled it back in. But you couldn't get mad at anybody. We were just having fun!

BILL HADER
Having Robert Hays and Julie Hagerty playing their love story—you like them, and I watch it now, and I go, "Oh, their performances are kind of what holds it together, in a weird way." Without them, I don't know how else it would've worked. Alec Berg, a guy who I work with on *Barry*, always talks about that scene, that one moment that's kind of serious, where they're in the airport and Robert Hays says, "You can't leave, I love you," and it ends with him saying, "What a pisser!" Alec says, "You need that scene. Once you have that scene, you know that they actually care about each other, and you know what's at stake."

Jim: After we saw the screen test, we knew Bob was Striker, and we knew Julie was Elaine. There was never any doubt in our minds.

ROBERT HAYS
Later, when we were filming, Beth, who had introduced me to Howard Koch, was so proud that she'd gotten that together—she would come by the set, and the boys would come up to her and say, "Thank you, thank you, thank you!"

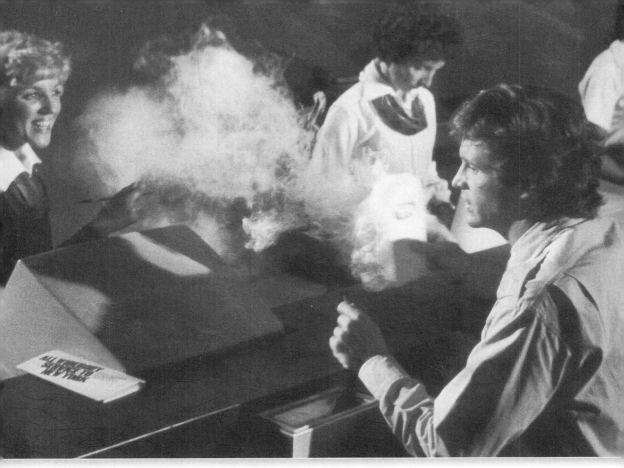

"Smoking or nonsmoking?"

CHAPTER 4

MADISON

I was doing community theater and I was always interested in acting, but I was also interested in sports. I was interested in a lot of things. I was a pretty normal guy. I wasn't like the guy who grew up in a dark theater watching movies. Seeing Kentucky Fried Theater at the University of Wisconsin made me think I could do this. You don't have to be a card-carrying industry person. It had a huge impact on me.

WILLEM DAFOE

Jim: After the disastrous show at the Wisconsin Student Union South, we were completely dejected. I sort of disappeared during that time. I was a few years older, and I had the full-time job as a private investigator in Milwaukee that I really liked. I also had a girlfriend named Terri. If you saw her you'd understand.

David: Meanwhile, the Monday morning after the Union South disaster, we were shocked to see a review of the show in the student paper by a writer named George Hessleberg. He actually liked it!

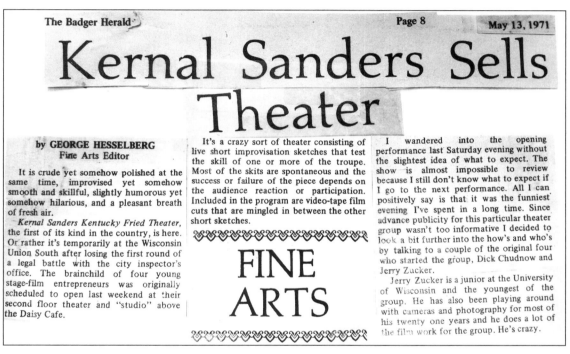

The Badger Herald · Page 8 · May 13, 1971

Kernal Sanders Sells Theater

by GEORGE HESSELBERG
Fine Arts Editor

It is crude yet somehow polished at the same time, improvised yet somehow smooth and skillful, slightly humorous yet somehow hilarious, and a pleasant breath of fresh air.

Kernal Sanders Kentucky Fried Theater, the first of its kind in the country, is here. Or rather it's temporarily at the Wisconsin Union South after losing the first round of a legal battle with the city inspector's office. The brainchild of four young stage-film entrepreneurs was originally scheduled to open last weekend at their second floor theater and "studio" above the Daisy Cafe.

It's a crazy sort of theater consisting of live short improvisation sketches that test the skill of one or more of the troupe. Most of the skits are spontaneous and the success or failure of the piece depends on the audience reaction or participation. Included in the program are video-tape film cuts that are mingled in between the other short sketches.

FINE ARTS

I wandered into the opening performance last Saturday evening without the slightest idea of what to expect. The show is almost impossible to review because I still don't know what to expect if I go to the next performance. All I can positively say is that it was the funniest evening I've spent in a long time. Since advance publicity for this particular theater group wasn't too informative I decided to look a bit further into the how's and who's by talking to a couple of the original four who started the group, Dick Chudnow and Jerry Zucker.

Jerry Zucker is a junior at the University of Wisconsin and the youngest of the group. He has also been playing around with cameras and photography for most of his twenty one years and he does a lot of the film work for the group. He's crazy.

First review: somebody actually liked it!

Jerry: Then we got a call from the building inspector. The one who shut us down at the Daisy Cafe. He felt so bad about it that he wanted to suggest a new location: the Shakespeare and Company Bookstore on Regent Street. They had a storage room in the back, just big enough to hold an audience of seventy. It looked like a great space to build a theater.

David: I quit my construction job and moved to Madison in March. Jerry, Dick, and I dismantled the stage and control room at the Daisy Cafe, and loaded it all onto a U-Haul trailer. Dick drove it over to Regent Street. And there, just like we'd done before, we constructed another entire stage and control room, the third one in two months, this latest in the former back storage room of the bookstore. We spent the early spring and summer of 1971 hammering and nailing.

Jerry: We were always pretty industrious—do it yourselfers—but I doubt much of it was up to code. When we were finished, the building inspector came back. He seemed as happy as we were. He just said, "Great, you're fine. Glad it all worked out in the end."

David: This, despite the fact that the ceiling was constructed of flammable cardboard.

U-Haul rental: Dick, David, gas station guy, Jerry.
We documented everything.

Jerry: We'd work on building the theater during the day and rehearse the show at night. It was six of us: David, Dick, me, Chris Keene, Lisa Davis, and Bill West. It was a very happy time.

David: We advertised in the student paper, the *Daily Cardinal*, put up posters around campus, and one night painted an entire block of plywood at a State Street construction site.

Jerry: We had to paint over a previous graffiti that read, "ON THIS SITE: A BLOCK LONG ERECTION." It was a better joke than our ad.

David: Definitely something in the water in Madison.

Jim: I was a junior in high school when a friend and I decided to drive out to Madison to check out the University of Wisconsin campus and attend a football game. We

got to the stadium about an hour before kickoff and took our seats right next to the student card section as they were rehearsing. When their very bossy leader yelled out a number on a megaphone, each student would hold up his or her card to collectively form a huge "W" or a badger or some other iconic UW symbol. At the end of the rehearsal, the head guy ordered through the megaphone, "Now, no matter how exciting the game gets, no matter how many points we score, **I don't care if we're down by three touchdowns in the last two minutes and come back to win—DO NOT THROW THE CARDS!"** Immediately, as if on cue, five hundred kids threw their cards in the air and left. Talk about inspiration. That moment was my spiritual connection with the university. Not sure if there was ever an academic one, but certainly there was a strong spiritual one. Ten years later and just one block away, we opened Kentucky Fried Theater in Madison and continued to throw the cards. And I think pretty much that's what *Airplane!* went on to do—throw the cards.

David: Finally, we were ready to open in July. For some reason we called the show *Vegetables*, and this time we made sure to assemble enough material, video and live, for a full ninety-minute show, including an actual planned intermission.

Jim: I came up to watch for the first time. When I saw the show, I was blown away; it was so cool and so good. I realized what I'd done, and I think I sort of pleaded with the guys to let me back in, because I wanted to be a part of it. It was just so funny and unique. I don't know what happened to Terri, but the guys welcomed me back.

The Shakespeare & Company Bookstore on Regent Street.
They had a storage room in the back.

David: The reviews ranged from great to fantastic. *The Daily Cardinal*, just screamed, "See this show! For your own good, see this show!" My kind of review.

Jerry: We started selling out. Which means every night we had seventy people who would be telling us what they thought was funny or not so funny with either laughter or silence. That was an important time for us, the beginning of learning what worked in front of an audience. It's something we would've missed out on if we had been able to put our sketches on YouTube. We could hear and feel the reaction—we could see their faces. Stand-up comedians do that every night.

David: We heard people laugh or not. And the "not" was as valuable as the laugh, because we learned, "Oh, that didn't work, so we won't use that in tomorrow night's show." Editing 101.

Jim: This was the early seventies. Vietnam was still going on, you had all these political elements: Nixon, Watergate, feminism, Black Power. And we just steadfastly ignored all politics. And I think that's part of why people liked it. We were refreshing, and we found other things to make fun of. We found things to laugh at despite your political leanings. Everyone loves a good fart joke.

Jerry: Exactly! The politics of the time weighed so heavily on everybody that I think people were just happy for a couple of hours of not thinking about it. People were as sick of the antiwar movement as they were of the war.

David: We instinctively knew that media was where it was at, so we did TV and movie satire. That set us apart. I think we saw Nixon jokes as being cheap, too easy.

Jim: We'd go to UW football games with our Sony Portapak, which was a battery powered reel-to-reel deck you could strap on your back with a camera attached.

Jerry: We thought it was the greatest thing ever invented. A technological marvel. We were untethered. Now we could go anywhere!

David: Forty pounds of equipment which today is contained in a cell phone.

Kentucky F

By GERALD PEARY
of the Fine Arts Staff

The greatest nights in the theatre (and this certainly includes an evening with Kernel Sanders Fried Theatre, Madison's wonderful new company) are never characterized by our total involvement in the dramatic experience. Rather part of us is always on edge, always slightly nervous, always outside the presentation.

The reasons are simple: the more impressed we become with what we see, the more we keep wishing (and in a slightly annoyed way) that our friends were also in attendance and sharing the excitement with us. The more we keep resenting the thousands of philistines out walking the streets who have never even heard of the show, much less ever plan to attend. The more itchy we become for the presentation to end, so that we can rush outside and shout to an ignorant, morally impoverished world, "SEE THIS SHOW! FOR YOUR OWN GOOD, SEE THIS SHOW!"

Jim: Back in those days, there wasn't a net behind the goal posts, so after a touchdown or a field goal, students would try to catch the football and throw it up and out of the stadium before the ushers got it.

Jerry: It was much more entertaining than the football game.

Jim: We did an announcer play-by-play as our camera followed the ball. Afterward, we interviewed the kids and the ushers.

Jerry: The audience loved it. They were all rooting for the kids in the end zone.

David: This came on the heels of antiwar demonstrations, riots, assassinations, and even a recent bombing on the UW campus. It was such a revolutionary time in America, and all we wanted was to make people laugh.

GEORGE HESSELBERG (Columnist at Wisconsin State Journal)
They were very funny. The "seriousness" was everywhere at that time, the antiwar feelings and all. There was a big hole in the humor blanket, and here are these guys . . . just being funny! Their arrival on campus—their timing—was perfect.

Jerry: It was just silliness. Our humor was never angry or mean-spirited.

Jim: And we were lucky in so many ways. One day we got to the theater in the morning and the padlock was hanging by a thread. Somebody had obviously tried to break in and steal our videotape equipment. All we had was that padlock on the door, but somehow that little thing held. Over the years, we've talked about what a tremendous break that was, because it's not clear what we would've done if somebody had stolen all our stuff.

David: No one thought to insure it.

Jerry: No one could afford it.

Jim: Would we have given up? Would we have started over?

Jerry: There were a ton of times like that, moments that felt like, if this one thing didn't happen, we never would've ended up where we are. So many of our mistakes were miraculously corrected. Somehow our naivetéé always seemed to work to our advantage. Either this was all meant to be, or we were the luckiest guys alive!

CHAPTER 5

LESLIE

While we were shooting, I was laughing at it myself. I really enjoyed it. But I never knew it was as funny as it really was. I went to see the first screening, and I hear people laughing. I'm in the scene . . . what are they laughing at? Because I did not know. And I was doing things that were funny. But I couldn't see it. The dumbest lines, like, "Don't call me Shirley." I had no idea that would stick with me forever.

LESLIE NIELSEN

David: Michael Eisner agreed from the beginning that we could cast serious actors. There was zero drama surrounding the four tough-guy roles. No persuasion was ever necessary. But the hardest one to cast was Dr. Rumack. We were getting rejections from all of our top choices. Years later, I happened to read Vincent Price's obituary. It said his greatest career regret was turning down *Airplane!*

Jerry: We also offered the role to Vince Edwards, who played a superfly intense doctor on a 60s hospital show called *Ben Casey*. It was a great piece of good fortune that they both turned it down. At some point we remembered "that guy who had been the captain of the ship in *The Poseidon Adventure*," famous for seeing an enormous tidal wave and exclaiming, "Oh my God!"

Jim: We had to look up his name; he was that obscure. I think we might've run the name past Jeffrey Katzenberg, but by this time the studio didn't seem to mind what we were doing.

Jerry: They were also very preoccupied with the first *Star Trek* movie. That turned out to be a big help. I think our entire budget was less than the amount that *Star Trek* was over budget. Anything we were doing just seemed like less of a problem.

David: So we got very excited, because this captain of the *Poseidon* guy, or whoever he was, didn't seem to have a humorous bone in his body. We couldn't wait to break the

"I am serious, and don't call me Shirley."

news to our casting director, Joel Thurm, who had been brave enough to agree to have his name associated with casting Stack, Graves, and Bridges in a comedy.

Jerry: And we greeted him in the morning all ecstatic with the news that our choice for the doctor was . . . Leslie Nielsen!

Jim: He finally snapped.

Jerry: His jaw dropped and he exploded. "Leslie Nielsen?! Leslie Nielsen is the guy you cast the night before!!"

Jim: Mind you, we had only three weeks to go until shooting started.

"'I don't know where I'll be then, Doc,' he said, 'but I won't smell too good. That's for sure.'"

JIMMY KIMMEL
They cast it so well. That's one of the brilliant things about it, that, as a kid, I didn't really realize. But in looking back, we now think of Leslie Nielsen as a comic actor, which he wasn't at all. But because of that movie, he became one. And just the seriousness of these disaster movies we were so in love with in the seventies. *The Towering Inferno* and *Airport* and all these movies with George Kennedy in them.

"I just want to tell you both good luck. We're all counting on you."

Jerry: But Leslie turned out to be a fish in water with our style of comedy. He loved it. He was actually a comedian stuck in the body of a leading man, a closeted clown. He later admitted that when he read the script, he called his agent and said, "Don't tell them, but I'd pay *them* to do this movie!"

Jim: When we first met Leslie, he said he'd done an episode of *M*A*S*H*, thinking it gave him some comedy credentials, but we looked at him and said, "Well, we'll just forget you said that."

> **BARRY DILLER (Former Chairman, Paramount Pictures)**
> Given its ridiculousness, I thought that every part of it was perfectly cast. Leslie Nielsen was a stroke of genius.

Jim: He was the perfect person to deliver those lines. The way he says, "Good luck, we're all counting on you," and his response to, "A hospital? What is it?" "It's a big building with patients, but that's not important right now." His timing was impeccable.

Jerry: What we shared with Leslie was a sense of anarchy. For whatever reason, he loved giving the finger to authority figures. He relished the idea of playing the guy everyone is supposed to respect, and then saying and doing really stupid things.

Jim: He had perfected the art of pretending he had no clue he was in a comedy.

BILL HADER

When Alec Berg and I were doing *Barry*, there was a running bit where I'd walk up to him and say, "I just want to tell you: good luck, we're all counting on you." Any major dramatic moment. We're just about to blow up a car, and there's tension on set, and I'd walk up and say, "I just want to tell you: good luck, we're all counting on you." And then when he was leaving for the day, I'd walk over to him, and he would actually start laughing because he knew what I was about to do. "I just want to tell you: good luck, we're all counting on you."

ROBERT HAYS

God, Leslie was so funny. Of course, everyone was funny! But before that, Leslie had done a few TV comedies, like a *M*A*S*H* episode, he'd been a leading man in movies, and he'd played a lot of bad guys on TV, but he'd always wanted to be really goofy, and he needed somebody to give him a shot. And those guys, they not only opened the door for him, they pushed him through. That's the way he always said it, anyway.

Jerry: Before we met Leslie, he had appeared in hundreds of dramatic film and television roles. I think that the little fart machine he always carried with him might have been his way of coping with a career filled with heavy drama.

David: Bob Hays cracked up a couple of times right before takes. We couldn't figure out why. Then we found out Leslie would wait for just the right moment and squeeze the fart machine.

Jerry: A friend of his made them for him. I do remember he was selling them on the set. After a while the whole crew had them and all you'd hear was constant farting sounds. I could never get mine to work right, but Leslie really had a way with his. He played it like a virtuoso, producing every possible kind of fart sound.

Jim: Why wouldn't we expect Leslie to be an anarchist off camera as well?

KAREEM ABDUL-JABBAR

Leslie was a crazy guy, always trying to disrupt everything. He had a device on him that would make farting noises, which he loved to press whenever we were doing dialogue. At first, I thought he just had some sort of intestinal problem. He made everyone around laugh.

Jerry: Leslie knew he looked like the person he was making fun of: a tall, handsome, straight, White guy. But underneath, there was a rebellious little kid in there who needed to get back at someone.

ARNE SCHMIDT (First Assistant Director)

I got a look at Leslie's fart-maker thing, and it was basically two baby-jar lids. One lid was normal and the other lid had a hole punched in it, so when you squeezed the hole against the palm of your hand, it'd make a farting sound. So he'd walk around with this in his palm, and he just made farts all the time with it. At first he was doing it, and you know, he's an actor and it's funny, and you've already done lighting and everything, and it's just a few seconds on the set or whatever, no big deal. But then he started selling them to the crew. So now, while the crew is lighting the set, all you could hear were farts. So, I threatened to confiscate their fart-makers if they didn't knock it off!

JULIE HAGERTY

Leslie had that little magical machine of his, and in front of the executives he made it do that . . . noise. And he looked at me and went, "Julie!" And I wanted to die! If you were doing a rehearsal, he'd make the sound, and then you'd start giggling. He got us all. And he even carried it along to the press tour! Leslie was just so naughty. But he had so much fun making that movie. He was like a duck to water. I mean, we all had fun. It was pure joy!

JOHN FRAZIER

One day Julie said, "Let me borrow one of those things." Somebody on the crew had been hitting on her, and she got a little tired of it. So they were in close quarters, and she had her little fart machine, and she was talking to this guy, and she let one rip from the machine . . . and it just purged him. He never came back! I think she might've kept one in her purse from then on, like pepper spray.

Jerry: It makes sense that we connected so well with Leslie. Like us, he came from a small town, in his case, the far north of Canada—I think it was Regina, or Moose Jaw or something like that—but he had dreams of something bigger and saw an opportunity. We identified with that.

Jim: I didn't.

David's Eulogy of Leslie Nielsen
Delivered at the Funeral, Fort Lauderdale, Florida
November 30, 2010

It was summer 1979, a full three weeks before the start of shooting for *Airplane!*, and our casting director had finally had enough. Lloyd Bridges, Robert Stack, Peter Graves, and now Leslie . . . who?

At least audiences had heard of the first three, but this guy—it was true, when it came time to select an actor to play Dr. Rumack, my brother Jerry, Jim Abrahams, and I remembered, "This one guy, he's been in hundreds of television shows, and I think he played the captain of the *Poseidon*. What's his name?" Our research revealed that the actor's name was Leslie Nielsen. Jim, Jerry, and I were thrilled when he agreed to meet, not because he was "funny" but because of his long résumé of serious films and TV. To us, he was hysterical. The long list of straight dramatic acting roles demonstrated to us that he would be perfect. When we watched those movies, we laughed.

At our first meeting, he mentioned proudly that he had done an episode of *M*A*S*H*. We assured him we wouldn't count this brief comedy experience against him. But when he read the *Airplane!* script, he "got" its unconventional nature and offbeat style. We heard later that he told his agent, "Take whatever they offer; I'd pay them to do this."

Arguably the best role was that of Dr. Rumack, played by the guy no one wanted or ever suspected would be funny, much less believed would go on to have a second career starring in feature films as a goofball comic. Leslie was great in the role because he never "winked"—let on that he knew he was in a comedy. This was essential to the style, and Leslie had a natural instinct for it.

In all the movies we did together, we hardly had to shower him with any verbal praise. He always knew he was doing okay because, "I could hear David laughing during the take," he would say. And I was! Tough to just sit there silently during "Nice beaver!"

Offscreen, he wasn't so much of a joke-or storyteller but a chronic prankster. The stories are legion about the fart machine, which he kept hidden and sprang on any hapless stranger who approached him. He used it on set, on talk shows, anywhere he could find a victim. One time, at a press junket in

Charlotte, I remember watching Leslie let loose with the device on a crowded elevator, the other occupants squirming up against the walls in an effort to distance themselves. And just like the scenes we put him in, he never broke character, never let on that he knew he was being funny.

Leslie got the biggest kick out of his newfound status as an international comedy icon—almost as though that, too, was some kind of prank he had pulled. But mostly, he just really loved to laugh. Doing goofy things on and off the set made him happy, which was almost always his demeanor. And in turn, he made all of us happy. I think we all got along so well because we were all anarchists at heart—grown-up kids who still got the giggles from poking fun at authority figures.

As the years went on, I always tried to find a place for him in whatever movie I was doing. And he was always delighted to accept. And when each movie came out, he always turned out to be the funniest thing in it. A director couldn't ask for a better track record.

In the movie business, friendships tend to be intense—and brief. You live with someone every day for three months, and then, despite promises of keeping in touch, getting together, calling, you go back to your separate and individual lives. Looking back on it, I think I wanted Leslie to know that we valued him beyond that—and how much we all appreciated him, as a talented performer and a friend.

We invariably would get to discussing our history together, reminiscing a bit and renewing our good-natured debate about who the hell was luckier to have met the other, Leslie Nielsen or the Zucker-Abrahams-Zucker team. The truth was, all of us knew how grateful we were to have each other in our lives, both professionally and personally, and we expressed it to each other often.

Leslie was grateful for everything in his life (most especially his wife, Barbaree), almost as though he didn't feel he deserved any of it. Maybe that's why he was so happy.

And maybe that's why he was so good at making everyone else happy.

CHAPTER 6
DIAL-A-FART

TIRED OF PRAYERS, WEATHER, TIME?

KENTUCKY FRIED THEATER

1330 REGENT ST.

PROUDLY ANNOUNCES

DIAL-A-FART

251-7646

Begins Friday Night, Jan. 14, at 12 Midnight

ADDITIONAL NOTE:
One last performance of "Vegetables" will be presented this Saturday night at 8:00 p.m. only.

**Free Doughnuts and Sneak Preview of New Show.
For Reservations Call 255-3646**

Their work . . . When I thought about the kind of movies I wanted to make or work on, that was it. When I saw not just *Airplane!* but *Kentucky Fried Movie*—at that time, I was probably fifteen years old and a huge martial arts fan, and they did a parody of *Enter the Dragon* ("A Fistful of Yen"), which was one of my favorite movies. I just sat there and laughed hysterically, and it just kind of all clicked: "Wow, you can take something that you love and make fun of it like that? This is brilliant!" Because I wasn't offended by it. It was like . . . I dunno, I had the same excitement watching the parody that I did watching the movie!

KEENEN IVORY WAYANS

Jim: One of the great things about Kentucky Fried Theater in Madison was that on the other side of the back wall of the stage was a donut factory, and the whole audience could hear this "pop, pop, pop" when the batter would go into the grease to make the donuts. And after the show, everybody would get stoned and have fresh, warm donuts from the donut factory.

David: One night, someone had the bright idea of bringing trays of donuts, freshly baked from the factory, onstage at the end of the show. At first we just handed them out to the front rows and people were passing them back, but evidently not fast enough, so we started tossing the donuts to the middle and back rows. Then, of course, somebody in the audience thought of throwing one back at us, and then all of a sudden it's a free-for-all donut fight.

Jim: We actually have a video of that! We also came up with some fun ways to promote the theater. Dial-A-Fart was a prime example of that. We published an ad in the paper.

Even St. Christopher couldn't bear to watch.

Jerry: We rented this big, heavy recorded message machine from the phone company. In those days that was a big deal. In our outgoing message, we explained the history of farting, with an assortment of examples. In a few days, so many people were calling that it tied up the entire exchange. The phone company had to shut it down. And this was years before we ever met Leslie Nielsen.

Jim: Let's face it. We are all blessed with a God-given ability to write fart jokes for thirteen-year-old boys. I actually have a second home in Eagle River, Wisconsin, that's been paid for, 100 percent, by residuals from fart jokes.

Dial-a-Fart has phone woes, ties up lines at Ma Bell

By HERBERT GOULD
of the Cardinal Staff

Dial-A-Fart hit Madison with a big noise but the telephone switchboard came up with a bad case of indigestion.

Dial-A-Fart, an invention of Kentucky Fried Theatre, was started early last month as a promotion for upcoming shows. When a listener dialed 251-7646, he heard a series of rare utterances, such as "the Edwin Sinclair Memorial Fart" and "the rare, beautiful Beatrice Vogel Twitter."

However, Dial-A-Fart became so popular that it began to tie up telephone facilities in the central office, according to a Wisconsin Bell Telephone Co. spokesman. The telephone co. received numerous complaints on service within the 251 exchange.

IN CASES SUCH as this, a telephone representative explained, "We reserve the right to discontinue service."

Consequently, the originators of Dial-A-Fart were notified last Wednesday that the line which carried their recorded message would be discontinued. Service was halted later that day.

A member of Kentucky Fried Theater (KFT) explained that Dial-A-Fart was first conceived over a bowl of chili at the Union. "We heard Dial-A-Prayer and decided 'why not'?", a KFT member revealed. He added that the group had hoped to use other telephone messages as future promotionals, including "Dial-A-N—Obscene Phone Call", "Dial-A-Dirt" and "Dial-An-Orgasm."

HOWEVER, the phone company's decision to cancel service may put a damper on KFT's recorded message advertisements. A Wisconsin Bell spokesman felt that KFT would have to install many more lines in order to continue using recorded messages for advertising, which would up the costs of future Dial-A-Farts considerably. "We're stymied right now," commented a member of KFT.

Public response to Dial-A-Fart seems to have been overwhelmingly positive. Wisconsin Bell only voiced concern about keeping their lines free for use by all customers.

LE PETOMANE, world famous flatulator, whose ability to blow out a candle at six feet and

David: The *Vegetables* show was a hit, and we continued it into the fall. One night, Chris Keene called in sick and we had to scramble to find a piano player. The only one we knew was a med student we grew up with in Milwaukee named Bob Goisman. We had about an hour to quickly teach him the show. He learned his parts, and minutes later we went onstage. He was a great piano player. The problem was, he had never seen the show before, and at every joke he cracked up, like he was in the audience rather than an actor onstage. So we started laughing at his reactions, and it was hard

JAMES S. ABRAHAMS

INVESTIGATOR

LAW OFFICES
deVRIES, VLASAK & SCHALLERT

710 NORTH WATER STREET
MILWAUKEE, WISCONSIN 53202
273-2900

for anybody to keep a straight face. Fortunately, the audience got into the spirit of it and loved the show.

Jim: He had so much fun, he actually considered quitting med school and joining the show permanently.

Jerry: Fortunately for the Goisman family, that didn't last long.

David: Then, in January, we started a new show, *The Entire History of the Whole World*.

Law firm: Jim (top left) trying his best to blend in

Jim: I was living a double life. I still had my job in Milwaukee, so during the week I was working for this incredibly conservative law firm as their private investigator. They were litigators and defended insurance companies.

David: An entirely different planet.

Jim: An entirely different galaxy. They made straitlaced people look like party animals. Everyone wore suits and ties, had short hair, and was clean shaven. It was the ultimate "play it straight" job. Then, every Friday afternoon I'd change into jeans, jump into the law firm's Ford Fairlane 500, smoke a joint, and drive the seventy miles to Madison to do the theater. Suddenly, I'd be surrounded by long hair, army jackets, pot-perfumed air, bearded faces, no bras, kids wanting to have fun, and the show. Madison was the Midwest's Berkeley of the early seventies. We'd do the show, eat donuts, just have a ball! The antithesis of playing by the rules. It was anarchy. And then on Monday, I'd hop back into the Ford Fairlane 500, go back to the law firm, and be the straitlaced guy they thought I was.

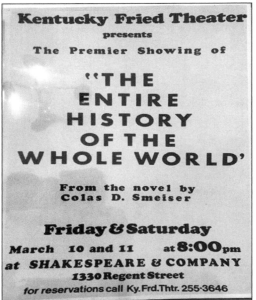

Kentucky Fried Theater
presents
The Premier Showing of
"THE ENTIRE HISTORY OF THE WHOLE WORLD'
From the novel by
Colas D. Smeiser
Friday & Saturday
March 10 and 11   at 8:00pm
at SHAKESPEARE & COMPANY
1330 Regent Street
for reservations call Ky. Frd. Thtr. 255-3646

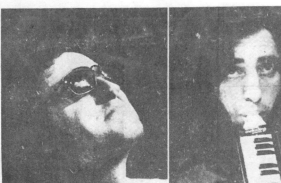

10   Wednesday, December 15, 1971   THE MILWAUKEE JOURNAL

TV, Movies, Live Comedy—All at Once

Special Correspondence

Madison, Wis. – Every Friday and Saturday night for the five months, 140 people paid $2 each to crowd a dark storage room. There, for two hours they simultaneously watch three television cameras, three movie screens and seven young actors put on "Kernel Sanders ucky Fried Theatre." It may well be one of the exciting developments in Madison theater since the nude parts of "Peter Pan" attracted a lot of attention a few ago, much of it from the e.

Police Not Interested

ntucky Fried Theatre, ever, is not attracting the or getting national

eotape machines, television monitors and other electric apparatus) and their in $800 budget exhausted, show officially opend to out crowds.
    The building, itself, took actors a month of steady work to transform. But the bare age room became an authentic theater, with a workable stage lights, and built-in screens monitors and speakers.
    The "room" is in the back Shakespeare & Company, version of a general store ing penny candies and New Republic.

Others Join Troupe

The lineup, after Chud and Abrahams, includes brothers Jerry and David Zu Lisa Davis, Chris Keene

The *Milwaukee Journal*, December 1971

Jim: I was actually getting away with my duplicity. Occasionally, my job at the law firm would include picking up witnesses and driving them to court. Of course, I was warned not to talk to them about the facts of the case, so I'd make shit up. One time, I was driving a young woman to court and I explained that prior to her testimony she would have to rinse her hands in a cauldron and circle it three times while singing Elton John's

"Tiny Dancer." (It was number one at the time.) The opposing lawyer saw me enter the courtroom with the young woman, so when she got up on the stand, he asked her what I had told her about the trial. She promptly told him, under oath, about circling cauldrons and singing "Tiny Dancer."

David: Busted!

Jerry: But so worth it!

Jim: Huge, hairy eyeball from the lawyer I was working for. I don't think I won over many points with the judge either. And then, as if that weren't enough, I woke up on December 15 to a big, front-page feature article in the *Milwaukee Journal* about the theater. I was outed.

Jim: This was not the image DeVries, Vlasak, and Schallert had been cultivating in the Milwaukee legal community. When I got into the office, they were having a big staff meeting. The look they were giving me was very reminiscent of the look I had gotten from my parents for the past twenty years.

Jerry: When we first started the theater in Madison, we were open to anything, "Sure try it, see if it gets a laugh." But as time went on, a style was emerging. We became more and more aware of what our "brand" was. "*This* isn't our kind of humor; *that* is. It might get a laugh, but it doesn't fit. It's not who we are." Eventually, the style became a passion, and we didn't want to stop. But we also realized that we weren't going to make a living doing a show in Madison, Wisconsin.

DICK CHUDNOW

We were very successful in Madison, but we were only able to charge a dollar for admission. We talked about taking the show to Milwaukee, because it was a bigger town. But I had lived in L.A., so I said, "Look, it's a waste of energy to go to Milwaukee. Why don't we just move it to L.A.?" And they were, like, "Oh, that's a big move, I don't know if we want to do that." But David, who was the most adventuresome, was willing to do stuff, and he said, "I'll go out with you, and if we find a place where we can do it, then we'll move."

David: I think it was during *The Entire History of the Whole World* show that we saw some sketch groups on *The Tonight Show*. They all appeared fairly regularly, doing what we thought was a rather conventional brand of sketch comedy, and we started to think, *We're much funnier; why couldn't we do this?* It was Mrs. Zubatsky's law: if you have a better idea, put down your laundry, move to L.A., and get on *The Tonight Show*.

"Oh, it's nothing to be alarmed about. We'll get back to you very quickly."

David: In March of '72, Dick planned to fly to L.A. and find a theater, no matter what. When I mentioned this to Dad, his response was, "Here's plane fare, you need to go, too." That was another fortunate thing. The first night Dick and I were in L.A., we were invited to dinner at the Beverly Hills home of our cousins, Jack and Shirley Brody, along with a dozen other relatives. After dinner, we showed some of the video bits from the show. Not such a good idea as I remember, since one of the videos featured the soundtrack to Walt Disney's *Lady and the Tramp*, dubbed over a grainy 1940s porn video of a woman being sodomized by a Doberman.

Jerry: You showed that?

David: I'm trying to recall what I was thinking at the time. But when I told Uncle Jack that we were looking for a theater, or a building we could turn into a theater, he had an idea for us. He was an anesthesiologist at the Beverly Glen Hospital and on the hospital board. They owned a vacant building a block east. It had been used as a drug rehabilitation center, and he suggested it as a possibility. So the next day, Dick and I drove over to check it out. It was a complete mess, but I thought it was perfect. There was a large room, which was more than big enough for a theater, and even a second-floor apartment where we could all live!

> **DICK CHUDNOW**
> I believe in serendipity, that if things are going to happen, then things like this will happen for you. So David's uncle said, "If you want to fix that up so that it's up to code, as far as plumbing, electricity, and everything, then you can have it for $600 a month." And it was a huge place!

"I've never been so scared. And besides, I'm twenty-six and I'm not married."
"Well, to be honest, I've never been so scared. But at least I have a husband."

Jim: David was raving about this perfect building when he returned from L.A., but I was still on the fence about whether or not to go. Steve DeVries, the head of the law firm I worked for, called me in one day. He wanted to know more about what was going on and if I was leaving. I asked his opinion. He said, "Quit waffling. Make a decision. You're old enough. If this is what you want to do with your life, then just do it." My dad was gone by then, and my mom was living in Washington, DC, so it was something I really needed to hear from an adult.

Jerry: I thought all the lawyers were against it.

"Stan, go upstairs to the tower and get a runway diagram.
Terry, check down on the field for emergency equipment."

Jim: They probably were. But DeVries was a great guy. He said, "It's time for you to get on with your life." That helped. But truthfully I think the overwhelming reason why I decided to move to L.A. with everyone was my lifelong inability to say no.

David: The year before, when I told Dad I wanted to quit the real estate firm and move to Madison to do the theater, he simply said, "Well, when you're twenty-one, you're as smart as you're ever going to be. So you might as well try it." I used to think my dad was so smart because he always had something wise to say. And he was, but a lot of that was just having lived a long time.

Jim: Picking L.A. was relatively easy. *The Tonight Show* had originated in New York, but when Carson moved in 1972 to L.A., it solidified our decision. Plus, the average temperature in New York in March is 36 degrees, in L.A. it's 72.

Jerry: I remember thinking, *If we could be on* The Tonight Show, *just once, I could die and have lived a good life.* I mean, I'd always have *that.* I could always tell people, "I was on *The Tonight Show.*"

David: And your tombstone could read, "Jerry Zucker. He was on *The Tonight Show.*"

Jerry: Or "Jerry Zucker—in death as in life, he's just not that deep." I also thought it would be more pleasant to starve in Los Angeles than New York.

Jim: Plus, Chudnow said, "I don't care *where* you guys are going, *I'm* going to California." And Dick was the star of the show. For me personally, I didn't care which coast. I just knew that I had narrowly missed being involved the summer before, and I really didn't want to miss out on whatever lay ahead.

Jerry: That June of 1972, each of us agreed to put up $3,000 to start the theater in L.A., so we had a total of $12,000 to make it work. It would have to last us three months, because that's how long we figured it would take us to build the theater and start selling tickets.

Jim and Joan, circa 1966

Jim: I still had one lingering reservation about the move to California. For several years in college I had dated a girl named Joanie Dickinson. She was bright, fun, beautiful. We were in love. After she graduated she moved to Denver, and eventually we broke up. But I was still in love. So I gave her a call and asked if she would meet me for lunch at the airport in Denver. I was so nervous. At the airport restaurant, I explained that I had hooked up with some guys from Milwaukee, we had started a theater group in Madison, and we were going to move to L.A. But, I said, I'd pass on the whole thing if she would come back to Milwaukee and marry me. I still have this indelible memory of the plane back to Milwaukee taking off. I looked out at the speeding tarmac and thought, *Gosh, I guess I'm moving to California.*

CHAPTER 7

HOLLYWOOD

A lot of comedies in the last thirty years have wanted to be *Airplane!* But most of those movies took the wrong message from *Airplane!* They were gag, gag, gag, gag, where *Airplane!* is really structured, driving the story along all the time. In a weird way it's like a Beatles movie. It looks like the easiest thing in the world, but there's a lot of sweat and blood that went into it. Seeing the movie for the first time taught me a great lesson: You've got to play comedy as if it's deadly serious. You've got to play weirdness as if it's the most normal thing in the world.

PATTON OSWALT

Jerry: In Milwaukee, we rented a U-Haul truck, loaded up all our belongings, and left for Los Angeles. It was June 1.

David: Mom told us later she cried on the driveway as we pulled away. But Dad had consoled her: "Don't worry, honey, they'll be back in six months."

Jerry: No, that's why she cried, because she thought we'd be coming back.

Jim: My mom's guesstimate was three months. She told me not to give up my apartment lease. She'd given up on her dream of me going to medical school and was clinging to the hope that I could at least keep the Ford Fairlane 500. Our first stop was Madison, where we took apart the stage and control room, salvaged every two-by-four and sheet of plywood, and loaded everything—including seventy chairs, video equipment, piano, and carpets—onto the U-Haul truck.

Milwaukee June 1: "We're going to L.A.!"

Jerry: On the way out of Madison, we drove past my college graduation ceremony. Our sister, Susan, is the oldest, and was the first to graduate, so we all went to that. Then David was the president of his senior class and gave a speech, so we all went to that. By the time it was my turn, nobody was interested, including me.

David: We drove in caravan, Dick in his car with a friend, Jerry and me in each of our cars.

Jim: And I drove the U-Haul, since all I had was my Honda 350 motorcycle. It fit nicely on the truck with the chairs and equipment from the theater.

Jerry: That was before cell phones, so every morning we'd pick a place on the map, meet there at night, and look for a cheap motel.

"Hey, Larry, where's the forklift?"

David: We stayed in two rooms, two beds in a room, but since there were five of us, we had to rotate nights when two of us had to share a bed.

Jim: One night, David and I were sharing a bed. The next morning, we woke up and our arms and legs were completely entangled in each other. David opens his eyes, and out of a dead sleep, says to me, "What does this mean?"

David: Another time, we were in one of those diners along the way, and the waitress comes up to us and says, "Hey! Are you guys the Kentucky Fried Theater?" And we all lit up, and we said, "Yes! How did you . . . know?" How could she have possibly known? We had such dreams of being famous—a sense of destiny—so when the waitress said she recognized us, we rationalized, well, maybe word about KFT had traveled all the way to this tiny diner!

Jerry: As it turned out, Jim had put the waitress up to it.

David: When we found out, we were so aggravated! We all kind of laughed, but Jerry and I were not all that happy about it.

Jim: Gosh, I didn't know until now that you guys were so upset.

Jerry: We got speared on our own ambition.

David: We were embarrassed.

Rock Springs, Wyoming

Jim: I'm sure that wasn't my intention. It was probably more of our whole philosophy: let's not take anything—including ourselves—too seriously.

"We have clearance, Clarence." "Roger, Roger. What's our vector, Victor?"

Jerry: Here's what it was. David and I had bigger egos and more wild ambition about the whole showbiz thing than Jim. I think Jim had decided he was going to do this because he liked it, and it seemed better than not doing it. But David and I were hell-bent on making it, and Jim always found creative ways of bringing us back to reality.

Jim: For me, the stakes weren't all that high. My life had already been pretty humbling—especially with the downgrade from medical or legal scholar to college dropout to private eye. A failed theater venture would probably have fit nicely on my résumé. Plus, it's not like we had families at home we had to feed, or that we were going off to war. If for some reason it didn't work out, my plan was to travel around the United States and write a book about the best jogging and fishing parks in America. Did you guys have a Plan B?

David: Definitely not. I mean, if someone ever asked me what I'd do if we didn't make it, I'd just respond with a stupid joke like, "Well, I always have my dad's mattress business to fall back on." But in reality, I never considered for a minute we wouldn't make it. Never entered my mind that it was impossible, or even that there were long odds. I thought there was nothing that could stop us, that we had an original style and material better than anyone else. There was nothing else to do but this.

Diamond in the rough, but still a junkyard

Jerry: I didn't have a fallback position. I didn't think that far ahead. I've always been an optimist, and this was a great adventure. Life was good. Why ask questions?

David: The last leg of the trip west was Las Vegas to L.A. Once there, we got off at the Overland exit off the 10 freeway and stopped at the Beverly Glen Hospital to pick up the keys to the building that would become the new Kentucky Fried Theater. Then we drove a block east to 10303 West Pico.

Arrival on Pico Blvd. Jim wishing Joanie had said yes.

Jim: The outside was all green and purple peeling paint. Inside was worse. Everything was covered in graffiti. It looked more like a crack house than a medical facility.

David: I think Jim may have been a little disappointed, since I had exaggerated to everyone how great the place was. Back in Madison, he seemed to be on the fence about quitting his job and leaving, so I had painted a rosy "streets are paved with gold" picture of the building. I had talked it up the same way to Chris Keene, but with no success.

Jerry: It was an indoor junkyard. The kind of thing you'd expect to see just before the wrecking ball hit. I think there's a picture of Jim sitting on the curb, in the overgrown weeds, in shock.

Jim: I honestly don't remember being disappointed. Mostly I remember thinking, *So this is what smog is.* I had never been to L.A. before and I would ask Chudnow about smog. Did you need to use your windshield wipers? Could you drive through it? Did you need to turn on your headlights? Finally, I had the answer. It wasn't that bad.

David: But in my mind, this was paradise. At worst a "before" picture. I couldn't wait to get started.

Jim: Then we walked upstairs into the apartment. There were three bedrooms and a small dining room which could possibly fit a bed. The walls were covered with obscene graffiti, there was no water or electricity, the sinks and bathtub were caked with grime, and the whole place reeked from dog shit on the kitchen floor. But at least I knew what smog was.

"Let me see your tongue."

Jerry: But the crappy mess was just going to take a lot of crappy work. Finding a building with that much space on Pico Boulevard, for like $600 a month, was another monstrous piece of good luck.

Jim: Well, for Jerry it was very much like the college apartment he had just left in Madison.

Jerry: No, the Madison apartment had toilets.

> **DICK CHUDNOW**
> The building was on Pico Boulevard, which, if you don't know L.A., is a major thoroughfare into town, and it was on a big lot with parking, a block away from 20th Century Fox. It couldn't have been in a better location. Only about a mile from the UCLA campus. It was amazing that we were basically just given this place for $600, because we lived there! All of us lived upstairs for $600, in L.A.! It took a while to get it cleaned up, though. Jerry and David were sort of construction guys. We basically painted and cleaned up, and we got it ready.

Jerry: At the time, they were using it to store hundreds of extra hospital beds, so for the first week we slept on those. We bought a Coleman stove to cook on. Does anybody really care about this kind of detail?

David: They don't, but I do. The beds were stacked four high. We had to climb up to the top and be careful not to roll over in our sleep. The very next day, we began hammering and nailing. I knew carpentry from my days in construction, and Jerry could do electrical work and plumbing. How, I never knew.

Jerry: For some reason that always fascinated me, and I was good with my hands. Not with women or anything useful, but I liked figuring out how stuff worked.

David: Jerry sewed curtains for the stage and even a couch that he stuffed with foam rubber.

Jerry: Well, I'd, um, hang out there with my mixed martial arts friends before our rugby games.

Jim: Dick and I would follow instructions. Plus I was the designated grocery shopper and cook.

David: I made our beds, literally, out of two-by-fours, and then we put mattresses from the drug rehab center on top of the plywood.

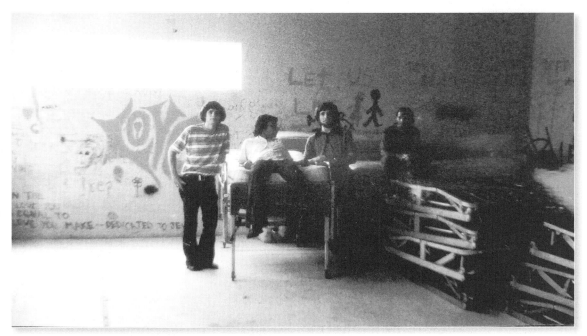

First night in L.A.: The place was filled with hospital beds.

Jim: How we all didn't die from hepatitis C is a miracle. After a week, we moved into the apartment and started work on the theater.

Jerry: Jim would knock off work at about three to go to the market and buy dinner. Every afternoon he'd cook a roast or something, and we'd all have dinner outside, on the rooftop space off the kitchen.

Ready to renovate, June 1972

The first week: Jim painting windows

Jim's car: Bob's MG

Rooftop meal: There was no dining room.

Jim: L.A. was so different. Beaches. Perfect weather. Vanity license plates. They didn't have those in Wisconsin back then, so even they were a discovery. When I realized I was jeopardizing my life just having a motorcycle in L.A., I bought an old Chevy. I got vanity plates that said, "Bob's MG." People would pull up next to me at red lights and say, "Hey, buddy, that's not an MG." And I'd say back to them, "Well, I'm not Bob."

David: Occasionally, we'd get invited to a party. At one in West Hollywood, I realized I still had my measuring tape clipped to my belt. Jim got introduced to a girl with bright green hair, tattoos, and a lot of piercings, and all he could think of to say was, "What do you hear from home?"

Jim: Of course, today, she'd just blend.

Jerry: And movie stars. The first one I ever saw was Walter Matthau. I walked out of the AVCO Theater in Westwood, and there he was, just standing there, like a normal person would stand outside of a movie theater. It was so strange.

Jim: Once, we were invited to a rehearsal for *Laverne & Shirley*. We were sitting in the audience, which was pretty empty, and they ran a scene for the first time. Everybody laughed. Then they ran the scene a second time. Not as many laughs, but there were two guys standing over in the corner who were laughing really hard. And they ran the scene again, and these guys in the corner laughed just as hard. This kept happening. Eventually, we asked our friend, "Who are those two guys?" And he said, "Oh, those are the writers."

PETER FARRELLY

I remember when I came out to L.A. to work with them, I'd lived there for about a month, and I knew more places to go than they did . . . and they'd been there for years! They'd be, like, "Where are you going?" "Oh, I'm gonna go to the Crush Club." "Where's that?" "You know, the Crush Club! It's Friday night!" No. They didn't know it. They never got out! They were exactly the same guys: they'd work, they'd go home, they'd shoot hoops, and they'd go to bed.

Jerry: We did have a party one night, out on the rooftop deck, and for some reason we decided to hire an accordion player. Not like Weird Al or anything, just an old polka guy. People found it strange, but nobody said anything. They just assumed that that's what people from Milwaukee did.

David: We put out a bunch of inedible hors d'oeuvres, stuff like slices of raw potato or lemon peel on a fancy toothpick. Jerry even made a big Jell-O mold in a Pyrex oven dish with a whole raw fish floating inside. I think we eventually served real food.

> **PETER FARRELLY**
>
> I wanted to work with ZAZ, because they were telling and living the whole story. I loved what they were doing. Like, the first time we met, they gave us the address, and we showed up, and the office door said, "Dr. Milton J. Flausner, DDS." We were, like, "What the fuck . . . ?" So we're walking down, asking people, "Do you know where the ZAZ office is?" But no, nobody knew where it was. And finally I opened that door, since they'd given me that address . . . and that was it!

Jerry: We were having a blast. But our main goal was getting the show up and running before we ran out of money.

Jerry operating nail gun: it was so loud he had to use ear muffs.

Construction: Famous Jewish carpenter legends.

Jim: We were pretty confident about the material. We had two successful shows in Madison, and between them we had plenty of great jokes. We just planned to use the best bits. I think the only thing we were not confident about at that time was replacing Chris Keene.

Jerry: Keene was a brilliantly talented comic actor who also played the piano. So we had bought an old upright piano in Madison, put it right on the stage, and integrated it into the show.

David: We even used the piano as a prop. In the courtroom, it became the judge's bench.

Jim: When we needed accompaniment, he would just hop over, play what he needed to play, and then he'd be on to something else. Keene's sense of humor perfectly matched ours.

Jerry: We pleaded with Chris to come to L.A. with us, but he was struggling to make the decision. I think there was a girl involved. We even offered him a full partnership.

Jim: We thought the show would fall apart without him.

David: I wrote a long letter to him, telling him how the show was going to be a hit, how we were going to be on national television and eventually do movies. I laid out exactly what was going to happen in the next ten years. I thought it would be so convincing he would change his mind for sure. So, I'm walking from the theater to the corner mailbox, and strangely feeling worse and worse with every step. By the time I got to the mailbox I was literally shaking. I turned around, went back to the theater, and threw away the letter. I wish now I'd saved it!

"They bought their tickets. They knew what they're getting into. I say, let 'em crash."

CHAPTER 8

STUCKER

In the middle of the summer of 1980, I heard the trio of goofballs that made *Kentucky Fried Movie* had just made a disaster movie spoof titled *Airplane!* I was a big fan of disaster movie extravaganzas and movie spoofs. So a disaster movie spoof by those Kentucky Fried idiots, was a run—don't walk—cinematic experience. And on July 11th (yes, my records are that exact), I went to The Mann's Old Town Mall theatre to see their latest lewd, crude, rude, and shrewd monstrosity. And I can honestly say, I had never seen a motion picture that managed to cram in as many jokes and gags per-foot-of-film as "*Airplane!*"

(nor have I ever again).

QUENTIN TARANTINO

"And Leon's getting laaaaaarger!"

David: It's impossible to watch *Airplane!* and not notice Stephen Stucker. Time and again, people comment on "that guy." He totally goes against the grain of the movie. What's he doing there? When we watch it now, he *is* the second half of the movie.

Jerry: Stucker was the only one who could write for Stucker. Every joke in *Airplane!* was written into the script over the years. Almost nothing was improvised. But we couldn't write the kind of outrageous lines we needed for Stephen, so we'd call him and read him the setups, and he'd fire back all these great punch lines. There was no one else like him.

David: Back in the theater days, Steve would sneak up behind our friend Bob Weiss (a film producer), jiggle his stomach, and say, "Would anyone like a rooooooooooollllll and coffee?"

> **JIMMY KIMMEL**
> Maybe my favorite quotable bit from the film is "And Leon's getting laaaaaarger!" Because it's so silly. And so unnecessary, and so unrelated to anything else that's going on.

> **BILL HADER**
> Stephen Stucker was such a scene-stealer in *Airplane!*, and it's so unfortunate that he passed away so young, because for a movie that has so many amazing lines, so many people quote his stuff. He's like Fred Willard in *Best in Show*, where almost every line is a killer.

Jerry: I have a distinct memory of the moment we first heard about Stephen Stucker. We were at a party with our friends David Steinberg—the personal manager, not the comedian—and Arnold Lipsman, a publicist.

Jim: Steiny was an early inspiration for me. My first memory of him is from when I was eleven. I was playing in a basketball league. My teammates and I arrived at the gym a little early and stood along the sidelines as the game before ours was ending. With ten seconds to go, one kid got fouled and went to the free throw line. If he made the shot, his team would win. That was Steiny. As the ref handed him the ball, he took a deep breath and said to the ref, "Would you say this is a pretty high-pressure situation?" The ref looked at him like he was nuts. "If I miss, will I get depressed—have emotional problems?" Totally flummoxed. "Will my teammates be able to forgive me?" The ref had no clue. It was life changing. It touched my soul. I remember thinking, I gotta meet this guy. Later in high school we wound up being friends and are to this day. A couple nights ago Steiny and I went out for dinner. When the waiter came to take our orders Steiny said he was torn between two dishes. He asked the waiter to make the choice and surprise him.

Jerry: We mentioned to Arnold and Steiny that we were having a hard time finding a funny piano player. Both of them immediately said, "Stucker!" and started laughing hysterically. "Oh, you've got to meet Stucker!"

David: We arranged for him to come to the theater and audition. I remember seeing him for the first time from the second-floor kitchen window. An orange VW Beetle drives up, and this tall guy gets out wearing two-tone leather hot pants. My heart sank.

Jim: I was twenty-eight at the time, and I'm sure I had never known an outed gay man in my life. But this guy just pranced in, wearing skin-tight black and gold leather hot pants, thong sandals, and this black lamé shirt that was wide open, with lots of jewelry.

David: The old piano from Madison was sitting in the middle of all the construction, covered by a tarpaulin. Stucker walked right up to it, threw the tarpaulin aside, sat down, and started playing, and he was brilliant.

Jim: He played Elton John's "Take Me to the Pilot." It was as though the piano were levitating. I had never seen or heard anything like it.

DICK CHUDNOW
This guy walks in wearing basically a leotard cut down to the navel, with his hairy chest showing, and he's entirely in sequins. I can't remember if his face was sequined, but the entire outfit, chest and everything, was in sequins! The gayest guy I've ever met. And one of the most hysterical. Stucker was just out there.

Jim: He was as outrageously funny as he was a gifted pianist. He was from Cleveland, and he'd been a soloist with the Cleveland Symphony Orchestra.

David: He wasn't what we were looking for at all. I mean, not even close. But we may have figured that at the very least, he'd be a terrific piano player. And, in comparison, everyone else who auditioned just seemed dull. He was too funny for us to not take the chance.

Jerry: We were so committed to the idea of playing everything straight, and then Steve comes in, and he was just this outrageous and uncontrollable personality! Even the way he stood; his feet were always in a ballet pose. That was his default position. He was so different, but exactly what we needed.

Jim: It was an adjustment, not for Steve, but for us. In one early rehearsal, Dick actually had to kneel down, grab his feet and try to straighten them, saying "Steve! This way." We were trying to get him to be a little bit more like us. Wrong!

David: By early August, we had made enough progress on building the theater to be able to start rehearsals. Our construction became focused on creating a control room and box office, and decorating the lobby. Instead of the usual headshots of cast members, we put up giant pictures of us as kids.

Jerry: We also sold posters. One was a romantic image of Jim and a girl holding hands on the beach with a slightly altered version of the famous Fritz Perls quote: "I am not in this world to live up to your expectations, and you are not in this world to live up to mine. And if by chance we find each other, it's beautiful."

David: The actual theater space was a stage and three white walls. Pretty plain. So we put up two plaster cherubs on opposite walls, three feet from the stage, to represent an ornate, 1920s rococo movie palace. I don't know if anybody got the joke, but it was there.

Jerry: I think there were a lot of jokes that nobody got. We were good at that. I'm not being self-deprecating; we just tried a lot of strange things.

Jim: In the restroom, we made a metal insert in the toilet bowl that had electrical sensors in it, sensitive to pressure. It was connected to an electrical board and lights

I am not in this world
To live up to your expectations,
And you are not in this world
To live up to mine;
You are you,
And I am I;
And if by chance
We should find each other,
We'll fuck our brains out.

over the tank. The idea was that, if you peed on certain parts of it, it would light up and ring bells like a pinball machine. But I don't know that it ever worked.

Jerry: No, it never worked. It was an incredibly stupid idea.

David: But it was constructed. We were actually going to do it. I know the word "insanity" is overused, but this, I mean it's hard to believe we ever did this. Later, I think we used it as a reminder that "You don't need to do all that if the show is funny."

Jerry: But the idea was always "Leave no stone unturned." We wanted the satirical insanity to start the minute you walked in the door. Even the program—nothing in it was true.

Lobby decor: theatergoers in front of blowup photo of Jerry

Open for business.

Kentucky Fried Theater

presents

V·E·G·E·T·A·B·L·E·S!

10303 West Pico Boulevard
556-2663

WOOD

You can make many things of wood. The wood from cigar boxes can be turned into pins, buckles, and buttons. Dogs, penguins, and other animals can be whittled from small pieces of wood. Larger pieces can be combined with the smooth ends of orange crates to make homes for your animal friends. Birdhouses, bookcases, and magazine racks are good wood-working projects. Wooden spools, button molds, and dowel sticks can be easily made into a child's toy.

When you are out of doors, look for interesting pieces of wood. Driftwood, old roots and burls can be carved into centerpieces or lamp bases. Small limbs that have fallen on the ground but have not rotted make excellent hike sticks.

Ask someone to show you how to saw wood and clamp it safely into a vise, how to hold a nail when driving it with a hammer. If a hammer head seems to loosen a little, hold it upright and strike the end of the handle on a bench or block.

ROUND AND ABOUT LOS ANGELES

Things to do after the show:

★ Visit a dairy and learn how milk is handled and prepared for delivery.

★ With others, plan a series of window displays on home safety.

★ Tell what constitutes a colony of bees and how it lives.

★ Play a game using the language of another country.

★ From a list of the main occupations of people in Los Angeles, choose several which interest you.

★ Take part in choral reading.

★ Walk across the room in such a way that your friends can guess the type of character you represent.

★ Discuss with your dentist what you can do to make your teeth more attractive.

★ Help plan and start a library.

PAUL BASTA (Technical director) 25, began his offstage career in Reno, Nevada, where his father was chief engineer with the NASA Mercury Space Program. He moved to Los Angeles in 1960 after his parents and two sisters were tragically killed in a fire. He received his bachelor of science degree in electronics at UCLA where he did exploratory research in the field of Fibro kinetics. During his current film graduate work at UCLA, he has served as technical advisor for several theatrical productions including "My Sister Eileen," "She Stoops to Conquer," and "Flames in the Attic."

KFT Program: not really a program

Jim: "Things to do after the show" was taken directly from the *Girl Scout Handbook*. I don't recall what we were doing with a *Girl Scout Handbook*. To this day I wonder what people reading that in the audience thought.

Jerry: The cast was listed "In order of appearance"—Clean Cut, Orderly, Messy, Disheveled, etc.

David: Our mindset was to make fun of convention. That's just how we were.

Jim: We set up 8mm film projectors so that when people walked into the theater, loud music would play to a projected loop of Frisbee throwers on one wall, tossing to people catching them on the opposite wall. On the front screen an audience on another film loop watched this back and forth like a tennis match.

David: By this time Lisa Davis, from the Madison show, had come out, so we had our full troupe in L.A., and we started rehearsing. Stucker added a lot of bits that only he could do.

Jim: Ann-Margret was a big star back then, married to an actor named Roger Smith. There was a famous incident in Las Vegas where she was performing and she fell off the

"Auntie Em, Uncle Henry, Toto, it's a twister, it's a twister!"

"Where did you get that dress? It's awful! And those shoes and that coat . . . geeeeez!"

stage and was injured. So Stucker would stride out onstage, sit down at the piano, and say, "Ladies and gentlemen, live from Las Vegas, Ann . . . Margret!" And he'd get up from the piano and impersonate her singing a song from *Bye Bye Birdie*, and then suddenly he'd lose his balance and fall off the stage into the first row of the audience, and scream in a high voice, "OHHHH!!! Roger! Roger! My face! My face!" He was just so outrageous.

David: In September the theater was finished, we were done rehearsing, and finally we were ready to open the doors. We scheduled a preview, and with the help of David Steinberg and Lipsman managed to attract a full house.

"There's a sale at Penney's!"

Jerry: The show was great in a Midwest college town, but this was L.A. Steve was hysterical, but so different than anything we had done before. Was this all really going to work?

Jim: But as it turned out, Stucker was fantastic. From his opening overture through his crazy poems, everything he did, he was unquestionably the star. People just loved him. They roared every time he raised an eyebrow. I don't think anybody knew the rest of us were onstage. And we finally said, "Oh, now we get it."

BOB WEISS (Producer on *Kentucky Fried Movie*)
I was always up for a good laugh, and not knowing really anything about KFT other than that someone had recommended it, I went down to Pico Boulevard. I believe it was the weekend they had their official opening. I didn't go with anyone the first time. I just took myself, and I was blown away by the show. The show was outrageously funny, and Stucker was hilarious. The guys couldn't figure out who I was, because I kept coming back to the show. They later told me their best guess was that I was either some big producer or a narc.

Jerry: We learned a lot from Stephen's success in the show. We weren't in Wisconsin anymore. We had to expand our vision of what we were, loosen up a little. He was such a bright light. We were the cake; he was the frosting. The combination worked. The same in *Airplane!* He wasn't one of the characters we were making fun of. He was making fun of everyone else. We dropped this outrageously flamboyant gay man into a sea of cardboard straight men and let him wreak havoc. We never would have written that part if we hadn't witnessed his magic firsthand.

Jim: For one of the sketches, the whole cast would be onstage, and we'd sing John Lennon's "Imagine," but we'd change the lyrics to things like, "Imagine no insurance salesmen," and imagine no this and imagine no that.

BOB WEISS

One of the great things about the theater was the interactivity. Things like an hour into the show the lights come up, and all of a sudden a ringing phone is lowered down from the ceiling. And it kept ringing until somebody picks it up, and the guy goes, "Huh? Yeah." You hear him talking, you don't know what's being told to him. But then he hangs up the phone and announces, "It's a fifteen-minute intermission." And then the laugh comes. A huge laugh.

A phone lowered: *"I'm supposed to tell you there's a fifteen-minute intermission."*

KFT troupe, August 1972: Jerry, Lisa Davis, Jim, Steve, Dick, David

David: At "Imagine no insurance salesmen," Jim would walk offstage, and as he left he'd hand a business card to a guy in the first row.

Jim: And then we'd say, "Imagine no homosexuals." And everybody in the audience, you could see their eyes dart right to Stucker . . . but then Jerry would look down and slink off the stage, as if he'd just been outed.

David: Mind you this was 1972, when attitudes were just beginning to evolve.

Jim: That first preview was a complete success, but the first audiences were so small that we felt almost awkward performing. I remember one night there were more of us onstage than people in the audience.

Jerry: How can you do a show in front of just ten people?

> **DICK CHUDNOW**
> I think David went to the UCLA campus to put up posters and, of course, to meet college girls. But word of mouth is the best kind of publicity, and people told other people.

David: So we took the whole group of them on a tour of the theater, backstage areas, our upstairs apartment, etc.

Jerry: We placed a few ads in college newspapers, but it was mostly word of mouth. We also got some good reviews, particularly a very enthusiastic one from the *L.A. Times*.

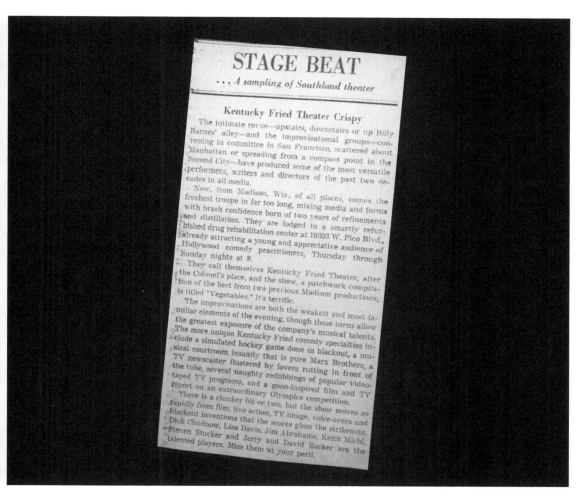

David: And one from the L.A. *Free Press*.

THE
Burning
BUSH

JACK S MARGOLIS

Mankind has reached the end of its language tether. I saw something Sunday night that was so funny, that by intermission I was laughing so hard and so long that I was gagging and choking and tears were running down my care-worn face. It's a group called Kentucky Fried Theatre. and I have no words that can describe them adequately. "Funny. zany. outrageous. innovative. brilliant ..." forget it. These words have been weakened through senility.

The group is made up of five men and a woman. Jim Abrahams. Dick Chudnow. Lisa Davis. Steven Stucker. Jerry Zucker. and David Zucker.

I've decided that I'm not a critic, and I can't really do justice to the shows that I see. I can only hope that Chris Van Ness. whose opinion I respect. and other critics in LA who are also very good. like Charles Champlin and David Sheehan. go to see Kentucky Fried Theater. and do a review of it.

But I do know this: I've been a comedy freak all my life. I've made a good living writing it. most of my friends are comedy writers or performers. and there's no other world I know more about than the world of comedy. And Kentucky Fried Theater made me laugh more and longer than anything I can remember.

The six members of the group. along with Keith Michl who does the technical stuff. built the theatre themselves and all live together over it.

They're all young. but not once did they do anything which could be considered sophomoric or amateurish.

This has been a really good week for me. I worked hard. went to some great parties. and balled some super chicks (one of whom said. "I'm sure some chicks have blown your mind. but have you ever had one who's blown your nose?" I said. "No." She said. "Open your mouth." I did. and then she put her mouth over my nose and blew into it. I recommend it highly.) But the best part of the whole week was Sunday night. when my friend Alan Mandel took me to see Kentucky Fried Theater. They open officially October 7. and will be doing shows every Thursday. Friday. and Saturday night after that. They're located at 10303 West Pico Blvd. (near Avenue of the Stars) and you can call 556-2663 for reservations ($3.00). It'll be the best two hours you're ever likely to have.

Jesus. I've just realized something. If something comes along that I like better than Kentucky Fried Theater. what in hell can I say about them?

KABC TV News, LA: the controversial billboard.

David: Despite the rave reviews, our audience remained pretty small.

Jim: Then there was the Arab oil embargo. Gas prices skyrocketed to eighty-four cents per gallon. I worried whether people would still be able to afford to drive to our show.

Jerry: We couldn't afford to advertise in the *L.A. Times*, so we tried to drum up a little free publicity. There was a billboard in the empty lot next to the theater. We rented it for a month. In big, bold letters, it said, "This is it! Kentucky Fried Theater!"

Jim: And then we got a bunch of our friends together and staged a huge demonstration. The "protesters" marched in a circle around the empty lot, chanting "Save. The. Sign!" They claimed that a big corporation was planning to tear down the sign and plant a tree in its place.

David: The story played on the KABC news and on the front page of the *L.A. Times* Calendar section. Suddenly, our Friday and Saturday night shows were packed.

Jerry: We used to do a series of blackouts in the show. For the first one, the announcer would say, "A fried egg!" And I would basically just hit the floor and start quivering, and then flip over on my back and quiver some more.

David: And then the announcer would say, "A fountain." Stucker would come out, do a ballet pose, and then spray a stream of water through his teeth into the first row. For the third blackout, the announcer would say simply, "A pair of shoes," and when the lights came on, in the middle of the stage there'd be a pair of shoes on a chair. Right around this time, our friend Rich Markey came out from Milwaukee, and he'd hang out with us backstage.

> **RICH MARKEY**
> One night they couldn't find the pair of shoes, so in a panic they told me, "Go onstage, just stand there and don't do anything!" The announcer said, "Rich Markey." When the lights came up, there I was . . . who's that guy? And it was a bigger laugh than before. I did that for the next six months.

Jim: There's another bit where a couple onstage is watching a prerecorded newscast that's playing on the video monitor. Pretty quickly they start to make out and ignore the newscast. The newscaster starts watching *them*. As the couple's passion builds, the newscaster is joined by two technicians. The couple and the guys on TV all become equally aroused, and they all climax in unison.

Jerry: Mallory Sandler, who was our cousin, and I played the couple watching the newscast. One night, Mom and Dad were in town visiting and were joined in the audience by Mallory's parents. Although the skit was mostly a lot of very over-the-top hugging, the ending was a simulated blowjob, and I was dreading doing *that* in front of the family. And then I made the giant mistake of telling Jim about it. When the sketch ended, there was no blackout. I looked toward the wing and suddenly there's Jim—walking onstage—and introducing our parents to the audience. He had them stand, and gave a little speech about how nice it was that their kids were working together.

David: There was a lot of sexual humor in the show. Guys kept telling us that if they brought a date to the show they'd always get laid afterwards. They'd thank us.

Jim: Once you sat through that show with a date, there couldn't be any more inhibitions.

David: I remember how great we felt at midnight on Saturday.

Jim: Yeah, after the second show.

Jerry: Jim had a friend who was a dentist, and he would come to see the show and say, "You guys don't know how lucky you are. People hate coming to see me. They complain about the pain and are usually slow to pay. But you guys get paid in advance, they laugh the whole time, and after you're done they stand up and applaud."

David: And through all this, Steve stood out; he was the wild card. Audiences loved him. He was having the time of his life. But being the star of the show also had its drawbacks.

Jim: He'd had a pretty conservative upbringing in Cleveland, and my guess is that somewhere along the line, he couldn't take his role as a straight guy anymore. He came out to California and outed himself.

Actors Trod the Billboards

*"I think that I shall never see
A billboard lovely as a tree.
Indeed, unless the billboards fall
I'll never see a tree at all."*
—Ogden Nash

BY DAVID LARSEN
Times Staff Writer

You've heard, of course, about the group that wants to preserve wooden outhouses.

It's called the Birch John Society.

Well, now there's a group out in the Rancho Park area that supposedly wants to save billboards and ban trees.

Demonstrators were out in force Thursday, about a dozen of them, marching with placards around a vacant lot at 10303 West Pico Blvd.

The billboard on the lot isn't really being threatened.

But just in case somebody gets a bright idea and plans to replace it with a tree, they should be prepared to pack their trunk, to say nothing of the branches and leaves.

Actually, the whole thing was staged as a spoof by cast members from the adjacent Kentucky Fried Theater to celebrate the opening of their new production, "My Nose."

"We're so used to our billboard," explained actor Jerry Zucker. "If they ever tear it down for a tree, next thing you know there'll be children playing and birds singing. There goes the neighborhood."

Woodman, spare that billboard.

EVENING OUTLOOK

99th Year—22nd Issue   FOUNDED 1875
1540 Third Street—EXbrook 4-6731 UPton 0-5527
Member of Audit Bureau of Circulations and Subscriber to United Press International
Classified GL 1-1381 United Western Newspapers, Inc.
SANTA MONICA, CALIFORNIA, —Saturday, Oct 27, 1973—19A

36 PAGES—10c

Three Star

★ ★ ★

theater
by dave berman

Schizophrenia on stage

Anyone new to the Los Angeles theater scene who found himself at "The Casting Couch" at the Next Stage in Hollywood one night and "Vegetables," a multi-media revue at the Kentucky Fried Theatre in West Los Angeles on the next, would come away schizophrenic over the quality of work done here.

Probably neither are typical. "The Casting Couch" is terrible and "Vegetables" is excellent. The truth lies somewhere in between.

Choose your own adjectives — brilliant, fresh, zany, crazy, sharp, biting, clever, hysterical, raucous, riotous, etc., etc.—"Vegetables" is all of them. It's got more laughs per penny than any other show in town.

Launched nearly a year ago by a group of young University of Wisconsin students who converted a drug rehabilitation house at 10303 W. Pico Blvd. into the Kentucky Fried Theatre, it plays Thursdays, Fridays and twice on Saturdays to packed houses. Ever seen a line standing outside a small theatre? You'll see it at KFT.

Word has gotten around. The young, hip crowd, the kind that frequents nearby Westwood movie theatres, is out in force for an evening of pure fun.

And that's what they get. You never want it to end and when it does, after 90 minutes, it seems all too short.

The Zucker Brothers — David, Jerry and Steve — along with Jim Abrahams, Keith Michl and Mallory Sandler lampoon television, movies, commercials, newscasters, sportscasters, Broadway, sex, rock and roll, Middle America and themselves. Politics gets little attention, unless you see mediocrity and, banality as part of an overall political mentality (perhaps it's just the reflection of it).

Refreshingly, all their subjects are devastated — but without malice. Maybe it's because satire demands familiarity and the fact that we're familiar with the satirized subject implies some sort of subliminal affection for it. (If we hated TV commercials so much,

why don't we shut them off the first time and forget them? Instead, we learn them by heart and the satire works because of it.)

The evening opens with Steve Zucker — a madcap mugger sans pareil — sitting down at his upright piano, adjusting his rearview mirror, and meandering through a medley of off-key Broadway hits, leaving them beyond repair. Among other things, there's a "slide show" of the group's drive West, a parody of our media mania wherein the newscaster gets caught up with what his audience is doing while it's watching him, a mime of Adam meeting Eve for the first time and a ballet to "Tales of the Vienna Woods" with underarm deodorant spray cans providing counterpoint.

The execution is perfect: the characterizations are fresh and quickly created, the timing is right, the delivery clear and the pace slows down only long enough for the audience to catch its breath before it's off and running again.

You can't afford to miss this

Jerry: On the rare occasions when he thought an audience wasn't responding to the level he had come to expect, he would turn and glare at them while pretending to file his nails with an emery board. I think once he gave them the finger. But they laughed. They thought it was part of the show.

David: One night he did a lot more than flip off the audience. The night of the Sparkletts bottles.

Jerry: A group of dentists had bought out the entire house for a night; it was an older crowd.

Jim: They brought in their own wine and beer and maybe liquor, which they served during the intermission out in the lobby.

David: The reaction was quiet. A struggle to get laughs. In particular, I don't think they got Steve. And he hated when he wasn't getting laughs, approval. Steve wasn't someone you ever thought had a mean bone in his body. But there was a lot of stuff he held in. He was a sensitive guy.

Jerry: His parents never came out to see how he lived or watch him perform. And sometimes all the pain he held in would explode out. Maybe he saw a hundred disapproving fathers out there.

David: When the show finally ended, Steve was beside himself. He stayed onstage after we had gone into the greenroom and we could hear him screaming.

> **RICH MARKEY**
>
> He was yelling at the audience and cursing at them angrily and just really maniacally, screaming at them, "GET OUT! GET OUT! YOU MOTHERFUCKERS! I HOPE YOU ALL CRASH YOUR CARS AND DIE!" That kind of stuff. The audience was still filing out of the theater, but a few couples were straggling behind. I heard a guy say, "Don't talk like that in front of my wife!" And one of the guys really tried to back him off. And the wives pulled whatever remaining husbands were left out of the theater, so now there's nobody left in the audience.

David: Of course, we became alarmed. I ran around to the lobby and found a line of confused audience members exiting the theater. At this point I could hear, in addition to Steve's screaming, the sound of crashing glass.

Jerry: It was the Sparkletts bottles. The big five-gallon ones we used for the water dispenser in the lobby. In those days, they were made of glass, not plastic. I should add that although we had half a dozen of those glass Sparkletts bottles, we only used one, which Jim would fill each week from a garden hose.

David: That's, of course, back when the tap-water quality in L.A. was very high.

Jerry: Anyway, Steve was outside on Pico Boulevard, throwing glass bottles down on the concrete, one by one. There was glass and water everywhere.

David: Meanwhile, I'm out in the lobby trying to explain this to people, saying, "Nothing to worry about; it's all part of the show," with the sound of shouting and crashing glass in the background.

Jerry: Jim and I managed to get Steve back to the green room before he reached the point of physically assaulting the audience.

> **RICH MARKEY**
>
> Stucker ran out the backstage exit, with Jerry and Jim trailing after him. Cars were pulling out of the parking lot . . . and he was throwing five-gallon Sparkletts bottles at them! The first one landed in the middle of the street and shattered into a thousand pieces. Cars were swerving, trying to avoid it. I grabbed a broom and started sweeping up all the glass from the street.

David: By the time I got there, Jerry and Jim were trying to console Steve, who was sitting on the steps leading up to the stage, quietly sobbing.

Jerry: Apparently what had set him off was one of the dentists, most likely thinking he was joining in the spirit of fun, took a can of shaving cream and sprayed it on one of the balloons that Steve kept tied to the piano.

David: I sat down next to him. He put his head on my shoulder, choking back sobs, and said, "David, they put shaving cream on my balloon." After a glance at Jerry and Jim, I responded calmly with, "Well, under the circumstances, what else could you have done?"

Jerry: Everybody laughed. Even Stucker laughed.

Jim: Afterward, when all the dust had settled, he sat there, teary eyed, and he said, "It's just so hard being me."

JULIE HAGERTY

I loved Stephen. I adored him. He was a genius, brilliant and talented, and it was a great loss that we lost him when we did. We became great friends. Some years after *Airplane!*, Stephen and I drove cross-country together. I had bought an old Ford Cortina station wagon, but then I had to figure out how to get it home. I didn't know anything about buying cars, and neither did he. He was wearing hot pants and black Army boots and carrying a long cigarette holder. And I thought, *"Oh, lord, and we're driving cross-country? This isn't going to be conducive to stopping in some of the states we'll be in...."* Talk about a road movie. We'd stop and get Mile-High Pies. And back then you could smoke, so he had his cigarette holder with him all the time. At one point, it was nighttime, and he was driving and I was sleeping in the back. I don't know why, but we were in a hurry! So all of a sudden the car is bumping all over the place, and I wake up, and he's driving, he's smoking his cigarette, and he'd brought a battery-powered TV, so he was watching that while he was driving. I said, "Pull over! I'm driving!" I absolutely loved him, but when we got to Ohio, he wanted to stay with my mother, so I said, "Fine, you can stay with my mother. But I'm going on to New York!" So he stayed with my mom for a couple of weeks, ironing. He loved to iron.

CHAPTER 9

THE TONIGHT SHOW

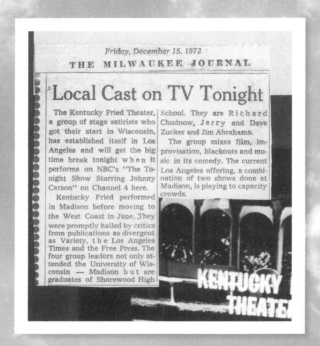

David and Jerry Zucker and Jim Abrahams came to Harvard to screen a rough cut of *Airplane!* When the screening came along and I met them, it really was just revelatory. I mean, I was good at getting through classes as a writer, but I'd never really thought about the fact that movies had writers, and that filmmakers were paid money to do this. It was a complete light bulb moment for me, one where I went, "Oh! This is something that maybe I should try!" Really, that catalyzed this whole progression that led me to make a short movie at Harvard and then set me off on a journey to Los Angeles, where I thought, Well, I'll give it a couple of years and try to be a writer and see what happens. Cut to many years later when it all worked out! That movie was completely responsible for starting me on my career journey.

CARLTON CUSE

Jerry: In December 1972, after doing the show for three months, we finally attained that impossible goal we had set for ourselves back in Madison: we made it on to *The Tonight Show*.

Jim: At the time, we considered ourselves not movie writers or directors, but a performing group. We were focused on that. In Madison, *The Tonight Show* had been our dream, but it turned out to be more of a nightmare.

Jerry: Before the show, I went up to the balcony to watch the rehearsal. I turned to my right, and there was Johnny Carson. He asked me if I was nervous. I said, "Yes." He smiled and said, "Don't be. You'll be fine." It was such a brief moment, but I felt like Gandhi had spoken to me.

David: Carson introduced us, but Mickey Rooney talked too long and they ran out of time. We got bumped. It was okay with us, because we got to meet George Foreman. They had to pay us for the night we got bumped, and then we got paid again for the night we were actually on. I think it was two or three hundred bucks.

Jim: So the next night, Joey Bishop was the guest host, and he gave us this terrible introduction where he says something like, "I've never met this next group but I hear they're from Milwaukee, and they're playing here at some little theater on Pico Boulevard. This is their first appearance ever on television, so I'm sure they must be scared shitless. Please welcome . . . the Kentucky Fried Theater!"

Jerry: It went downhill from there.

David: It wasn't so much that we were particularly terrible. We got big laughs from the studio audience. But our material was geared to our theater, and not to a television audience. All those other sketch groups that we thought we could top were looking better and better.

Jim: For decades, when I went back to Milwaukee, I had to apologize to the people who'd stayed up late that night.

Bewildered: *Tonight Show* guest host Joey Bishop reading the KFT introduction. *"They must be scared shitless."*

"Nervous?" "Yes."
"First time?" "No. I've been nervous lots of times."

Jerry: People would say to us, "Hey, we saw you on *The Tonight Show*." Then after a long pause, they'd add, "So, yeah, you were on that."

David: After appearing on a few more television shows, and audiences being underwhelmed, we made a joint decision with the networks not to appear on any more TV shows. I remember that there was a discussion among us to possibly try writing a movie script, but we had no idea what form that might take, so for the time being we focused on the theater.

Jerry: The show was humming along and we hated to turn people away, so we started adding more seats.

Jim: Because of fire code laws, you were only allowed to have 130 people in the theater, so we had a second version of the theater that could seat 140.

David: . . . with an additional row of seats in the center aisle.

Jim: Which was entirely illegal. Every once in a while, a fire inspector would come and inspect the building to make sure we were compliant with fire regulations, and we had this drill where we could almost instantly hide those extra ten chairs.

Jerry: We were like the guys changing tires at a NASCAR pit stop. We could do it that fast.

David: Actually, we hid an entire room! The entrance to it was disguised as a cabinet inside the greenroom. It was supposed to be a firewall.

BOB WEISS

After I'd seen the show ten times or something, I worked up the courage to talk to them because I was trying to figure out a way that we could work together. I remember meeting with them in the greenroom. And of course we were all trying to be adults, and trying to come off as, you know, professionals. So we're sitting there trying to move the ball forward, and all of a sudden somebody runs in and goes, "The fire marshal's here!" BOOM! He was still in the lobby, but the guys didn't wait to explain; they had already jumped out of their seats and started grabbing chairs. I thought it was a joke because all of a sudden they're all running around in a Chinese fire drill. I poked my head into the theater. Chairs were disappearing, aisles were being created, doors were being cleared. One of the guys threw chairs into a cabinet door in the greenroom which concealed a hidden room.

Jim: It was not very safe.

Jerry: It was completely safe. As long as there wasn't a fire.

David: Within a minute, we had cleared the center aisle of all the chairs and stashed them behind the false cabinet.

Jerry: It turned out the guy just needed to check the date on the fire extinguishers. He didn't pay any attention to the seats. But it had been a while since the last guy was there, so we needed the practice.

David: It was a good thing they never came back after we put the risers in the audience. That wasn't exactly legal either. Like the cardboard ceiling in Madison.

Jerry: I wonder what the statute of limitations is on this stuff.

David: Three to five years, I think. Unless it involves a death.

Jim: At least all of Jerry's electrical work was done to code. I think.

David: And luckily no one died.

Jerry: Wait. There was a code?

David: We were always living in fear of the fire marshal. There was this one guy who kept coming back. A real hard guy. Finally, Jim had enough and just told him outright. "Look, you're comin' in here every week, and pointing out all sorts of trivial shit, and frankly, this is just harassment!" To my surprise, the guy just mumbled something and left. And never came back. I was stunned.

"What a pisser!"

Jim: I guess I was just venting twenty-five years of frustration with authority figures. He had actually just pulled me aside and asked me why I didn't become a doctor like my parents wanted.

BOB WEISS

That was a tremendous icebreaker. There was no posing after that. Until then, we were all trying to posture a little bit, but after that it was revealed the emperor really wasn't wearing any clothes. It would have taken God knows how many meetings and personal interactions, but instead there was this shared experience, funny as hell, and it was perfect.

David: That was about the biggest crisis we had, until we had a *real* crisis.

DICK CHUDNOW

It's not like people weren't telling me, "Oh, don't get married." As a matter of fact, I had a rash on my wiener, and I thought I had syphilis or something, but I went to the doctor, and he said, "No, it's just an allergic reaction. Are you going out with anybody?" I said, " Yeah." He said, "Well, don't get married to her. You're allergic to her." This is the doctor! So everybody said, "Don't get married!"

Jerry: Everything happened very fast. He met this woman, they got married, and announced she wanted to be in the show.

Jim: It was a little scary, and a little sad. After all our years together as friends, roommates, goof-offs, and business partners . . .

Jerry: In addition to the fact that none of us thought she had any talent, we would have had to replace Mallory, who had just replaced Lisa Davis in the show. Mallory was absolutely terrific, and we all loved her.

DICK CHUDNOW

My wife wanted to be part of the troupe. But she had no stage experience. I was in love. I couldn't say, "Sorry, I'm sticking with the guys." Even though I had seen what happened with Chris Keene, who stayed in Milwaukee and kind of regretted it, nothing was going to sway me.

David: Dick said, "Either she's in the show, or I quit." It was an ultimatum, and it came on a Monday when we had a show to do on Friday!

Jim: As hard as it was, we had to let Dick quit. But now we faced the problem of replacing—in the space of less than a week—a guy who was in practically every scene! And although Stucker was the frosting, Dick was the cake.

> **PAT PROFT**
> KFT was one of the hottest comedy tickets in town. It was an easy fit. We worked together a lot over the years. Same sense of humor. Midwestern humans not tainted by either coast.

Jerry: So that night we went to the Comedy Store to see Pat Proft, a brilliant stand-up and writer from Minnesota whose style of humor was similar to ours. We had seen him there a few times before, and he really made us laugh. After his set we asked him if he wanted to join the show.

Jim: He was genuinely funny and really comfortable onstage. Actually reminded us of Keene.

Pat Proft's first night: It worked!

"Alright, give me
Hamm on five, hold
the Mayo."

Jerry: Tuesday through Thursday, we worked Pat in. It was pretty intense. He had to learn the entire show in three days.

David: We thought Pat would be great, but we still had no idea what to expect. How the audience would react to a show without Chudnow was still a question. So it came time for the eight p.m. show Friday night, and we were all pretty nervous.

Jim: The show turned out to be amazing! One of the best audience reactions we ever had.

Jerry: I think that's not uncommon. When everybody is nervous about a new show or a big change, it creates a lot of energy and the audience can feel it. So, the following Monday, we had a meeting with Dick. We knew now it was possible to do the show without him, but we still wanted him back—under a few conditions. But there was one that he just couldn't accept.

> **DICK CHUDNOW**
>
> It came down to a vote where they said, "It's either her or us. You have to make a decision." They didn't want her coming around anymore. They likened it to a Yoko Ono situation.

David: He wasn't willing to come back under those conditions.

> **DICK CHUDNOW**
>
> And it turned out to be a disaster. It was too hard living in L.A. with her, so I moved back to Milwaukee. And that was a good thing. But there was a long period of depression. I was driving an ice cream truck after that, and I would drive along the streets of L.A. and see billboards for *Kentucky Fried Movie* or *Airplane!* That was hard. That took therapy to get over.

Jim: I think Dick would tell you that he went through hell after that. But the happy ending to the story is that he moved back to Milwaukee, and he opened a very popular comedy improv club called ComedySportz, where he still thrives.

David: I remember going back to Milwaukee to visit a few times, and we'd get together with Dick.

"I had to ask the guy next to me to pinch me to see if I was dreaming."

DICK CHUDNOW

It was the worst thing to happen and the best thing to happen, because if it hadn't happened, then I never would've gotten back to Milwaukee to start ComedySportz. Had I not left, I would've still been out in L.A., trying to get parts in movies and doing that struggle and probably doing more drugs than I was already doing! So it was a good thing. We have thirty-one cities now, and it's growing all the time. It's great because it's improv, and improv people are "yes, and" people. They say "yes" to everything. It's just a joy to be around them. So it all worked out well.

David: At first, when Dick left, it seemed like a disaster. A lot of problems do, at the time. But, taking the long view, it brought Pat Proft into our lives, who not only was great in the shows, but became our most important collaborator: head writer of the *Police Squad!* TV series, cowriter of the three *Naked Guns*, cowriter on *Hot Shots!*, *Hot Shots! Part Deux*, and the *Scary Movie* series. I'm working with Pat to this day.

Jim: The first weekend that Pat Proft was in the show, an incredible *L.A. Times* review came out. Up to that time, our audiences were sometimes full and sometimes not. From that moment on, there was never an empty seat.

DICK CHUDNOW

Eventually, we all got back on good terms. You know, it was hard for all of us. I remember Jim sent my father a letter saying, "He shouldn't be doing this, it's a mistake." Which didn't matter. But we were both at the high school reunion. And I saw Jerry when I went to L.A., and David, Jerry, and I—Jim couldn't make it—we all had lunch. I mean, I think they're all geniuses!

FRIDAY MORNING, JULY 6, 1973

STAGE BEAT
A Kentucky Fried Theater Delight

By now you've probably heard of the young semi-improvisional new group called "Kentucky Fried Theater," and if you've resisted seeing them out of the natural human perversity that stiffens in the face of such adjectives as "zany, innovative, outrageous," etc., you're missing out.

From the first moment Steven Stucker swirls out in ultraregal recital fashion, affixes a rear-view mirror on his upright so that he can view himself, and thunders out several heraldic Broadway overtures in increasingly elliptical, clinker-studded, mad-genius-gone-amok fashion through KFT's narrative of their drive west from Madison, Wis., in which they brave the trials of fatigue, distraction, fear and surreptitious flatulence, you're swept up in an hour-and-45 minute program that seems to last 30 seconds.

For charge, subtlety, economy, satirical bite, discipline—all those faintly academic terms which attempt to describe comedy elevated to art instead of refracted as manic dumb-show—this group is far superior to any like it. They move swiftly into the center of their situations and characters, and once their moment has been reached, out. No hanging on for extra laughs. No self-indulgence. Even the improvisations are astonishingly taut and brilliantly effective.

Of all the reasons for the collapsed spirit of American comedy through the last decade or so, one certainly has to be the disruption of a mass audience with a stable sense of self-identification. KFT comes out of Middle America. Sensitive to the burgeoning influence of the mass media, their humor is based largely on movie themes and the suffocating banality of most TV ads (one shows a man extolling, in perfectly straight narrative, the ease of shaving with a certain cream without having to use water, in the meantime cutting his face open until his eye falls out) and seems to point to a fresh common denominator for our experience, blasting a hatch open to relieve the stale air of our everyday lives.

Aside from extremely well-written material, a mixed-media presentation that for once is used to advantage instead of distraction, Stucker, Jim Abrahams, Dick Chudnow, Keith Michl, Jerry and David Zucker and Mallory Sandler, are excellent performers who dig the audience as much as the audience digs them. Be the first on your block to call 556-2663 and hurry on down to 10303 W. Pico Blvd. Thursdays at 8 p.m. and Fridays and Saturdays at 8 and 10:15 p.m., and receive, for a limited time only, your ticket stub back at no extra charge.

—LAWRENCE CHRISTON

CHAPTER 10

ZERO HOUR!

I was in high school when the movie came out, but I knew I'd seen something totally new. Within the first few seconds—with the tail of the plane looking like the fin in *Jaws*—the whole audience was hysterically laughing—and it never stopped! Everyone in my high school was quoting it. I'd never had an experience like that watching a movie.

MOLLY SHANNON

Jim: In the show, we did a lot of spoofs of TV commercials, so we'd leave our video machine on overnight to record the late-night movies in order to capture the dumbest commercials. In the morning, we'd clear off the tape to see what we got. It was like seining for fish.

David: What we did capture one night, and completely by accident, was an obscure 1957 airplane disaster movie called *Zero Hour!*, starring Dana Andrews, Linda Darnell, and Sterling Hayden. It was a melodrama about a World War II pilot with PTSD who has to land a passenger plane whose pilots had been stricken with food poisoning. Instead of being interested in the commercials, we got absorbed in the movie.

Jim: Coming across *Zero Hour!* was kismet. The first of many gifts we received from that movie was the exclamation point at the end of the title. Not only did we use it in *Airplane!* but also in *Police Squad!*, *Top Secret!*, and *Hot Shots!*

David: The exclamation point was the first joke.

Jerry: *Zero Hour!* was intensely serious and unintentionally hilarious. In order to satirize something, we have to find it laughable, but we also have to have affection for it. We loved *Zero Hour!* And it was actually a very well-constructed plot. You could actually use it to teach film structure. What a gift!

Jim: One gem in the middle of the movie was the signature line: "We need to find someone back there who not only can fly this plane, but who didn't have fish for dinner." Arthur Hailey actually wrote that! We didn't have to change it. It was ideal. Imagine being kids who spent 100 percent of their lives looking for things to spoof and then coming across a line like that in *Zero Hour!* I've often thought that's how Jonas Salk must have felt when he discovered his polio vaccine.

Jerry: Jonas Salk saw *Zero Hour!* but just never saw the possibilities.

David: We thought about overdubbing it, like Woody Allen had done in *What's Up, Tiger Lily?* But then we figured, why not just remake it with straight actors, in black and white, and on a prop plane?

Jerry: We knew nothing about screen writing, no clue how to write a story with three acts, character arcs, etc. But in *Zero Hour!* it was practically all there for us. All we had to do was add the jokes.

PARAMOUNT PRESENTS

DANA ANDREWS
LINDA DARNELL
STERLING HAYDEN

ZERO HOUR!

CO-STARRING ELROY "CRAZYLEGS" HIRSCH · GEOFFREY TOONE
JERRY PARIS INTRODUCING PEGGY KING WITH CAROLE EDEN
PRODUCED BY JOHN C. CHAMPION · DIRECTED BY HALL BARTLETT
SCREENPLAY BY ARTHUR HAILEY, HALL BARTLETT AND JOHN CHAMPION FROM A STORY
BY ARTHUR HAILEY A PARAMOUNT RELEASE

"We had the fish. Why?"

Jim: I can go this way or that about the existence of God in my life. But finding *Zero Hour!* is definitely in the pro column. You can get a DVD of *Zero Hour!* today, and on the jacket it says, "The movie that inspired *Airplane!*"

David: We were merely the little boy saying, "The emperor has no clothes." But more than that I think we saw in *Zero Hour!* a blank canvas where we could put in jokes.

Jim: It was as though someone had given us a Christmas tree and we just had to hang our ornaments on it.

BILL HADER

I was probably about ten years old when I saw *Airplane!* at my grandparents' house. I just remember that, even at that age, I knew it was an anomaly. I was, like, "Why is this so funny? Why does this work so well?" It was the first time I'd seen something like that, something that wacky, where it just seemed like the people acting in it weren't comedians or weren't in on the joke, so I went, "Oh, that's the way you should perform comedy: without a wink to the audience. So that the people in the movie don't know they're in a funny movie." I just thought it was phenomenal.

ADAM MCKAY

MAD would kind of reference things in the movies and just make them a little bit different. But *Airplane!* borrowed the idea of parody which *MAD* magazine was doing and took it to punk rock level. I don't use that phrase lightly, but I would say it's almost punk rock in certain parts of the movie. Things were always on the edge of anarchy and really playing with form. It's a parody, but they went further.

David: Two decades before, *MAD* magazine was our first exposure to parody. I think that was the root of *Airplane!*

Jim: They had a feature called "Scenes We'd Like to See," where they'd make fun of a movie in one page. They would set up the scene in different columns—very realistically.

David: The characters and background would be completely straight, to set it up.

Jim: Then in the last column, they'd pull the rug out from under it all, and there would be the joke. That was an influence for us, because that's exactly what we like to do: set it up with real, serious actors, serious sets, and serious music, which allowed us to make our joke.

Jerry: *MAD* would do a joke in the foreground, but then you'd notice some other joke going on in the background, or in the margins.

David: That concept really made an impression on us—background. I used to watch old black and white movies from the 1930s, and my mind would wander to the extras in the background. That was what interested me. I would think, *Gee, all these people are dead now.*

Jerry: Thank you, David. I think Jim and I can take it from here.

Jim: There was a movie in the early seventies called *Harold and Maude* where they did a wonderful background joke. There's a scene where Ruth Gordon is in a kitchen talking to a girl, and out the window in the background, you see Bud Cort lighting himself on fire.

David: It was a huge laugh, partly because the audience enjoyed discovering that stuff on their own, and not having it pointed out for them. If they had cut to it, it wouldn't have been funny at all.

Jerry: *MAD* magazine had a character called Marginal Marvin who would always be in the margins, outside the panels. Characters would say things like, "Help! I'm stuck in this stupid magazine."

David: Yes! It was as if they were teaching us never to respect convention. To literally go outside the margins. Like at the end of a movie, of course, the credits would roll. But we saw no reason to stop there. So we dropped in fake credits.

PROPERTY MASTER	STEVEN LEVINE
SUPERVISOR OF PRODUCTION ADMINISTRATION	BETTY MOOS
AUTHOR OF A TALE OF TWO CITIES	CHARLES DICKENS
CAMERA OPERATOR	FREDRICK J. SMITH
FOREEZ	A JOLLY GOOD FELLOW
NEW YORK CASTING	GRETCHEN RENNELL
CRANE GRIP	LLOYD BARCROFT
DOLLY GRIP	JON FALKENGREN
POLI-GRIP	MARTHA RAYE
WHAT THE HELL IS A GRIP?	PERSON RESPONSIBLE FOR MAINTENANCE AND ADJUSTMENT TO EQUIPMENT ON THE SET.
GENERALLY IN CHARGE OF A LOT OF THINGS	MIKE FINNELL

Jim: And then, at the very end of the credits, there was the usual stern FBI warning: "Any attempt to reproduce, copy this movie, etc., will result in criminal prosecution." And Jon Davison added, "So there!"

Jerry: The FBI called Paramount; they were not happy. They had a point. They were trying to prevent film piracy, and here we were mocking them.

David: But it was too late to take it out. It was already playing in eighteen hundred theaters.

BOB WEISS

As silly, zany, and chaotic as *Airplane!* appears to be, it took real discipline to pull it off. It was a specific tone that they had to hit for it to work. As they defined their style, they actually evolved a set of rules that provided boundaries.

David: The first inkling I had that comedy might have thought or discipline behind it was when I saw *The Dick Van Dyke Show*.

Jerry: That was the first sitcom I remember watching as a kid. I had to ask Mom to remind me when it was on. I don't think I really understood everything that was going on, but I was mesmerized by the laugh track.

David: Weren't a lot of those laugh tracks fake?

Jerry: I'm sure it was, but it didn't matter. I just liked hearing all those people laughing, the idea of someone saying something funny and then everybody laughs. It was intoxicating. Also, his occupation was a comedy writer. That was his job! A show about people who got paid for writing comedy!

ADAM MCKAY

It's all about that sense of, "Oh, these guys are for real. These aren't guys who are trying to get commercial laughs to pay their bills. These are guys who really love this stuff." You can just feel it. They know what they're doing and have a specific point of view for their comedy. It's a remarkable thing. I mean, talking about it right now makes me want to go watch *Police Squad!* again. In fact, I'm going to! And I'm sure I'll laugh just as hard now as I did then.

David: I remember one specific episode where all of the other fathers in Richie's class came to school and told the class what they did for a living, and Dick Van Dyke agonized over how he could do it because his job was so odd. But of course he ended up speaking to the kids and described how comedy works. I remember he said, "Comedy

Zero Hour!

Airplane!

depends on surprise." It was the first time I thought, *Hmmm, there's a science to this. There are rules.* Decades later, at some party in Malibu, I actually met Dick Van Dyke. I told him the story about how this episode made such an impression on me. He had no recollection of it.

Jim: The first rule, and even the idea that there *were* rules, came to us through my friend Alan Mandel. He came to one of the early previews of KFT and met with us after the show. He was an interesting guy—carried his wallet in his hand instead of his back pocket so his ass wouldn't have a bulge.

Jerry: Not really that big a thing, but it seemed very Hollywood to us, so the next time he came over we stuffed our back pockets with golf balls. He never noticed.

David: In one sketch, Stucker was being the clown, but the actor who was supposed to be the "straight man" was also being funny. Alan said, "You can't do that. That's a 'joke on a joke.'" We said, "What?" He went on, "You have to pick one person to be funny, and the other person has to be serious." Because of that encounter we started thinking about what we were doing and why things were funny. Or not. We proceeded over the next few years to add fourteen more rules.

Jerry: It became sort of a shorthand so we wouldn't need to have the same discussions over and over again. We'd just say what rule we thought was violated.

Jim: Of course, these were just *our* rules for *our* comedy, guidelines for us.

David: When Mike Myers made *Austin Powers* he probably ignored most of these rules and made a very funny movie. Same with the Wayans and *Scary Movie.* We were by no means unique in having rules. Laurel & Hardy, Preston Sturges, and even Mark Twain had their rules.

Jim: To me, the fifteenth rule is the most important: there are no rules.

THE ZAZ FIFTEEN RULES

1. **JOKE ON A JOKE** Two jokes at the same time cancel each other out. If the joke is in the background, the foreground action should be serious, and vice versa. Focus on one joke at a time.

2. **ACKNOWLEDGEMENT** Sometimes referred to as "winking." Don't acknowledge the joke, or that you made a joke. Actors in the foreground must ignore jokes happening behind them.

3. **MERELY CLEVER** A "clever" joke isn't good enough. It has to get a laugh.

4. **BREAKING THE FRAME** Don't remind the audience they're watching a movie. Jokes about the movie itself, the movie business, or comedy itself are a strict no-no, although it's possible to sneak one in if you don't dwell on it. See Rule #11: That didn't happen.

5. **TRIVIA** A joke using references so arcane that few people will ever get it.

6. **JERRY LEWIS** A comedian who is doing every possible crazy thing he can to get a laugh. As a result, when something was over the top, we would just say, "Jerry Lewis."

7. **AXE GRINDING** When the joke is overshadowed by some message, it gets unfunny fast.

8. **KNOCKING DOWN THE POSTS** Conceptual jokes are fine, but people don't laugh at concepts; they laugh at verbal or visual punch lines. In *Airplane!* the gag of the soldier leaning out the door as his girlfriend runs alongside is merely *referencing* the same scene we've seen in hundreds of films where it makes sense—on a train. Fortunately, we decided to put old-style railroad posts on the runway and have the girl knock them over. People clearly get the concept of the scene, but they don't laugh until she knocks down the posts.

9. **STRAW DUMMY** A hollow setup for a joke where the target has been invented by the writer. You can't satirize something that doesn't exist. Like a block-long, nuclear-powered bus.

10. **CAN YOU LIVE WITH IT?** Once a joke is made, it can't be allowed to hang around (Rule #14). Like a personalized license plate, how long can "LV2FART" be funny?

11. **THAT DIDN'T HAPPEN** Something that totally defies all logic but is on and off the screen so fast that we get away with it. Robert Stack in *Airplane!* yells, "They're on instruments!" Cut to the cockpit—the actors are playing musical instruments. Seconds later, the saxophone and clarinets have disappeared. If it's done right, no one in the audience will ask where the instruments went.

12. **UNRELATED BACKGROUND** A joke happening in the background, though unacknowledged, still needs to be related in some way to the action in the foreground. This rule was put into effect after the release of *Airplane!*, when we were desperately trying to figure out why no one laughed at the spear striking the wall behind Robert Stack and a watermelon crashing on the table behind Lloyd Bridges. It made us laugh so hard when we wrote it, filmed it, saw it in dailies, as well as in the finished film. Unfortunately we were the only ones. It was craziness without an actual joke. We left it in, and probably in some way it adds to the irreverent tone of the film, but it never gets a laugh.

13. **TECHNICAL PIZZAZZ** Special effects and big action don't necessarily mean funny.

14. **HANGING ON** Don't play a joke too long. When it reaches its peak, get out. The film should move off a joke before the audience does.

15. **THERE ARE NO RULES** We try to follow these rules as closely as possible, realizing that perhaps what is most important is knowing when to ignore them.

CHAPTER 11

LANDIS

They were all smart guys, they had lots of ideas, but they really didn't know anything about filmmaking. I mean, nothing. You have to learn about coverage and montage and film language and just very simply things like that. It's carpentry. Although they learned. And quickly, I think.

JOHN LANDIS

Jerry: We wanted to write a comedy based on *Zero Hour!*, but we had no idea what an actual movie script looked like, and we didn't know anyone in the movie business. But one night David happened to be watching *The Tonight Show*, and one of Johnny Carson's guests was a twenty-one-year-old kid named John Landis who had just made a low-budget comedy horror movie called *Schlock*.

David: I immediately tracked down Landis's number and called him to ask him how he did it. So he answers the phone, and I start to introduce myself. But all he said was, "How did you get this number?" I told him, "I called the distributor, listed on the ad in the paper, and they . . ." He exploded, "They *gave* you my number?!" This was not much help in calming him down, so I quickly said, "Look, I don't want anything from you, I'd just like to invite you to our show, Kentucky Fried Theater." This stopped him long enough to reply, "Oh, yeah, I've seen that driving down Pico."

Jim: So Landis came to see *Vegetables*. We chatted after the show and agreed to have lunch the following day at the old Hamburger Hamlet on Sepulveda in Culver City.

JOHN LANDIS

We had lunch. I thought they were funny, and they said they wanted to make a movie, so I said, "Do you have a screenplay?" And they literally said, "What's that?" I mean, that sounds ridiculous, but it's absolutely true! And I said, "Well, you have to have a screenplay! What do you want to do? What's your movie?" And they said, "What does one look like? What's the form of the script? How do you actually write it?"

David: And he said, "Oh, why don't I just give you a script of mine, so you'll understand the form."

JOHN LANDIS

I had written *An American Werewolf in London* in 1969, so I happened to have a couple of copies of the script in my car. I said, "I'll give you the script, and you can copy the form. You'll see, it's easy." So I gave them that script.

Jerry: I loved it! It was the best movie script I had ever read. Partially because it was the only movie script I had ever read. But now at least we knew what one looked like.

Jim: Truthfully, I have no recollection of reading it. We literally just used it for the template to do slug lines, dialogue, etc. And then we proceeded to start writing *Airplane!* Years later, when I saw *American Werewolf* I remember being happy I hadn't known the ending.

The air blast was supposed to blow the guy's beard off on the far left—it wouldn't budge.

BOB WEISS

ZAZ and I met Landis independently. He walked into my office looking for a job. He'd been a stunt man and accountant. I started using him at Video Systems, where we made instructional videos teaching truckers safety and training films for the LAPD. Later on, I recruited David, Jerry, Jim, and Landis for a video called *Recognition of Injuries*. That was the first time we were all together. The special effects guy who did the aorta bleeding effects was Rick Baker, who went on to win many Oscars for makeup.

Jerry: So, we started writing *Airplane!* in the little dining room above the theater. At some point, we realized we were using a lot of *Zero Hour!* Like the entire plot.

Jim: There were very specific legal parameters for doing parody. You're allowed to take characters and occasional dialogue—the lawyer told us that—but not the full story.

David: It was around that time that we first showed the script to Landis.

> **MATT STONE**
> We had a meeting with John Landis at one point, and he told us that when they first showed him the script (for *Airplane!*), he was, like, "Guys, this isn't a parody, this is plagiarism!"

David: So we figured we had to buy the rights.

Jerry: It wasn't very difficult back then. The studios didn't see any value in those old B movies. It was found money for them.

Jim: The option was $2,500. We could afford that. Plus we were able to remake the movie without worrying about being sued for plagiarism. What we certainly didn't appreciate at the time, and for several years, was how perfect the story in *Zero Hour!* was for us.

Jerry: Or the importance of telling a good story in a comedy. Even in a crazy satire, or perhaps *especially* in a crazy satire, the jokes work so much better if you actually care about the danger all these people are in, and whether the lovers will get back together—how this whole situation is going to resolve. If you play the stakes as real, the jokes come as more of a surprise. What could be better for comedy than two people trying to make a relationship work on an airplane with no pilot? Thank you Arthur Hailey, Hall Bartlett, and John Champion!

"WEIRD AL" YANKOVIC

Although it draws from many sources, *Airplane!* is primarily a parody of a relatively obscure movie from the fifties called *Zero Hour!* I'm sure most of the people seeing the movie didn't catch the references—and it absolutely didn't matter. It was here that I learned perhaps the most important lesson about successful parody writing: it needs to be funny even if people aren't familiar with the original source material. (Another important lesson: gravely serious people saying ridiculous things is always funny!)

"The life of everyone on board depends on just one thing: finding someone back there who not only can fly this plane, but who didn't have fish for dinner."

BOB WEISS

I came over to sit in on a writing session. They'd gotten a copy of *Zero Hour!* and would go through it scene by scene on their video recorder, and *very* carefully. They were like comedy surgeons. They'd take the serious parts of the movie, and that was the skeletal structure of the narrative of the story for *Airplane!* Then they'd take lines and setups and supply the punch lines. And what was great about that style of comedy is the audience did a lot of the work themselves. What they had to do was emulate the archetypes, and the audience was ready for it because they shared the references. There were literally hundreds, thousands of hours of television and movies that everybody watched. But it was very smart, because you didn't have to see the original movie to enjoy the jokes.

David: The important thing for us was not to face a blank page.

"Flying is no different than riding a bicycle. It's just a lot harder to put baseball cards in the spokes."

Jerry: We hated the blank page.

David: We needed what we came to call "materials," and in this case that meant *Zero Hour!*, *Airport*, *Airport '75*, *Crash Landing*, and a few other obscure black and white 1950s movies. They provided us with all the straight lines we needed, like, "Looks like I picked the wrong week to quit smoking," and "Surely you can't be serious."

Jerry: I'm pretty sure we watched every airline disaster movie ever made.

Jim: There's nothing more fun than the three of us watching a movie, and somebody says, "How about this?" And then another guy says, "Well, yeah, and then we do this!" Creating a joke, to me, is still the most fun part of the whole movie business. We'd just laugh. Our friends were all going to an office, school, business, or something. And we'd go to work every day, write jokes, and laugh. Then I'd return to my apartment on the beach. Can you imagine?!

BILL HADER

It's hilarious when you watch *Zero Hour!* now, because it really is just three dudes watching a movie and riffing on it and then going, "You know what? Let's just do this!" Now that I've been a comedy writer, I mean, that's the kind of thing you'd normally talk about but never go and do, because you'd be, like, "Well, that's insane!" And there's this rule where, you know, it needs to be grounded. But they're great jokes! They're just perfectly constructed bits. And you can tell it's just three guys trying to make themselves laugh, which is always where the best comedy comes from.

Jerry: We wanted to spend all our time writing, so we decided to stop performing. We created an entirely new show with Pat Proft, Steve Stucker, Mallory Sandler, and Bo Kaprall, a friend of Pat's from Minneapolis. We called it *My Nose*, forcing the *L.A. Times* to print, "My Nose: Runs continuously."

Jim: We built a giant nose above the box office, so people would have to stand under it when they bought tickets. Then we hooked up a speaker inside it that made a loud mucus-filled sneezing sound, accompanied by a spray of water that landed on people standing in line.

David: But they kept coming.

Jim: *My Nose* was a success, like *Vegetables* had been, even though we weren't in it. Maybe *because* we weren't in it. But it didn't matter to us; we were writing a movie!

David: When we still thought of ourselves as a TV sketch group, we had the idea of doing a national show with comedy sketches and musical acts. Essentially, it was the idea for *Saturday Night Live*. We took it to our William Morris agent, and she said, "Nah, that's not a good idea."

Jerry: Stupid!

"There's some trouble on your husband's flight."

". . . but what other choice have we got?"

Jim: Not her. Us, for listening!

David: But smarter than the agents was Lorne Michaels, who had the same idea and brought Dick Ebersol, head of NBC late-night programming, to see the show. He saw the possibilities.

> **DICK EBERSOL**
> **From *Live from New York: An Uncensored History of* Saturday Night Live by TOM SHALES**
> Lorne pitched an idea based on *Kentucky Fried Theater*. I decided right away that it wasn't for me. I just really didn't dig it. But Lorne and I hit it off.

David: Sometime, soon after, Michaels brought Ebersol to see a performance of *My Nose*.

> **DOUG HILL and JEFF WEINGRAD From their book *Saturday Night: A Backstage History of* Saturday Night Live**
> Lorne and Ebersol saw each other again in January 1975, spending an evening watching a performance of Kentucky Fried Theater in a ramshackle warehouse near Century City.

David: Whatever Ebersol thought of the show, soon after that evening *Saturday Night Live* did become a reality. But for us, it felt great to be writing a movie, and even better not to have to be onstage anymore. And now we had weekends off, which was a strange new experience after three years!

Jim: We'd get to the theater at ten in the morning. And like all writers, we'd drink coffee, talk about current events, talk about sports, procrastinate as long as we could, and then we'd write for a couple of hours and go home. It was wonderful.

David: Although we weren't onstage anymore, the experience of the live show definitely influenced the pacing of *Airplane!*

Jerry: Our desire for pace was definitely forged by our fear of silence, but I do remember that in the early drafts of *Airplane!* there were way too many long, serious speeches. We just loved all that cool, hard-hitting dialogue.

> **BOB WEISS**
>
> *Forbes* did a listing of the top ten funniest movies based on the number of laughs per minute. *Airplane!* was number one, *The Hangover* number two, *The Naked Gun* number three.

Jim: And we wrote without the slightest thought about how complicated the gags might be or how much they might cost to film.

David: We'd write things like, "The beating heart jumps out of the beaker, across the desk, and falls off the edge," and "Striker struggles with controls, sweating profusely. Water is gushing down his face ridiculously."

Jim: One advantage of doing a spoof of a B movie is that the effects only have to be as good as the ones in a B movie. You can still see the tiny wires pulling the bouncing heart and the wires holding up Hays when he's juggling. At the premiere of *Airplane!*, when Stucker first saw the miniature of the plane, he yelled out so the whole audience could hear, "It's just hanging there!"

> **JOHN FRAZIER**
>
> The bouncing heart on the desk, we made that. We had a little armature inside the heart, and I think it had a little monofilament on it, so we could bounce it with the little gadget we had inside of it. The boys were just, like, "Whatever you can give us, that's what's going on the screen!" So that's what we did. And the scene with Bob Hays when he's trying to land the plane and he's starting to sweat, I had put a ring around his head with little holes in it, and I could control the water coming out of the thing, and we could hide it in his hair. I remember Jon Davison saying, "What would we have done if Bob Hays had been bald?" I said, "Well, he wouldn't be sitting here if he was!"

David: Our first idea was to call the movie *The Late Show* and do segments of *Zero Hour!* broken up by commercials. That was really an early, early version of what would eventually be *Airplane!* And as if that weren't bad enough, we had Beaver Cleaver flying down the plane.

Jerry: Oh my God, do we have to tell people that?

David: No.

Jim: After about three months, we had a completed screenplay that we couldn't wait to get out to the world, but we needed some feedback, some person who could give us a professional opinion.

David: Through a friend of Mallory Sandler, an actress named Barbara Mallory, we met her husband, Lloyd Schwartz, who with his father, Sherwood Schwartz, had produced *Gilligan's Island* and *The Brady Bunch*.

LLOYD SCHWARTZ

I first crossed paths with the guys waiting in line at their *Kentucky Fried Theater* show. It was absolutely packed. It was *the* place to go. I remember their crazy piano player, Stephen Stucker, playing this overture that had pieces of every famous show in it. I thought, That's so bold! It was *all* bold stuff. I grew up in Los Angeles, grew up in television, and that's been my whole life, but these were guys who came from Wisconsin, and did it their own way, and I just said, "God, that takes such courage!" It's easy for me; I've been here.

Jerry: Lloyd was really smart, and it was very kind of him to read our script and come in and talk to us.

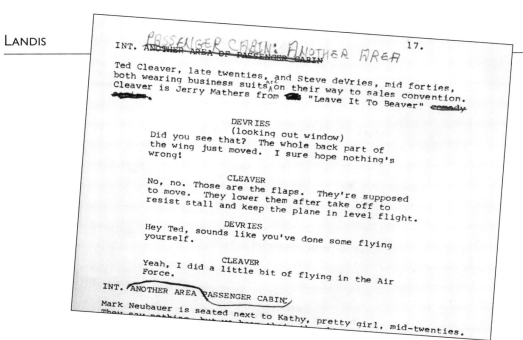

INT. ~~ANOTHER AREA OF PASSENGER CABIN~~ PASSENGER CABIN: ANOTHER AREA 17.

Ted Cleaver, late twenties, and Steve deVries, mid forties, both wearing business suits are on their way to sales convention. Cleaver is Jerry Mathers from ~~the~~ "Leave It To Beaver" ~~comedy~~.

> DEVRIES
> (looking out window)
> Did you see that? The whole back part of the wing just moved. I sure hope nothing's wrong!

> CLEAVER
> No, no. Those are the flaps. They're supposed to move. They lower them after take off to resist stall and keep the plane in level flight.

> DEVRIES
> Hey Ted, sounds like you've done some flying yourself.

> CLEAVER
> Yeah, I did a little bit of flying in the Air Force.

INT. ANOTHER AREA PASSENGER CABIN.

Mark Neubauer is seated next to Kathy, pretty girl, mid-twenties.

Early, early script: June 1975, featuring Beaver Cleaver

LLOYD SCHWARTZ

They brought me the script for *Airplane!*, which at that point was called *The Late Show*. I remember reading the script, and the first thing up was when the two announcers are talking to each other at the airport. I said, "This can't happen!" That was my note. Well, it happened in *their* world, you know?

David: After he read the script, Lloyd said, "This is pretty good, but the airplane story gets interrupted by the commercials." So the next draft had fewer commercials, and the next draft after that none at all. No longer *The Late Show*; it now became *Kentucky Fried Airplane*.

Jim: Now we faced the problem of actually getting it made. At the time, none of us had ever even been on a movie set, so we talked to John Landis about directing it.

Jerry: John said, "Sure, but how are you going to finance it? Making the movie is fun; trying to raise the money is horrible." Before we knew it, we'd been at it, trying to sell the script, for a year without any results. And we couldn't figure out why. That's how clueless we were.

David: This was very, very depressing—a low point for me, because I thought we had this great script, and now we had to go back to doing the theater again!

Jim: David told me about a dream he had during that time: he was standing at the head of a big conference table, in front of a dozen suits, pounding the table and shouting "You can't stop us!" On the other hand, my attitude was to prepare for the worst and then be pleasantly surprised when anything better happens. Plus I was living on the beach in Malibu for $350 a month; it was seventy-two degrees every day in January, so I wasn't that crushed.

Jerry: I don't remember that as some horrible, crushing moment either. Probably because it didn't just end one day, it kind of faded out over time. We were young, and the theater was still packed. Whatever we were doing was better than the alternative, because there was no alternative.

David: During this time, Lloyd Schwartz was doing a Saturday morning kids' show called *Big John, Little John.* I think he felt sorry for us. He thought we were talented because he'd seen the KFT show a couple of times and figured we were good enough to be TV writers. So he gave us a job writing an episode for *Big John, Little John.*

"Captain, how soon can we land?" "I can't tell." "You can tell me. I'm a doctor."

Jim: The humor was as you would expect, quite mild. We were bored and frustrated. It was a long way from our style of comedy.

David: It was like doing a college term paper. So we handed it in, but not without hiding a little gem in the middle of the script.

Jim: Almost immediately, the phone rang.

LLOYD SCHWARTZ

They were very free-form kind of guys. So they turned in the script, and mind you, this is the most innocent, G-rated, Saturday morning kids' show material, and I'm reading this classroom scene involving two cute eight-year-olds, and suddenly I come to a line: "Valerie rubs a ruler in her crotch and asks Little John to smell it." I had to explain to them, "Guys! This script goes straight to the network! And the network guy is a former priest! The show could get canceled!" They, of course, did this all to amuse me, and looking back on it, it *was* funny. But at the time I had to sit them down and explain that I have to deal with the corporate world.

David: Around that time, Pat and Bo wanted to leave to write for TV. So we decided to create a new show, which was actually a compilation of the best of all the shows that we'd done, and reflecting our frustration we called it *Beating a Dead Horse*. We were so done with this. But we were to do the theater for two more years. The big nose was replaced by a movie-theater-style marquee.

Jerry: You built that whole thing and mounted it yourself.

Jim: David was desperate, trying to imagine he was already in the movie business. Think Richard Dreyfus in *Close Encounters*, madly building that mud mountain in his living room.

Jerry: An idle mind is the devil's playground. We did stupid little things to amuse ourselves.

David: One weekend, we had two family friends visiting from Arizona. They were in L.A. for an orchestra competition, so they had brought their French horns with them. We couldn't let this opportunity pass. The audience files in, the lights go up, and these two guys played an entire overture on the French horns. No laughs, just a completely confused audience.

Jim: During the blackouts between sketches there were only a couple of seconds to rearrange chairs and exchange actors. One weekend we had a stand-in actor. The problem was we never rehearsed the blackout choreography with him. So when I leaned over to place a chair we banged foreheads. A second later when the lights came up I started to speak my lines but there were 150 people in the audience looking at me with the same horrified expression as my parents did when I told them I couldn't be a doctor or a lawyer. That's when I felt blood streaming down my face. It was like my aorta ran through my forehead. I ran off the stage, got a lift to the emergency room, and took twelve stitches to my forehead.

Jerry: Whenever we had a visitor in the greenroom, right before we went onstage Jim would say, "Okay, it's time," and we'd all kneel around the coffee table, become very somber, and bow our heads in prayer. Jim would start, "Oh Lord, please grant us the energy to put on a good show tonight, an audience who will appreciate our jokes, and not be offended at the depictions of simulated sex, blowjobs, anal penetration, and words like shit, bitch, motherfucker, and suck my cock . . ."

David: I was always amazed at how long it would go on before people realized we were joking.

Jerry: Jim just kept going, getting more and more vulgar, until he just couldn't keep a straight face anymore.

"I could make a hat, or a broach, or a pterodactyl."

CHAPTER 12

KENTUCKY FRIED MOVIE

©2003 KFM FILMS.INC

I had a lot of regard for those guys, and having seen *Kentucky Fried Movie*, which I think is—well, if that wasn't the template for movies to come in the world of comedy, then *Airplane!* certainly was. I think movie comedies turned on the success of that film.

DAVID LETTERMAN

Jerry: Before we even started writing *Airplane!*, Ken Shapiro had turned his New York video show, *Groove Tube*, into a successful movie. So, we thought maybe we could do the same thing with Kentucky Fried Theater. Unfortunately, we again made the mistake of asking our agency, at that time William Morris, and they said, "No, you can't do that. It's already been done."

Jim: The agents were dependable. Rock solid.

David: Again we stupidly took that advice. It's like, if anything can be learned from this book, it would be "Stop taking stupid advice!"

Jerry: Don't sit at anybody's feet . . . unless it's like one of the Beatles or something.

Jim: Years later, I had another agent. I'd call him up for his insight about this or that. He'd invariably go off, "My wife is such a fucking bitch!" Then he'd tell me ten things he hated about his wife and hang up. At least he was entertaining.

David: This kind of thing was happening to us all the time back then.

Jim: We also had an agent named Danny Stevens in the early seventies. We had a bunch of meetings with him. He told us he was going to make us famous. One day, I ran into him on the beach, gave him a big hello, and he said to me, "Don't I know you from somewhere?" I said, "Danny. Jim Abrahams. You're my agent."

Jerry: Landis was the one who usually gave us the best advice, and he almost always recognized us.

JOHN LANDIS
One Saturday night, Bob Weiss and I went to see *Beating a Dead Horse*. Afterward, in the greenroom, they were talking about how their *Airplane!* script had gone nowhere, and I suggested, "Why don't you guys do a movie of sketches from your show?" Apparently they at one time had suggested that to their agent, who had discouraged the idea. I just blurted out, "You listened to an agent?!"

Jerry: I think at the time Landis was writing dialogue for a James Bond movie at Fox, just a few blocks up the street from the theater. He offered to help with our script and direct it.

David: By which point we were way past taking our agent's advice and decided, "Let's do this movie!" And so we began to put together the Kentucky Fried Movie script. We took the best of all our shows and added new material. But of course we still needed to raise the money.

Jim: We added new stuff like "A Fistful of Yen," a spoof of Bruce Lee's movie *Enter the Dragon*. And after a couple of months, we had a script. We shopped that script all over Hollywood, too, and nobody was interested in that one either!

JOHN LANDIS

There were a million crazy stories about trying to raise the money. I remember there was some guy in a big house in the valley. We all met in the pool house, which was his office, and within two minutes I knew this guy was full of shit, he'd never give us the money. He just wanted to tell us how wealthy and successful he was. So I wrote on the bottom of my shoe, to show Jerry: "This guy's a schmuck." And all of a sudden, maybe three seconds later, the guy goes, "What'd he write on his shoe, that I'm a schmuck!?" True story! And I'm sitting there, rubbing my foot on the ground really fast!

"And that, as much as anything else, led to my drinking problem."

David: All those meetings turned out to be a waste of time. We were getting an education in how Hollywood works. I think we always thought that if you created something great, people would line up to support it. That's the experience we'd had with the theater, so why would it be any different with a movie? But we learned you can spend years making people laugh, but it's another thing to convince anyone to say, "Yes! I will put actual money into this."

Jerry: We met a lot of people with deep pockets and short arms.

JOHN LANDIS

I also remember one lunch, at Musso & Frank, we were with a group of people that Bob Weiss got—three or four guys who were coming from out of town, doctors or lawyers or something—and the first thing that went bad was they said, "What do you recommend?" And I said, "The chiffonade salad!" Which is a famous Musso & Frank thing. And they hated it! So right away that was bad. And then we're just sitting there, and Bob is selling hard, and it became so clear to me that this was a complete waste of time, so I'm just sitting there thinking, When is this over?

BOB WEISS

One of the guys asks a legitimately good question: "What happens if you shoot something and it doesn't work? Or if something happens to the sets or the costumes? What do you do? You've only got a finite amount of money." I say, "Well, that's a good question. John?" And Landis says, "Truthfully? If something happens, I don't give a fuck. It's not **my** money!" I may have spit out the rest of my chiffonade salad. That was the end of that lunch.

Jerry: Then we had a meeting with this guy, a Bel Air real estate developer who had seen the show a couple times. He said, "Yes, I'm interested, this all sounds promising, but your budget is $600,000, so I'd have to bring some of my friends in as co-investors . . ."

David: At this point, we're thinking, *Great! Bring all the friends you like!*

Jerry: ". . . but I need to prove to them that you guys can actually pull this off, because you're an unknown quantity."

Jim: It was true. We had Landis, director of a microbudget indie movie; Weiss, producer of police instructional videos; and the three of us, who'd *seen* movies but had never been on a movie set.

HONG KONG

From *Kentucky Fried Movie*

David: So the real estate guy said, "Why don't you choose four sketches from the movie and shoot them on 35mm? Bring me a budget for that. I can finance it, then I'll show it to my friends. Once they see that, they'll agree to fund the $600,000."

"The sex record comes complete with . . . BIG JIM SLADE!"

The Ten Minutes: Landis and crew filming outside of the theater

Jerry: So we chose four scenes, ten minutes of screen time, and sent it to him with a budget of $30,000. A few days later, we meet with him.

David: And he says, "Well, I looked at the budget, and I decided I'm not gonna do it." When we left his house, we got into the car, we were driving away, and it was just silent. Gloom. And then one of us—or maybe all of us—said, "You know what? If we thought it was such a great idea for a stranger to invest $30,000, and we're so confident that it's gonna be great, then why don't we put our own money into it?"

Jim: And that's what we did. Jerry, David, and I each put in $5,000 we had made from the theater, and Jerry and David's parents put in the rest, and we shot these ten minutes, with Landis directing and Bob Weiss producing—all of us on spec.

JOHN LANDIS

So we shoot this thing, and cut it together on one of those old Moviolas, which by that time had been mostly discontinued, and I show it to the guys, and I say, "It's funny! I think it's good!" I was very excited, and of course, Bob was very excited, and we showed it to the studios, who just went, "Get the fuck out of here!"

David: So now, even with a film sample of how funny this movie could be, no one wanted to put any money behind it. That was another tough pill, because not only were we unable to raise a dime for financing; we now found ourselves with a $30,000 white elephant! That was another low point. Is this starting to sound like a string of endless low points?

Jerry: Only for you. Jim and I were always happy.

David: Yes, but good thing I wasn't, because in my misery I called up Kim Jorgensen to see if he would play it at his theater. At least we could see it in front of a live audience.

Jim and David with Lee Burch, editing the KFM ten-minute demo.

JOHN LANDIS

That night, we showed the ten minutes to a packed and very loud Saturday night audience, and it played brilliantly. It's funny when you see Kentucky Fried now, but it was really shocking at the time. It's not as shocking now, but there are still some things in it where you go, "Jesus Christ! Did I just see what I think I saw?" In any case, it played amazingly well.

Jerry: Kim Jorgensen was a guy we knew from Milwaukee. He ran the Nuart Theatre in West L.A.

Jim: The lesson we learned from the theater was: play it in front of a live audience to see if it gets laughs.

Jerry: Kim said he could show the ten minutes at the Nuart on Saturday night, but he wanted to see it first. We showed it to him that afternoon. He loved it! Laughed all the way through. And when the lights came up, he said, "What are you doing with this? Where have you taken this?"

David: We said, "Well, we took it around to the studios." He said, "Don't take it to the studios! I've got friends in the theater business in San Francisco who will love this!" Jorgensen asked how much we needed, and I think we told him five hundred to six hundred thousand. He said, "I can get you the money in two weeks!"

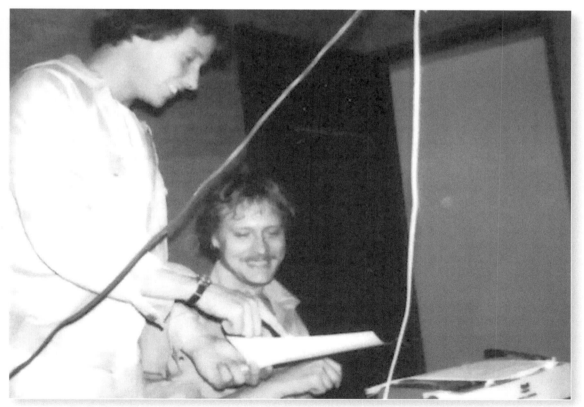

"I can get you the money in two weeks!" Jim with Kim Jorgenson

Jim: Two weeks later we got a call from Jorgensen: he got the money! We looked at each other, amazed.

David: It wasn't bullshit! We were going to make our first movie!

Jerry: What Landis had said was absolutely true: "Making the movie is fun, trying to get it financed is horrible."

Jim: Plus Jerry and I knew we'd get a few days reprieve from being on suicide watch for David.

David: If it hadn't been for UATC (United Artists Theatre Circuit) actually showing the ten minutes in a theater in front of live humans, they most likely would never have financed a movie from a script which featured racial humor, graphic sex, and dead children.

Jim: The goal was to tread the line of tastelessness.

> **QUENTIN TARANTINO**
> I remember going to see *Kentucky Fried Movie* at the United Artist Del Amo Mall Cinema. I will never forget my reaction to its closing vignette. It's the part when the couple is sitting on the couch, watching the news, and suddenly they start to hump each other. And as they hump, the news anchor notices it, and he and his crew watch and get off as well. I don't think I ever laughed as uncontrollably at a sequence in a film as I did at that scene. But I wasn't alone, the entire afternoon matinee audience was in deep hysterics—that losing control of your body type of hysterics. The literal definition of *'rolling in the aisles'*. What a climax!

Jerry: In 1976, everything on TV was network and heavily censored. The only place you could go to see anything remotely off-color was in a movie theater. The R rating was part of the sales pitch.

> **JOHN LANDIS**
> Kim said to us, "I want to be the executive producer, get this much fee, and get this many points." So that was the deal that was made, and Jorgenson ended up making a pile of money from *Kentucky Fried Movie*, which he used to buy the rights to his favorite book. When you look him up, two credits jump out: *Kentucky Fried Movie* and *Out of Africa*!

"A hospital? What is it?" "It's a big building with patients, but that's not important right now."

David: Audiences get the satirical intent of our jokes, no matter how edgy they seem. But jokes like the Black dudes and the pedophile pilot in *Airplane!* and many of the jokes in *Kentucky Fried Movie* would have a much harder time getting past today's studio executives. Luckily, *KFM* didn't need approval from studio executives to be made. Now, when the three of us show *Airplane!* and afterward do the Q&A, the question we always get is, "Could you make *Airplane!* today?" And my answer is, "Sure, just without the jokes."

CHAPTER 13

BEAVER'S MOM

I was a kid when I first saw *Airplane!* When the newspaper came spiraling out with the headline "Boy Trapped in Refrigerator Eats Own Foot," that was it! I decided I wanted to go into comedy.

ADAM MCKAY

Jim: We got the idea of subtitling the Black dudes after we saw the 1975 Blaxploitation movie *Shaft*, starring Richard Roundtree. When we left the theater we thought it was pretty good, but we couldn't understand a lot of the jive dialogue. The cast was 95 percent Black. So we thought wouldn't it be fun to put a couple of those characters in *Airplane!* and subtitle them with idiotic white guy translations?

"Okay boys, let's get some pictures."

AL WHITE

When I looked at the script, I couldn't make hide nor hair of the actual verbiage. But I got a sense of what they wanted. They wanted jive as a language, which it is not. It's a word here and a phrase there, originated by the jazz musicians back in the 1920s. So we had to first understand what they wanted, and then Norman and I tried to work together on it, but we couldn't seem to gel on what we each wanted to do, so I said, "Well, okay, you work on yours and I'll work on mine." So I went and got a couple of books—one was on Black English by J. L. Dillard, and another was on Black language—and I just saw what they had in standard English and tried to come up with what I felt was jive. I tried to jive it down, using actual words. So what we ended up saying does mean something. It's not a bunch of gibberish. It did actually mean something.

Jerry: In the original script we just wrote, "Mo fo, shi' man, wha' fo' mo." I mean, it was nothing, just enough to get the idea of what the joke was. So when Al White and Norman Gibbs came in, we explained, apologetically, that this was the best three white Jewish guys from Milwaukee could do.

```
INT. PASSENGER CABIN - ANOTHER AREA

Randy is taking orders from the two Black Dudes.

                         RANDY
            Would you gentlemen care to
            order your dinners?

                              FIRST BLACK DUDE
            'ey ma' muh fuh wha' fo',
            shi'.

SUBTITLES APPEAR:  I WOULD LIKE TO STEAK PLEASE.

                              SECOND BLACK DUDE
            Shi' no cain ma foh mess wi',
            ain!?

SUBTITLES APPEAR:  I'LL HAVE THE FISH, THANK YOU.
```

Early Script: the best three white Jewish guys from Milwaukee could do.

David: When Al and Norman did it for us in the reading, we cracked up. We just thought they were great. There was no question that we were going to cast them. In fact, they were so good together, I literally had no idea until a few years ago that the first time they'd ever met was while they were waiting to audition!

Jim: Of course, we thought the subtitles idea was funny but then that led to the idea: wouldn't it be great if someone you would never suspect had to translate it?

AL WHITE

In one of the scenes I say, "Mack herself a pro, Slick! That gray matter back, lotta performers down, not take TCB-in', man!" So "Mack" was taken from one of these books—the Black English book—and means "to speak." "Mack herself a pro": she said she was a pro, or professional. "Slick," that was his name I gave him. "Gray matter back": I needed a word to jive down the word "remember," but I didn't find it in either of the books, so I said, "Well, let me see: 'gray matter,' that's the thinking part of the brain, and 'back' for remember back. I can say, 'Gray matter back.'" And from there I'm just saying that a lot of performers stayed down and weren't taking care of business on the technical side . . . man! When we got to the set and sat down, I said to Norman, "Okay, what do you have?" And he went over exactly what he had, and I went over what I had, and then I said, "Oh, okay, well, when you get to that part where it says, 'See a broad a booty yak 'em,' I'll come in with, 'Lay 'em down and smack 'em, yak 'em!'" So we gelled it together right there, just before we shot. Jerry came over and said, "You guys ready?" and we said, "Yeah!" So we shot it, and he came back and said, "Can you throw a 'man' in there or something?" We said, "Yeah, we'll throw a 'man' in there!"

BARBARA BILLINGSLEY

I was cast because I'd been June Cleaver on *Leave It to Beaver*. I'm sure that was the humor of the whole thing: that I talked jive. I was sent the script, and I thought it was the craziest script I'd ever read, but my husband said, "I think it's funny!" Well, my part wasn't written, really. It just said I talked jive. So I went to see the directors, and I said I would do it.

Jerry: We were sort of obsessed with those sixties family TV shows. We watched all of them as kids, but particularly *Leave It to Beaver*. I mean, David and I were literally Wally and the Beave. And Barbara Billingsley was the perfect mom, and the most unlikely person to speak jive.

David: Just the thought of June Cleaver in that role made us laugh. She was simply the whitest White lady on the planet.

Jerry: We were so thrilled to meet her! I remember the day she came in—it was like we had been put up for adoption, and now we were finally getting to meet our real mom.

"Jus' hang loose, blood. She gonna catch ya up on da rebound on da med side."

BARBARA BILLINGSLEY

I met Norman and Al—they're the ones who wrote the jive talk—and we went to lunch and we discussed this whole thing. These fellas were wonderful, and they taught me. They could rattle jive off like you have no idea. But I could never get a clue as to how it was done. Like pig Latin, I could figure that one out. But it wasn't hard for me to learn. I have no idea why. You know, "Hang in there, blood." "Chump don' want no help, chump don' get no help." It just wasn't hard. Maybe they were good teachers!

KEN COLLINS (Second Assistant Director)

I think it was part of that attitude of really well-established people just sort of going with the flow and giving themselves over to the guys and saying, "Okay, I'll do what you want!"

AL WHITE

I ended up writing Barbara Billingsley's jive dialogue and instructing her in its proper elocution. She was very intent on getting it right. It was such a pleasure working with Barbara. My mother just loved *Leave It to Beaver*, and I asked Barbara if she wouldn't mind speaking to my mother. That was the crowning moment, because I called my mother, and I said, "Mom, I have Barbara Billingsley here, and she'd actually like to speak to you." She was so excited, and Barbara was so gracious. That was really wonderful of her to do that for me and my mother. Several years later, Barbara came to see me in *Gem of the Ocean*, an August Wilson play I was doing at the Taper Forum in Los Angeles, and she sent me a beautiful card, thanking me and telling me how wonderful it was to see me onstage and to have worked with me. I still have that card. She really was lovely.

KAREEM ABDUL-JABBAR

I loved the Ebonics scenes because they poked fun at a very real subject without diminishing it.

MAUREEN MCGOVERN (Sister Angelina)

I sang "Respect" to the two "jive dudes" while one was puking his guts out. They also shot me doing "I Enjoy Being a Girl," which has many verses, but it was left out of the film because it took way too long to get to the punch line. At one point while filming it, I lost my way in the lyrics and blurted out, "Oh, shit!" The song may not have made the final cut, but my "Oh, shit!" made a random appearance in the dailies, or so I've been told. Sure wish I had an outtake of that!

"*Shiiit, man. That honky mofo messin' mah old lady—got to be runnin' cold upside-down his head, you know?*"

"*Hey, home', I can dig it. He ain't gonna lay no mo' big rap-up on you, man.*"

BARBARA BILLINGSLEY

I went to New York to be on *The Today Show* because of that role. All kinds of things happened for me because of that role. And there are people who talk to me as much about that as they ever did for *Leave It to Beaver*. I got fan mail! It was crazy! My great-nephew, he's sitting in the movies, and he sees me, and he suddenly screams out, "Aunt Barbara!" He didn't know I was in the movie. But it was remarkable. It started my whole career again.

> **TOM PARRY**
> After *Airplane!* opened, I was in New York, it was playing in Times Square—and this was when audiences in Times Square were more likely than not to be African American—and I thought to myself, I really want to see this picture with an African American audience, because I want to see what happens when the guys start speaking jive. And I'm glad I did, because it was one of the biggest reactions I've seen ever to a comedy scene.

Jim: Watching a comedy movie that works, sitting anonymously in an audience, is one of the top perks for a writer/director. I remember going to watch *Airplane!* in an African American neighborhood. I was a little nervous when the Black dudes came up. Would it be offensive? But the audience genuinely loved it. Then I remember thinking, *Maybe this isn't merely a joke about jive talking and the stupid White guy subtitles.* I know we promised not to take ourselves seriously, but perhaps inadvertently we wrote a joke acknowledging the tone deafness of White America to the whole four hundred years of the African American experience.

David: Oddly, that joke got a huge laugh in Germany. Instead of jive, they dubbed them in a Bavarian dialect, which evidently northern Germans have trouble understanding.

Jerry: The airport PA announcements turned out to be easy to write, again thanks to Arthur Hailey, but hard to cast.

Jim: We were sitting and writing the script for *Airplane!*, and we thought, *Gosh, wouldn't it be fun to have the red zone/white zone people break into an argument?* But we couldn't think of an appropriate argument! So we walked to the local drugstore, and we just started looking through some cheap novels that were on sale.

Jerry: Of course, one of the books happened to be Arthur Hailey's *Airport*.

David: Of course, we started paging through it.

Jim: And there was this argument between this man and this woman that went, "Oh, really, Vernon? You want me to have an abortion?" "Well, if it's done properly, therapeutically . . ." So we just copied it from that book.

David: Word for word, even the names are the same! Betty and Vernon. We would never have come up with those.

Jim: To our credit we did write the line, "Listen Betty. Don't start up with your white zone shit again."

Jerry: Hailey just kept supplying us with great lines. By the time we figured out the joke, we were so attached to the setup lines that nothing else seemed right.

Jim: We've always known we were indebted to Arthur Hailey, but this really cranks it up a notch. And how perfectly insensitive is Vernon?! "But at least it's over quickly, and if it's done properly, therapeutically, there's no danger involved." Even in a *Roe vs. Wade* on-again, off-again world, Vernon remains the perfect numbskull.

OVER 5,000,000 COPIES IN PRINT

#1

THE NUMBER ONE NOVEL
OF THE YEAR
BY THE AUTHOR OF WHEELS!

ARTHUR HAILEY

AIRPORT

"Thought better of what?"

"Oh really, Vernon! Why pretend? We both know perfectly well what it is you're talking about. You want me to have an abortion. You've been thinking about it ever since I told you I was pregnant. Well, haven't you?"

He nodded reluctantly. "Yes." He still found Gwen's

door, no blank refusal.

He tried to make himself the voice of reason. "It's really the only sensible thing to do. Maybe in some ways it's unpleasant to think of, but at least it's over quickly, and if it's done properly, therapeutically, there's no danger involved, no fear of complications."

"I know," Gwen said. "It's all terribly simple. Now you have it; now you don't." She looked at him directly.

Arthur Hailey's novel: he just kept supplying us with great lines.

Jerry: Clueless people are always funny. So we used Hailey's dialogue and auditioned a lot of actors, but nobody could get it right. They all sounded like they were *acting* it, and we wanted it to sound like a disagreement between two emotionless PA announcers.

David: We kept bringing in different actors to read, but it wasn't working.

Jerry: No matter what direction we gave them, it never sounded like the real thing. Finally we asked, "Well, who actually did the airport recording?" And it turned out that it was the people who sold the PA system to the airport: a husband and wife team, and they'd just recorded it themselves!

David: They were, like, "Why hire actors? It's just 'red zone, white zone'!"

Jerry: So we asked them to come in and give it a try. They did it perfectly.

KEN COLLINS

It's really different now, but at the time we had access to the then TWA terminal at LAX.

David: We only had to close down thirty- or forty-foot sections of the airport.

DAVID LEISURE (First Krishna)

When we shot the scene with "The white zone is for loading and unloading only," my first daughter was born that night. So, I was shooting that scene and going, "Can I leave? Because I have a woman in labor I have to run back to." I made it in time, but that was just a weird six months of my life. Also, I hate to admit it, but I didn't get the joke. I didn't get it. I was, like, "This just looks like words to me. I don't see what's so funny." And it wasn't until I realized they'd used all these really, really serious guys and had them be really, really serious, which turned out to be funny, that I finally got the joke. I'm a little slow.

Jerry: Shooting at the airport presented a ton of challenges, because our cast of extras ended up getting mingled with people who were actually trying to catch flights out of LAX. And they were eating our food!

David: Of course, anytime we could, we used our friends and family as extras. In that opening scene at the airport, you can see our sister, Susan, and her husband, Bill, quite prominently. And then she appears as an airline clerk in the scene where Bob Hays gets the smoking ticket.

Jerry: I told our DP (director of photography), Joe Biroc, to put a light on her, and he looks back at me and says, "On an *extra*?" I said, "It's my sister." He says, "Gotcha!"

> **KEN COLLINS**
> At the time, extras were still unionized in Hollywood in the Screen Extras Guild, and there were a lot of regulations about how you had to pay them, so we kind of made a deal. We said, "You're basically going to have a regular job for a few weeks where you're going to be on this airplane, but sometimes there's going to be some . . . different stuff that happens. And sometimes there are going to be different people sitting in your seat or whatever." So we made a deal with people to give them regular employment but with the knowledge that sometimes they'd be displaced. So we essentially had a background repertory company that we put together for all the antics that were going to go on.

David: We put our sister and our mom in almost every movie we made. Between us they must have been in almost twenty films.

Jerry: Susan wasn't an actress, but she loved being in the movies. It made her somewhat of a celebrity back home in Vernon, Connecticut. She never missed a shoot. Often, she was featured in the background, but if we could, we'd give her a line. She never lost her enthusiasm for it. Our mother was a high school English teacher, but her first love was acting. She gave it up to raise us, so putting her in our movies seemed only fair.

David: It was nice to be able to give her real parts in movies, because it was a love of hers, and one could make a case that she gave it up for us. But Dad was not only *not* interested in getting in the movies; he had trouble even smiling for a camera!

Jerry: In *Airplane!*, Mom is the lady trying to put on makeup during turbulence.

David: I think she would rather have had an actual line.

Jim: My mom got a line in *Airplane!* She's the woman who's sitting next to Leslie on the airplane and says, "Oh, stewardess! I think the man sitting next to me is a doctor!" She introduced Leslie Nielsen's comedy career. He's wearing a stethoscope. She came out to LA about a week before to get ready for her part. And I remember her walking around the house for that entire week, saying, "Oh, stewardess! I *think* the man sitting next to me is a doctor!" And then, "I think the *man* sitting next to me is a doctor!" And then, "I think the man sitting next to *me* is a doctor!"

David: It was very special having our moms on set, especially with our "TV mom," Barbara Billingsley, and of course, we knew we had to get a picture!

Three moms: Louise Abrahams, Barbara Billingsley, Charlotte Zucker

CHAPTER 14

THE MOVIE BUSINESS

Kentucky Fried Movie was my sexual awakening. Several years after it came out we somehow had a VHS of it, and I'd never seen anything like it. Then came *Airplane!*, which changed comedy, and *Police Squad!*, which I felt was made just for me. I mean, I guess I'm just naming projects, but seriously it's amazing—just such a steady stream of absurd, silly, and totally unique comedy. You could watch any of those, plus *Top Secret!* and the *Naked Gun* movies, and you know in under a minute who made it. It was such a specific genre of comedy that no one really has been quite able to rip off, astonishingly.

SARAH SILVERMAN

David: The day the check cleared for *Kentucky Fried Movie*, we closed the theater. Finally, we were in the movie business!

Jim: And we dove headfirst into preproduction—whatever that was.

Kentucky **Fried Theater** 86'd to start cooking up a movie

After five years of sold-out performances to over 400,000 Los Angelenos, the Kentucky Fried Theater has closed its doors in order to devote full time to a feature motion picture, "The Kentucky Fried Movie." The last performance occurred Dec. 12.

Written by the same group of zanies who masterminded the Kentucky Fried Theater shows, the Kentucky Fried movie is slated to premiere in May of 1977.

Goodbye: *L.A. Times* notice, 1976

Preproduction: John Landis, Jerry, Bob Weiss, Jim

BOB WEISS

We needed to rent dollies, cranes, lighting, sound equipment, and we faced either paying a premium for being unknowns, or getting refused entirely. So the guys came up with the idea of naming our company Samuel L. Bronkowitz Productions, a name they just made up. Early on, I had to call a costume company to rent wardrobe, and I said to the woman, "That's for Samuel L. Bronkowitz Productions." She replied, "Gee, is he still making pictures?" It worked.

Samuel L. Bronkowitz Productions, Inc.

10303 WEST PICO BOULEVARD
LOS ANGELES, CALIFORNIA 90064

TELEPHONE
(213) KLONDIKE 2-1456

Since 1937

David: Once we were on set, we were definitely soaking everything in. This was a much bigger production than our small crew for the ten-minute film.

Jim: We were complete novices. I remember asking stuff like, "Who's that? What does she do?" Someone would tell us, "She's the script supervisor. She keeps track of what gets printed, and continuity." And one of us would ask, "What's continuity?"

David: This was material we'd written, but also performed, and we were very specific about how we thought our comedy should be done.

On the set of *KFM*: with Zucker nephews Ben and Jeremy Breslau. And Landis

Jerry: We were always tapping John on the shoulder, saying, "Uh, how about this?" or, "No, no, that's too over the top!" We didn't hold back. After a while, it was, like, "Whose turn is it to go and tell John?" You know, send someone into the fire. And we wondered why he was getting so irritated. Until we actually directed a film ourselves, and then we realized how incredibly patient he had been. God, that must have been annoying.

David: By and large, Landis respected our opinions, and he was very collaborative. But as the director, he was in control. I think we understood that to some extent, but we still had very strong views about how it should be done.

Jerry: John was a big personality, a great storyteller. He liked jokes to explode off the screen. Our style was more subtle. We wanted actors to stay within the tone that we were parodying. In the end, I think the combination worked well.

"We'll always be
grateful for Landis's
contributions."

Jim: John added things like the shower scene, which was one of the scenes that gave *KFM* its R rating—and probably half the box office.

David: Our mom had no problem with the R rating and was excited to have been in the courtroom scene. When her friends complimented her about her sons' having made a movie, she would thank them and say, "And you know, I'm in it!" Then, of course, the next question was, "Which part?" And she would always reply, "The shower scene!"

Jim: I remember shooting *Kentucky Fried Movie* and thinking, *Someday I'm going to have a family, and someday I'm going to have to explain this to my kids.* Cut to fifteen years later, and I walk into my family's TV room, and there's my ten-year-old son with several of his buddies, with the frame frozen on those gigantic naked breasts. No explanation needed.

Jerry: My kids are in their thirties and I still won't let them see it.

Jim: As collaborative as John was, and as many great jokes and scenes as he added, our takeaway was that if we write something, we need to direct it. There were dozens of

"Rams plagued by fumbles as earthquakes rock Los Angeles."

things in *Kentucky Fried Movie* that all worked out fine, except for the times when we said, "Um . . . we would've done that a little differently."

We would have done it a little different.

JOHN LANDIS
I had to be very Zen about them. Because I really think they're smart and I really think they're funny, but they didn't know anything about a montage or how you shoot a movie. So many times they'd come and ask things like, "Can't it be this color?" And I'd go, "No. We're on the set. We're shooting. The wall is that color."

David: The movie opened on August 10, 1977, without any big premiere, but the theaters were packed nationwide the first night.

Jerry: The next day we got a call from Salah Hassanein, the head of UATC. He was ecstatic. The movie made back their entire investment the first weekend.

©2003 KFM FILMS INC.

Jim: It got pretty good reviews.

Jerry: And some classic pans. Rex Reed said the film left him with the taste of bile on his tongue. Which explains that look he always has on his face.

David: Because of our experience on *Kentucky Fried Movie*, filmmaking was no longer a mystery. If it hadn't been for John and for *Kentucky Fried Movie*, I don't know if we would've ever been able to direct *Airplane!*

Jim: Earn as you learn.

David: It would've seemed beyond us. We found ourselves saying, "Hey, we can do this!" It turned out that our inability to raise the money for our original *Airplane!* script was a hidden blessing.

BILL HADER

I remember very vividly being in a video store and seeing the *Kentucky Fried Movie* box and it saying, "From the people who brought you *Airplane!* and *Animal House.*" Even at ten years old I knew their names, so I went, "Oh, man, I've got to watch this!" It was perfect for when you're a young boy and your friends are over. You've got to hide it, because it's contraband, but then you're, like, "Oh, man, you've got to see this!" I mean, few things were more exciting than *"Catholic High School Girls in Trouble"*!

CARLTON CUSE

I loved *Kentucky Fried Movie.* That movie was just crazy and amazing. As a teenager seeing it, it was a subversive, raunchy comedy unlike anything anyone else had done. It had a freshness to it that was completely striking.

Fistful of Yen: *Wizard of Oz* ending

REX REED

"The Kentucky Fried Movie" tries vainly to be a combination of "Saturday Night Live" and The Harvard Lampoon. The first line of the movie is unprintable in a family journal and the thing progresses from that sewage level to a series of take-offs on commercials, news shows, talk shows, game shows, kung-fu movies and sexploitation flicks. The format leans heavily on "Laugh-In," but is different in the profusion of vulgarity that would never be permitted on TV. The skits are stupid, resulting in a waste of time and money. Somebody named John Landis directed this trash with more energy than craft. Guest performers include Donald Sutherland, who is fast becoming the male Karen Black, Bill Bixby, and Tony Dow in his original role of Wally ("Leave It to Beaver"). They are all terrible. A trip to the Kentucky Fried Chicken chain would be more entertaining and would not leave you with the taste of bile on your tongue.

CHAPTER 15

BACK TO THE DRAWING BOARD

Honestly, *Airplane!* was sort of the *Star Wars* of comedy. We just remember being in the theater and thinking, like, This is a whole different kind of comedy. The tone of it was just something we'd never seen before and thought was so funny. And it really was like *Star Wars* for us. We went to see it several times, with different friends and everything.
It was a big deal.

TREY PARKER and MATT STONE

"There's no reason to panic."

David: After *Kentucky Fried Movie*, we went back and read our original *Airplane!* draft. We all realized this thing badly needed a rewrite; we couldn't just go pitch it right away.

Jerry: We had enough money from our small profit participation in *KFM* to live on for a while. Jim had moved out of the apartment above the theater years before and into his own place.

Jim: Imagine not having to share a bathroom with five other guys.

Jerry: But David and I stayed on a bit longer.

David: Until one day I was in my room talking on the phone with a girlfriend, and I noticed a strange echo on the line. It seemed to be coming from outside, so I walked into the living room and opened the window. Out on Pico Boulevard, a small crowd was gathered on the sidewalk, listening to my conversation, which was blaring over a loudspeaker.

Jerry: David was pissed, but at the same time, I think he appreciated the joke, so he just said, "Jerry, I realize this is funny, but I'm moving out."

David: Eventually, Jerry also moved out of the apartment. Since we no longer had the dining room at the theater to write, we decided to rent a bungalow in Santa Monica.

Jerry: It was on 4th and Ocean, the kind of thing that couldn't exist now because the land is much too valuable—a cluster of little one-story bungalows from the 1920s separated from each other with grass and walkways.

David: We had to tell the landlord we were living there and not just using it for an office. An old guy, Mr. Huffman.

Jim: Old? He must have been at least sixty! We spent almost a year there, rewriting *Airplane!* It made the perfect office. There was a living room, a bedroom, and a bathroom. And I had a toy poodle who used to fart a lot. Elaine. David and Jerry hated her.

Gassy poodle

Jerry: We probably shouldn't have gotten so pissed off that the dog was farting, but on the other hand, it could get pretty bad. Jim's sense of smell must have been diminished, or maybe an indication of just how much he loved that dog.

Jim: She was a toy poodle. How bad could those farts have been?

Jerry: Bad. I wish I could block out the memory.

Jim: You can't. She was named after my aunt, Elaine Elkon. Then we named Julie Hagerty's character after her.

Jerry: I would have been fine with another name. In any case, we worked at the bungalow Monday through Friday. We just wrote, without any pressure. It was a great time in our lives. We knew by then that the pacing was slow. Once again, we had fallen in love with all the great lines that we were making fun of.

David: Instead of just one little quick thing between jokes, we'd left these long speeches that I think were directly from *Zero Hour!* When we got back to work, with our editing experience from *Kentucky Fried Movie*, we looked at it and just couldn't believe that we'd put so much in.

Jerry: Losing all the excess dialogue was easy, and brainstorming new jokes was just pure creative fun. Of course, in those days it was all on a typewriter. I think most of the time it was Jim who'd type.

"By the way, is there anyone on board who knows how to fly a plane?"

David: It was always Jim.

Jerry: Well, I just know it was never me, because I can't type *or* spell. So that was out of the question. To make changes, David would literally cut strips of slug lines or dialogue and paste them onto the pages. Then he'd tape the pages together into a long continuous strip—a dozen feet long—and lay it out over the table and cut them into eight-by-ten sections.

David: And Xerox those. We'd all take them home and come back the next day with notes. Then we'd start over with revisions and it would become long strips again. From time to time, the pages would become such a mess of glue and cuttings we'd have to take it to a typing service called Barbara's Place. And they would type the whole thing fresh so we could start making a mess out of it again.

Jim: And if I might add, I'm not great at pitching jokes. So a lot of the jokes I initiated, I would just type them when I was transcribing a scene from *Zero Hour!*, and then I'd wait to see if David and Jerry would laugh.

David: Sometimes, Jim would type stuff into the script that he thought would never go in the movie, but just to get a laugh in the room. I remember reading "...and sit on your face and wriggle" and cracking up.

(ᴮᴰ) 61

157 CONTINUED: 157

                        ELAINE
     No.

                    DR. RUMACK
     All right. Unless I can get all
     these people to a hospital quickly,
     I can't even be sure of saving
     their lives. Now, is there
     anyone else on board who can land
     this plane?

                    ELAINE
     Well...

~~158   OMITTED~~

~~158~~ 157A INT. PASSENGER CABIN - NITE   159

     Striker, struggling with drinking problem, pours drink
     between his cheek and ear.

157B INT. COCKPIT - NIGHT

                    ELAINE
                  ~~(cont'd)~~
     No. No one that I know of.

                    DR. RUMACK
     I think you ought to know what
     our chances are. The life of
     everyone on board depends on
     just one thing: finding
     someone back there who not
     only can fly this plane, but
     who didn't have fish for
     dinner.

     CAMERA ZOOMS into CLOSEUP of Elaine's face as she realizes
     the severity of the situation.

158   EXT. AIRPLANE - NITE   158

     THUNDER and lightening.

160   INT. PASSENGER CABIN - NITE   160

     Passengers are listening to P.A.

                 ELAINE (V.O.)
     Ladies and gentlemen, this is
     your stewardess speaking.

ADAM MCKAY

I remember being in the movie theater and almost seeing white light. It overloaded me! And then my friends and I left, and we were just talking for days about the movie, and just every joke. "Looks like I picked the wrong week to quit sniffing glue," the dog attacking the guy to pick up the captain at his house. ... Those specific jokes that are almost like anarchy, where the structure of the movie almost falls apart but doesn't quite. We kept talking about it.

Jerry: I remember the first time we took the script into Barbara's Place. A few days later we got a call from the typist asking us if we were aware that we had named eight different characters Frank. We weren't. We just loved the name Frank.

Jim: We never thought, *Wouldn't it be funny if the pilot was a pedophile?* "Have you ever seen a grown man naked?" was just an outrageous line that developed into Captain Oveur's character.

Jerry: The setup for that joke is in *Zero Hour!* when the captain asks the question, "Joey, have you ever been in a cockpit before?" Someone stopped the tape and said that line . . .

Jim: It was actually a much more vulgar line than that.

David: I think it was, "Have you ever sucked a grown man's cock?" That was really the start of that character.

Jerry: In comparison, "Have you ever seen a grown man naked?" is really very mild—a real sign of maturity on our part.

Jim: We had written a hint of that earlier when Captain Oveur is at the magazine stand, casually browsing *Modern Sperm* magazine in the Whacking Material section. It's not like right away after seeing *Zero Hour!* we said, "Let's make the pilot a pedophile or the air traffic controller a drug addict or the guy who talks him down feel as though Christmas was a living hell or a dashing leading man who literally bored people to death." They all just sort of evolved.

David: We used every opportunity to make a joke, whether it was verbal, visual, or written, like cutting to the lighted sign in the cabin that read, "El No A You Smoko." That's literally the definition of "stupid."

MAUREEN MCGOVERN

I didn't get to keep the copy of *Boy's Life*, but years later someone sent a press pic of my Sister Angelina looking puzzled at *Boy's Life* partnered with Joey savoring *Nun's Life*. I have it framed in my office.

Jim: There were also lines like "I am serious, and don't call me Shirley," where we'd just burst out laughing.

Jerry: There was no pressure. Mostly, I just remember the three of us laughing a lot. And I can say, at least for me, it was the greatest joy to say something that would get a laugh from Jim and David.

Jim: Jerry, I think that all the time.

Jerry: On the flip side of that, when someone suggested a joke and the other two guys didn't laugh, we'd just move on. If David and Jim didn't laugh, I just assumed it wasn't funny.

David: We'd worked together for so long and grew to trust each other such that we didn't care about bombing in the room.

"Hey, Striker! How about a break? I'm getting tired!"

ADAM MCKAY
So much of comedy is about rhythm and timing, and when you watch the Marx Brothers and you watch *Airplane!*, it's like watching a Buddy Rich drum solo. Timing is timing. Timing is universal. And you can feel that crackling timing out of the Marx Brothers movies and out of *Airplane!* and *The Naked Gun* and all those movies. It's kind of undeniable.

TREY PARKER

It was so weird to find out that a big influence of theirs was the Marx Brothers. I still don't get that. I watched the Marx Brothers, and I'm, like, "How did this influence them? How do you get from the Marx Brothers to *Kentucky Fried Movie*?" I've tried to figure that out, and I cannot figure it out.

Jerry: We became Marx Brothers fanatics when we got to college. Their films were filled with brilliant slapstick, one-liners, songs, and even surrealism. They were true anarchists, provocateurs.

David: But still they had a discipline to them. Everybody around them was playing stuffy, pompous characters. Actors like Sig Ruman and Margaret Dumont. Not everyone was trying to be funny. We loved how they would build their gags to an impossible point where the punch line would go that one step beyond any logic. It put them in a class by themselves. They rose above the level of other acts, like the Three Stooges, who were just slapstick, physical comedians. That's why the Marxes are still funny if you watch them today.

Jerry: The Marx Brothers stood for a kind of freedom. They were an uncontrollable force in the midst of all those stuffy authority figures. They refused to take anything seriously.

Jim: Okay. All right. I've been sitting quietly for about fifty years of this conversation with you guys praising the Marx Brothers to no end. I've pretty much just bit my tongue. But frankly, I'm getting up there in years, and I really don't know how many opportunities I have left. So here it goes: I've never cared for the Marx Brothers. They were always too broad and cartoony and goofy for me.

David: You're saying this now?

Jim: In our early days I would try to say something about how obnoxious I found them. But you guys were so enthusiastic I just gave up. I know you're wrong, but I've learned to live with it. Can we at least move on?

David: Sure. Of course. So, the Marx Brothers, brilliant comedians in a class by themselves . . .

Jerry: . . . made fun of high society and we made fun of high drama. But both with a wrecking ball approach.

Jim: Oy. It's an entirely different kind of comedy altogether.

Jerry and David: It's an entirely different kind of comedy.

Jerry: If we had been gifted comic actors, our films might have been more in the Marx Brothers style.

David: But none of us had aspirations to act or play goofy characters. That's why we became writers, and we worked best when we worked together collaboratively.

Jerry: We were a very tight group; it was really more like three brothers. And somewhere along the line we made the decision not to take individual credit for anything.

David: I wonder if it was even a decision. I think we just never thought about it.

Jim: I think it was a rare moment of youthful wisdom.

David: The best way that a collaboration can work—and maybe the only way—is to not put any value on individual credit. I think we did it naturally. There were times when

"Air Israel, please clear the runway!"

an outsider would ask which one of us thought up a particular joke, and we'd say, "We don't remember," and we really *didn't* remember!

Jim: In success, there's plenty of credit to go around. In failure, it's like rats swimming from a sinking ship.

Jerry: But in fact, the three of us shared both the successes and the failures. And I think that really kept us from getting too carried away with either. It softened the sting of defeat and kept our egos in check when we were successful. We also had another rule: argue about something as much as you want, but don't get personal. You can say whatever you want, but you can't end the sentence with "You asshole!" So we never did.

David: I don't think the idea of "You asshole" ever even came up.

Jerry: Except when it came to the poodle.

Jim: Elaine! May she rest in peace.

CHAPTER 16

THE STUDIOS

When I was in the third grade, I realized that I had
memorized the jive scene from *Airplane!*

MAYA RUDOLPH

Jerry: After we finished the script for *Airplane!*—or thought we'd finished—we started the process of getting turned down by everyone all over again. By that time, we had met Jon Davison, who had produced low-budget films for Roger Corman. He agreed to be our producer—another piece of great luck.

> **JON DAVISON (PRODUCER)**
> I believe that Kim Jorgensen of Landmark Theaters suggested they get in touch with me. I guess they were shopping for a producer, and they sent me a script, and I was in preproduction on *Piranha*. And I said, "I can't do it for a year, because I'm doing this *Piranha* movie." And I got the impression that they weren't really gonna wait for a year. But as it turned out, a year later I think they were still trying to get it off the ground, so we reconnected.

David: Our first stop was UATC and Salah Hassanein, who'd had so much success with *Kentucky Fried Movie*. But to our surprise Salah turned it down, suggesting that we incorporate *Airplane!* into a *Kentucky Friend Movie* sequel as a "movie within a movie," as we had done with the Bruce Lee parody. After that, we tried shopping it everywhere. And I mean *everywhere*.

Jim: We tried to get it to anyone and everyone in town who could possibly read it, and one friend of ours said she had read it. We said, "Where'd you get a copy?" And she said, "I found it on the bus!" That's how many copies there were floating around. The worst-kept secret in Hollywood.

Jerry: We actually paid extra for thick, blue faux-leather script covers embossed with *Kentucky Fried Airplane!* in big white letters. A complete waste of money! It just screamed, "They're idiots!" But there was a guy, some producer from Canada, named Gerry Arbeid, who somehow got a hold of the script. I don't know how.

Jim: He must've found it on a bus.

Jerry: Maybe he was impressed by the cover, because he actually wanted to option it and made us an offer: if it got made, we would get paid $250,000!

David: He was going to get a director and cast it and make the movie. And he was offering real money. And we were kind of debating it, and I was agonizing over it, because I remember I was trying to rationalize, "Well, we could be on the set and we

KENTUCKY FRIED AIRPLANE!

We actually paid extra for thick, blue faux-leather script covers. It just screamed: "They're idiots!"

could kind of keep control over it." But Jim sat me down and said, "David, if we sell it, fine, but you're just going to have to sit shiva and let it go." Those exact words. And that was the best advice I ever got. Other than "Rome wasn't built in a day" from Dad.

Jim: And "Buy a tuxedo" from Howard Koch.

Jerry: It would have been like selling our baby to Michael Jackson. We just couldn't do it.

David: So we said no.

Jerry: We had a bunch of meetings at studios. We'd bring in an 8mm movie projector and show clips from *Zero Hour!* to try to explain the concept. We had a great meeting at Warner Bros. Mark Rosenberg, the head of production, loved the idea,

"Put all your metal objects in this tray please."

seemed to really get it. We were ecstatic. And then he read the script—or some reader did—and it was a pass. I don't know, if they're eventually going to pass, is it better to have a bad meeting and assume they're going to pass, or have a great meeting and then get crushed?

David: We were learning that in Hollywood no one actually reads anything. The heads of studios in particular will have someone way down on the totem pole read and vet incoming scripts. On top of that, comedy is hard to understand on the page, and *Airplane!* in particular was a difficult script to understand, because nothing like it had been done before. Looking back, I don't really blame anyone for passing on *Airplane!* It wasn't an easy concept to understand.

Jim: Yeah, I don't think it was a generational thing either. Woody Allen had been around, and Mel Brooks had been around, but there hadn't been anything comedian-less. So you could be twenty and not get it, and you could be seventy and not get it. I think it was just innovative, and people had to see it to really get it. It's like when they invented shampoo. I'm sure at the beginning people said, "A special soap just for my hair? That's crazy!" Then they tried it and their hair got much cleaner and they said, "Now I get it."

David: The point is, people just weren't "getting" the script, and we were getting nowhere. It was probably like Columbus trying to tell people, "If you sail west, you won't fall off the edge of the earth! It's round! There's land out there!"

Jim: "And your hair is filthy. Try this!"

David: Ken Shapiro had come to see the show (at Kentucky Fried Theater) and even substituted for Stucker on piano on occasion. We asked him to read the *Airplane!* script. When we went to his house for a meeting, he handed us back the script, saying, "This is *The Big Bus*," an unsuccessful 1976 disaster movie spoof. "It'll never work." As we backed out of his driveway, he sprayed a garden hose into our open car window.

Jim: We had been turned down by all the studios when somebody got the script to Bob Rehme at AVCO Embassy Pictures. A medium-sized studio, they had no physical studio lot, but at least had distribution.

Jerry: We were really excited about it, but they couldn't quite green light the project. They were on the verge of getting the money, about to get the money, really close to getting the money . . . but they didn't have the money. It was always, wait another week, or two weeks. We were frustrated, but then we got another offer.

"Sock it to me. Sock it to me. Sock it to me. Sock it to me."

Jim: We got a call from American International Pictures (AIP), another medium-sized studio, known mainly for cheap exploitation pictures. So we had a meeting with the studio head, a guy named Jere Henshaw. He liked the script, everyone was really nice, we agreed to the deal within a few weeks, and it was for us to direct! We couldn't believe it, we were all set to go, and we had the budget, a couple of million. We called AVCO and said thank you, but we're moving on.

Jerry: So we had our first production meeting with Henshaw.

David: And we began with, "We want to start casting, and the first person we want to cast is Robert Stack, as Kramer, who—" And Henshaw interrupts, "Wait a minute. Robert Stack? Robert Stack's not gonna be in this picture. This is a comedy, and we're gonna get comedians!" And we said, "Um . . . didn't anybody tell you the concept? Remember the meeting we had? Straight actors? Stack, Efrem Zimbalist, Vincent Price, Jack Webb . . ."

Jerry: And he yells at us, "Listen here! Lemme tell you something. *I'm* going to control casting, *I'm* going to control the sets, *I'm* going to control wardrobe, locations. I control *every single thing* on this movie!" And we looked at each other, stunned. All we could say was, "Is it okay if we take our water bottles?"

> **JON DAVISON**
> I went up there by myself to make one last pitch for the cast that we wanted, and Henshaw just wouldn't move off of, "Oh, it's gotta be Dom DeLuise!" He wanted to go down that road, so we actually walked away from the financing of the picture.

David: We called the lawyers and told them we wanted out. So that was the end of AIP. Two weeks later, Henshaw dropped dead of a heart attack.

Jerry: He did?

David: Well, I don't know exactly, maybe it was two years later, but it was certainly long enough for him to see *Airplane!* become a major hit. How great was that?

Jerry: Wow! That's a pretty serious thirst for vindication, David.

"No-frills passengers, please use baggage carousel seven."

Jim: When we first started the theater in Los Angeles, we tried to define each other's chief motivation and we decided that David's was vindication, mine was rebellion, and Jerry's was total irresistibility.

Jerry: It doesn't mean I actually was totally irresistible. I just wanted to be. Mostly women found me totally resistible. Evidently, clueless was not viewed as a romantic trait.

Jim: You wanted to be loved by everyone.

Jerry: No, just by more people than you and David.

Jim: I had a motorcycle that I kept parked behind the theater in L.A. As soon as we were done with the show, I'd sneak out the back of the theater, get on my motorcycle, go to my apartment in Santa Monica, smoke a joint, and watch sports. Sometimes I would rewatch a VHS tape of Gerald Ford falling down the steps of *Air Force One*, or the local newscaster who crawled under his desk when the earthquake hit. Jerry would go into the lobby after the show and hobnob with people, and David, during the show, would scout out the prettiest girl in the audience, and then he'd go and try to meet her.

David: One of them I followed out to the lobby, and then out the door, but before I could talk to her, she got into her car. I managed to take down her license plate number as she drove off. The next day I went to the DMV and got her phone number.

Jerry: They gave out people's *phone numbers*?

David: It was a different time.

Jim: Today that would be called stalking!

David: But then I dated her a couple of times, so it's okay!

Jerry: *That* made it okay?

"The Tower! Oh! Rapunzel! Rapunzel!"

Jim: Anyway, we went back to AVCO Embassy, and although Bob Rehme always loved the project, during our three-week AIP episode, they had actually gotten the money and quickly allocated it to another picture. We went back to the lawyers, and they just went, "Uh . . ."

David: We were out on the street again, square one. Rejections followed from just about every other studio. The worst one, I think, was from United Artists, which came with the comment, "*Kentucky Fried Movie* worked because of John Landis."

Jerry: But then, three weeks later—everything changed.

CHAPTER 17

MICHAEL EISNER

I've always been a person who believed if you hear something good, you should act on it and not just wait or put it in a notebook or something.

MICHAEL EISNER

Jerry: We were back to square one with no prospects of getting *Airplane!* made, and I get a call from Ned Topham of United Artists Theater Circuit.

Jim: Ned had been an executive producer on *Kentucky Fried Movie*.

Jerry: So Ned's on the phone, saying, "I just got a call from Jeffrey Katzenberg at Paramount. He heard about your script. Is it okay if I give him your number?" I didn't know who Jeffrey Katzenberg was, but he worked at Paramount, so I said, "Sure! Absolutely!" The next day I got a call from Katzenberg. He asked, "When can you guys come in?" And I said, "Whenever you want!"

David: I don't know that we had ever heard of Katzenberg or Eisner at that point.

Jim: Well, Michael Eisner at the time ran Paramount, and he had run ABC.

Jerry: So on Tuesday, we piled into the car with our projector and the script, and headed to Paramount.

Jim: At that stage in my life I thought, *Oh, you go to a meeting to find out that something's going to happen.* I never realized that you walked into a meeting with an agenda, an expectation, a goal. And I remember that David, Jerry, and I were driving to the meeting, we were all just having fun, and all of a sudden, Jerry got really quiet. And then we got to the meeting, and they said they were interested, and Jerry actually asked questions about the details of how we would do it. This was a revelation to me. I've spent the rest of my life going to meetings and figuring I should have some idea what I'd like to walk out of this meeting with. But up until that moment, that had never occurred to me.

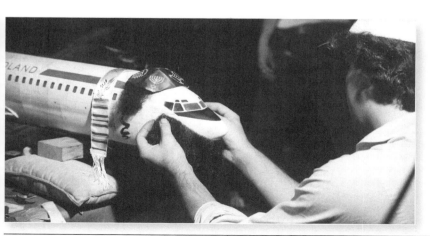

Air Israel in makeup

MICHAEL EISNER (PRESIDENT, PARAMOUNT PICTURES)

A person I'd known in New York, Susan Baerwald, and her husband had moved to California, and she got a job at United Artists as a script reader.

SUSAN BAERWALD

It paid thirty-five dollars a script at that time, and that was how I sort of bolstered my income a little. And I happened to come across the *Airplane!* script. And, you know, we read a lot of scripts, and not a lot of them make you laugh. But United Artists had passed on it.

MICHAEL EISNER

We had dinner with them, and I just started grilling her on how they liked L.A., and since she was a reader, I asked her, "Well, have you ever read anything that was any good? Because I know the stuff they send the people at home must be really poor." And she said, "It's all awful, but there was this one from these guys that did *Kentucky Fried Movie*." And it was a spoof of all those airplane movies, and it was based on *Zero Hour!*, which I had seen when I was fifteen.

SUSAN BAERWALD

It was rejected everywhere, but I can't imagine why. I wasn't aware of *Kentucky Fried Movie* at that time, but I came to know that it was very funny and had been a hit. And yet nobody had picked up on *Airplane!* The script was hysterical. I read millions of scripts. Good ones come along every two years.

MICHAEL EISNER

I didn't say anything. I just got up and I went to the phone—because in those days, you had to go to a pay phone—and I called Don Simpson. I said, "Don, by the time I get in tomorrow, I hope you own this movie." And I went back to the table and I finished the dinner, and that was that.

SUSAN BAERWALD

Later, Michael thanked me with two airplane tickets around the world. The guys also contacted me, and they said, "Well, we want to take you to lunch!" I was thinking Ma Maison or some fancy place. But it was Seafood Broiler in Burbank. If you don't know it, it was a sort of down-market seafood restaurant. A step below Red Lobster. Which is perfectly them.

". . . severe muscle spasms, followed by the inevitable drooling."

David: We entered Paramount through the old gate, the one Gloria Swanson drove through in *Sunset Boulevard*. We were in awe of being at a real studio. Up until this time we had been in the minor leagues, making an independent movie with a little budget. It would've been the same way had we entered the gates at Universal, Warner Bros., MGM, Fox, anywhere. This was a real studio.

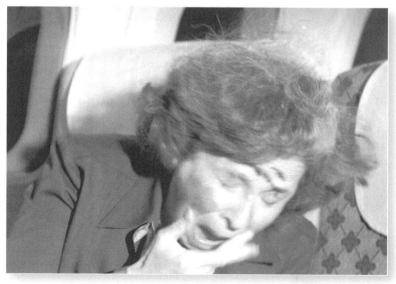

David and Jerry's mom: the makeup lady

Jerry: The offices were beautiful—classically designed with huge hallways filled with posters of all of Paramount's greatest films.

David: Art deco buildings from the twenties and thirties.

Jerry: But beautifully maintained. Not aging. Just always fresh paint, fresh carpet. With a lot of history.

David: Even walking down the hallways, we were in awe of the plush carpeting. We started singing as if we were the choir at a church service, "Para-mount! Para-mount! PAR-A-MOOOUUUNT!" We were just clowning around—probably while Jerry was thinking about what questions he was going to ask.

Jerry: As headstrong as we were, we still felt like we didn't really belong there.

Jim: Growing up in Milwaukee in the fifties and sixties bore no resemblance—I'm talking zero resemblance—to growing up in Los Angeles in 2023. I mean, nothing's the same. There were three TV stations, families ate dinner together, people got dressed up to go to the airport, there was a sugar bowl on the kitchen table and ashtrays in the living room, Father knew best. Everything from the moment you got up until the moment you went back to sleep was completely different. I guess I'm exaggerating a little. You can still get quality municipal bonds at 2–3 percent.

David: My wife and I and our two kids never had a family dinner together. But growing up in Milwaukee, it was every night.

Jerry: Maybe if you had learned to cook.

David: That was never gonna happen. But my wife did learn to order in.

ADAM MCKAY

It's hard to tell my kids now what that was like. There were three broadcast networks, and there was the movie theater down the street, and that was really it. So when this stuff hit, it concussed us! Everything was so straitlaced at that time, in movies and on TV, and it had a predictable tone to it, but these guys, we'd read their names in the credits, and we'd be, like, "Who are they?" And there was no real way to find out. There was no internet. They weren't in the encyclopedia. And we were kids! So we just had no idea who they were.

Jim: There was no social media, so kids would go out and play, and it was okay. It was all pretty mild, the stuff we did back then. We weren't trying to hurt anyone. We were just being creative. Like we'd go to the movies in the middle of the afternoon when there were only a couple of other people in the theater, then sit down behind some guy and ask him if he'd please move over one.

Jerry: It was a more innocent time, for sure. Mom and Dad weren't concerned that David was in a gang putting flares on train tracks to stop freight trains. They'd say, "Go out and play and be home by dinner." This was way before helicopter parenting came into vogue.

Jim's mom: *"I think the man next to me is a doctor."*

David: I should note that they did not find out about the flares until the police came to the house.

Jerry: Then they cared.

David: Yeah. But that blew over pretty quickly.

Jerry: Until he got caught for the next thing. They loved me too much to spend a lot of time worrying about David.

David: Well, there were a couple of other times when they didn't come to the house. Dad had to pick me up at the police station. Once, during a class, the teacher gets a phone call, nods, turns to the whole class and announces, "David Zucker and Glenn Crow, the *police* would like to see you." We were like rock stars. As it turned out, there were no charges, just a lot of interrogation.

Jerry: But David was always the ringleader. I was so proud.

David: Well, I think I just didn't accept authority well. It wasn't that I wanted to get into trouble; I was bored with *not* getting into trouble. And I had a knack for finding creative solutions to problems, combined with a need for attention. My sophomore year in college was the first year the university issued photo ID cards. A bunch of us said no way we're doing that; they're only going to use it to identify us in the weekly antiwar demonstrations! Of course, everyone caved and took normal photos.

Jerry: Except you. You went in dressed up as an Arab.

David: Yeah, with a thick mustache, dark sunglasses, and a turban. The photographer said, "You have to take off the sunglasses, you're unrecognizable." I replied in a stupid accent, "Zat ees zee idea."

Jerry: But you forgot that two weeks later you'd have to go in again and pick it up in person.

David: Yeah, Yeah, I had to dress up all over again. It was still worth it.

Jim: Years later, I had a photo of me Photoshopped. To this day, I send it when

I get a request for a picture. David, Jerry, and I got an award from Sherwood High School, and they actually put the picture on a plaque. I think we all connected over our shared sense of humor, but there was something more than that, I mean, between the two families. Our fathers were business partners.

Jerry: "A to Z in Realty."

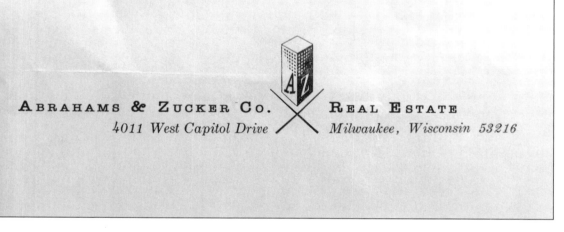

David: And they had a little jingle that played on the radio that we could probably dig up somewhere.

Jerry: Seriously?!

David: No, that's not true. But the families were close. Our sisters were best friends, and later became college roommates.

Jim: Every year my mom would make a one-week pilgrimage to New York to see all the new Broadway shows. Then she'd come back and tell us the stories and buy the albums. *West Side Story, The King and I, The Pajama Game.* My sisters and I would spend the following year singing the songs. We knew each album backward and forward. We loved it. But when I finally got to see the show or the movie, I remember thinking how odd it seemed that people would be having a conversation and suddenly break out into song.

"Honey . . . every . . . thing's . . . coming up . . . roses."

David: Later, we actually incorporated that into a sketch at the theater. Dad would always banter with people who worked for him, or with tenants in his buildings. He'd say the funniest things, but always deadpan. Maybe he got that from his father. There's a great old photo—I'm four years old, standing on a chair between Dad and Grandpa. Dad and I are wearing bowties, and to match us, Grandpa tied his necktie into a ridiculously large bowtie. Looking back at it now, Grandpa posing with a straight face was pure Leslie Nielsen!

Jim: Once in a while my sisters and I got bratty, and we would test my mom by threatening to run away from home. Her response was always, "Let me help you pack." My dad died when I was twenty, but I remember that he did have a good sense of humor. I remember in particular one time a friend of his had died, and he came back from the funeral, which I guess was an open-casket funeral. And I said to my dad, "How'd it go?" He said, "The guy never looked better in his life." I remember thinking, *Oh! It's okay to make fun of death!* That stuck with me, and it kind of opened

the door to dark humor. Decades later, we wrote "United Appeal for the Dead" for *Kentucky Fried Movie*, and I'd really like to think somewhere my dad is smiling.

Jerry: Our family was our first audience. They laughed when David or I made a decent joke, so we kept doing it. But no one ever said, "Hey, you boys should pursue this as a career."

Jim: The Zuckers have a pretty big family. So when we started working together I'd go over to their house, and a bunch of them would be sitting around the den or the living room chatting. It could get a little loud and a little hectic. But frequently I'd walk in and find Uncle Bob flat on his back on the floor, sleeping. Everyone would just walk around him or step over him. At first, I honestly thought they were putting me on. But they weren't. Uncle Bob just liked to take naps.

Jerry: In the Zucker family, all the men were talkers and nappers. I don't remember any athletes.

David: I imagine Jim's house probably wasn't too different.

"I could go on and on, but I would probably start to bore you."

Jim: I don't remember clowning around much at home. But with my friends, we used to do stuff like snagging our lines on the bottom of the lake when we went fishing when there were other boats around. Then we'd pretend we had hooked into a prize lunker, struggling mightily. The people in the other boats would put down their poles and cheer us on. Then we'd pretend the fish pulled us into the lake. Pretty big laughs actually. Once, I remember, we got applause!

Jerry: One thing we all had in common was that our parents just really wanted us to pursue anything but what we ended up pursuing.

Jim: To be honest, I think my parents just thought I was nuts. They probably had a pretty good case. One time, they sent me somewhere for vocational testing. The results that came back strongly suggested that I work with insects. My Aunt Ada probably summarized it best. She would always say, "I don't care what they say about you Jim, I love you."

David: But they were encouraging, weren't they?

Jim: Perhaps confused would be a better word.

David: I think our moms were very proactive in trying to steer us.

Jim: I gave my eighth-grade commencement address. Not a big deal, there were only twenty-five kids in my class. My mom wrote the address for me. It started by saying, "We approach eighth-grade graduation with mixed emotions." And then I remember thinking, *What the fuck are mixed emotions?*

Jerry: I remember Mom saying to me when I would argue about stuff, "You're going to make a great lawyer!" That was before they knew about ADD. And I guess she never noticed that my lips moved when I read.

Jim: You would've made a terrific lawyer. I think back to all the meetings we went to, when something was in dispute. David and I would just kick back, because you were making the point for us. All my parents wanted for me was to be happy—which of course meant be a happy lawyer or a happy doctor. When I was about seven, they started having me carve the Thanksgiving turkey. One by one each member of the family would come into the kitchen and say, "Oh look, he has the hands of a surgeon." My dad was a lawyer, and as a little boy I'd go to his office with him once in a while, and I saw all those books that I knew I could never read. And that pretty much ruled out jurisprudence. Then early in high school I took my first chemistry course—and there went my medical career.

 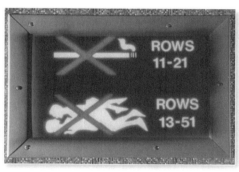

David: Dad found me a summer job at a chair factory, and I was in a spray booth, gluing cushions on chair backs. Occasionally, a fly appeared, I would spray it, and it would stick to the back wall. Then I'd label it with the exact date and time of death. Pretty soon everyone in the factory was crowding in to see the "fly museum." It disrupted everything, so I was moved to another part of the factory.

Jerry: Is that the job where you got fired after a week?

David: No, that was the drugstore across from the high school, where the job required the two things that were impossible for me: making change and finding things.

Jerry: I'm pretty sure we both inherited those genes from our father. Of course, once we were in the movie business, they forgot about all our areas of incompetence, and we became a source of great pride.

David: Although you did fool them briefly by majoring in education. Of course, you just used the opportunity to get laughs.

Jerry: Well, I had a captive audience. Or maybe it was like that story about the scorpion and the frog: "I can't help it, it's my nature." When I was doing my practice teaching at Madison East High School, we had to be evaluated a couple times a year. So one time, the professor took his seat in the back of the room, and I began my lesson by asking questions. When a student got the answer right, I honked a Harpo Marx horn and threw them candy. I had prepped them the day before to clap their hands together and grunt like trained seals. Amazingly, my professor actually thought it was a great teaching technique; all the kids had studied the night before so they could be part of the fun.

Jim: Little did he know you were just practicing for your real career.

David: It's hard to imagine what we would have ended up doing if we hadn't started working together.

Jim: My parents certainly were tenacious about encouraging my medical career. They were friendly with a wonderful guy, Dr. Jay Jacoby. He ran the department of anesthesia at Milwaukee County Hospital and set me up with a summer job working in the morgue. I'd help with embalming the dead bodies.

David: Yikes.

Jim: Every once in a while, a group of new nurses-in-training would pass through to watch an autopsy. I'd run up to the concessions area and get a hot dog and slather it with tons of mustard and ketchup and relish. Then I'd go stand in the middle of the nurses-in-training while the autopsy was going on and eat the hot dog. The condiments would splash on the floor and pretty soon someone would get woozy and pass out. When my parents found out, they weren't so amused.

David: So what exactly did you do there?

Jim: Embalming, for one. We would hook up an IV to the femoral artery of the corpse and give him a transfusion of embalming fluid. One day after we inserted the IV, a coworker and I went up to the commissary to get a bite to eat. Maybe we got second helpings. Maybe service was slow. I don't remember. But when we got back to the morgue all the fluid had run out, and the cadaver had filled up with air. He was actually sitting straight up on the table with an enormous inflated erection. I don't remember if he was smiling. But I actually do remember thinking, *It's too bad this guy is dead. He would have been so proud.*

David: In high school, I dreamed of one day making funny TV commercials. That's the height my directorial ambitions reached. All the movies and TV shows we watched originated from New York or L.A. Milwaukee was a place where things came *to*, not where anything came *from*.

Jim: There was always the sense that New York and L.A. were the happening places and Milwaukee was kind of in the sticks. I mean "I Wish They All Could Be Milwaukee Girls" wasn't going to work as song lyrics.

David: There was a reason that *Happy Days* and *Laverne & Shirley* were set in Milwaukee. Milwaukee *was* the joke.

"Flight 209, now arriving at gate 19 . . . gate 20 . . . gate 21 . . ."

Jerry: I remember occasionally hearing someone yell, "Hey, Milwaukee's on TV!" And we'd all run into the den because something that happened in Milwaukee made the national news. Can you imagine someone in Manhattan saying, "Quick, everyone come in here! They mentioned New York!"

David: There's definitely a very self-deprecating Midwest sense of humor that was born out of that and made it into our movies. Nothing was sacred. We weren't afraid to make fun of the big guys.

Jim: One of the classrooms at Shorewood High School on the top floor had a big domed ceiling. There was an echo. So the maintenance people strung a huge American flag across the ceiling to fix the acoustics. One day there was a substitute teacher, and one of my friends, Pete Pruessing, told her we started every day with the Pledge of Allegiance. So we all lay down on the ground facing the flag and said the pledge. Including the substitute teacher! It was fabulous! It was actually the second-most-talked-about thing at my fifty-year high school reunion. The first was everyone trying to remember where we'd held our fortieth.

David: We grew up around lots of people in Milwaukee who were funnier than we were. But they were all able to get jobs. No matter how funny they were in high school, all those class clowns eventually grew up to be real adults.

Jim: It's a shame Pruessing had such a successful career in healthcare. He would have been an excellent collaborator.

David: But I don't blame him for wanting to stay in Wisconsin.

Jerry: If I had really loved my kids, I would have raised them in Milwaukee.

CHAPTER 18

PARAMOUNT

Airplane! was not like anything else. And Michael Eisner, I think, felt that in his bones. Like, "Wow, this is really, really unique, and as such, is the kind of thing we should be doing!"

JEFFREY KATZENBERG

Jim: At Paramount, after you adjusted to the carpeting, in the hallways you saw pictures of film stars from years gone by. It was overwhelming. Plus just a couple of blocks down from the studio on Melrose Boulevard there was one of those do-it-yourself car washes. Whenever we had meetings after that, I'd try to get there early and wash my car. Kind of a two-birds-one-stone thing. That way if some meeting didn't go well, at least my car would be clean.

David: Our first meeting was with Jeff Katzenberg, who was at the time a vice president, but he seemed to be surprisingly open and friendly.

> **JEFFREY KATZENBERG (Vice President, Paramount Pictures)**
> I remember when they first came to Paramount and I met them for the first time. I had this genuinely little cubbyhole office. I think maybe it was eight feet wide and twelve feet long, with a little couch that the three of them and myself could barely squeeze onto. They brought in an 8mm film projector, and we closed up the blinds, trying to make the room as dark as possible, and because I didn't have anything on the walls, they projected *Zero Hour!* on the wall. And I can tell you, having had thousands—maybe tens of thousands, but certainly thousands—of pitches over forty years, that was a first . . . and there was never a second!

David: We delivered our spiel to Katzenberg, explaining how we wanted the film to look just like *Zero Hour!*, with serious actors, on a prop plane, and in black and white. He listened and watched very politely. I think the main thing was that he was supposed to meet us, hear the pitch, and bring us to Eisner's office. So we walked upstairs—on the way stopping to meet more executives: Don Simpson, Craig Baumgarten, and later Barry Diller, the chairman of Paramount Pictures. Many of the executives there went on to head studios or become successful producers, including Frank Mancuso, head of distribution, and Dawn Steel, head of marketing. But at the time, of course, we didn't know anything about them.

> **MICHAEL EISNER**
> I read the script before the meeting, so I was definitely wanting to make this movie. I picked it up because I loved airplane disaster movies—I could whistle the theme song of *The High and the Mighty* for you right now!—and I thought *Kentucky Fried Movie* was funny. It just seemed like a high-concept, funny idea with guys who had already done something that proved they had a lot of talent.

David: Michael truly believed in the concept—a crazy satirical comedy on an airplane. But at some point, he got wind of our intention to shoot the film in black and white on a prop plane and was dead set against it. We went into panic mode and asked Jeffery if we could present our case to Eisner. We just had to explain the logic, our vision of the film.

BARRY DILLER
The idea of it was so goofy and was so contrarian to anything else we were doing that it appealed to me from the first second that I heard it.

"I remember how I used to sit on your face and wriggle."

Jerry: We showed up at his office the next day and began our argument, explaining in detail why the movie had to be in black and white and on a prop plane, citing all our rules and theories about parody.

David: Eisner listened politely. He didn't argue with us. He just nodded. We were getting more confident. And then when we'd finished, he sat back in his chair and said, "Well, I have to say, you three have been very articulate, you've presented your position extremely well, and it sounds very logical and convincing the way you've explained it. And you may be right. You may go on to actually make this movie in black and white and on a prop plane, and it even may be a big hit. But it won't be at this studio."

Jim: We were stunned. I'm sure we looked at each other, a little embarrassed. Eisner saved the awkward moment by saying, "But don't decide now. Think about it over the weekend. Let's meet again on Monday, and discuss it." Of course, we came back on Monday, and we just caved.

Jerry: That was the best argument we ever lost in our whole careers. Eisner was absolutely right. We've thanked him many times since.

Jim: Early directing lesson: be steadfast in your vision but flexible enough to compromise. It's ticklish.

> **MICHAEL EISNER**
> I just didn't believe it in black and white. This was before *Roma* and *The Artist*. And I didn't believe it as a prop plane. Because to me we were parodying not the movie that they had bought, or *The High and the Mighty*, or any of those. We were parodying all the movies of the last decade, which were all in color and on jets. I thought you wouldn't be getting the full value of the parody. It would be too dated.

Jerry: He also wanted the film to resonate with people's current-day experience of flying.

David: It always reminds me of the story about the UCLA basketball coach, John Wooden. He had a rule: "No long hair, no facial hair." One day his star center, Bill Walton, showed up with a full beard, insisting "It's my right." Wooden asked if he believed that strongly. Walton said he did. "That's good, Bill," Coach said. "I admire people who have strong beliefs and stick by them, I really do. We're going to miss you." Walton shaved it right then and there.

Jim: You know, Eisner's also the one who once said, "If I had green-lit every movie I've passed on and passed on every movie I green-lit, my track record would probably be about the same." As successful as he was, I think he's a guy who did have humility and realism about himself.

> **MICHAEL EISNER**
> Of course, the guys had the last word. They made the sound of the engines on the plane that of piston motors! By the way, it probably would've been just as big a hit done their way.

It had to be a prop plane - or at least sound like one.

Jerry: We could always count on Eisner to be straight with us. The same with Jeffery. They trusted their instincts, but they listened.

Jim: Some years later, after *Top Secret!* flopped, Eisner and Katzenberg had moved to Disney, and they said, "If you have any more ideas, we still like you guys. Let's hear what your ideas are." We were still in shock from *Top Secret!*, and we were out of ideas. So we went to a writer friend who had an idea for a movie he called *Bachelor of the Month*.

David: So we pitched the idea to Eisner and Katzenberg at Disney. It was just terrible. But the funniest thing was Eisner's reaction.

Jerry: He turned to Katzenberg and said, "They're kidding, right?"

MICHAEL EISNER

It was so bad that I remember thinking they were testing me. And I'm not sure they weren't testing me now. Sometimes you deal with people. Like, I remember with Jim Brooks on *Terms of Endearment*, he started quizzing me on whether I'd really read the book. I'm not sure I didn't think this was a big parody in my office, that they were testing me as to whether, because they'd had a big hit, I would say yes to anything they came in with. That's what I thought. That's why I turned to Jeffrey.

David: So Katzenberg says, "No, they're not kidding, this is their pitch." And Eisner grimaced and said, "I hate it. I hate it!" So we just slunk out of there.

Jim: When we got out to the parking lot, we got to the car, and then we just started laughing hysterically. We couldn't stop. I think it was the final straw from *Top Secret!*

David: Years later, I directed Terence Stamp in *My Boss's Daughter* as a corporate boss rejecting a dumb idea brought to him by Ashton Kutcher, and I had him channel Eisner: "I hate it! I hate it!"

Jerry: I think we actually liked that he was so direct. It was an appropriate response, and he was right. The last thing we wanted was someone to say, "Great! Let me think about it," and then never get back to us.

Jim: In my experience with movie executives, one of the things that made Michael and Jeffrey, and Joe Roth, the former head of Fox, so outstanding was that, if the answer was no, they'd say no. I'm told that so many executives and people in the movie business today just keep you hanging around forever and don't return calls. But these guys, they'd say, "I don't like it, it doesn't work," and they let you go on with your lives.

TOM PARRY
The way the studio worked, there were about a half dozen senior production executives, and I was a young executive on the team. Our job was to usher projects through the pipeline. We were the point at which projects were submitted by agents, by producers, by writers, etc., and then we would advocate for the ones that we thought should be on the slate. There would probably be, in any given year, maybe 100–150 projects for which the studio would actually go under contract, otherwise known as being put into development, and out of those, maybe fifteen pictures would get made. Against that backdrop, we would have a production meeting every Monday and go through the list of projects, giving an update of where these projects were, what steps were next, etc.

David: They were also decent people on a personal level. In years since, whenever I had occasion to call Katzenberg, he would always return the call the same day.

Jim: When my house burned down in Malibu, Jeffrey was one of the first people to call me to make sure I was okay or to see if there was anything he could do to help. I'll never forget that.

Jerry: A few years ago, I gave a talk at Google that showed up on their YouTube channel. Eisner happened to be hooking up a new television set, and as he connected to the internet, there I was, talking about *Airplane!* And I said the things we always say about him, which is that we owe him our careers, and that he was right about a lot of things, and that we were really grateful. A few days later, I got a handwritten thank you note from him.

David: After the prop versus jet meeting with Eisner, the first order of business was to do work on the script, which Paramount still hadn't bought, and we weren't anxious to sell it to them, since we were still intent on directing it and didn't want to give up that control.

Jerry: So we just continued to develop it without signing a contract or accepting any money.

Jim: I'm relatively sure that, at that time, their notion—if they were going to get involved at all—would've been to buy the script from us and hire a director.

Tom Parry (right) with Jon Davison and another guy

David: At the time, we had no idea what the odds were against us. We were so naive that we didn't even realize that being in development at a studio was no guarantee, and that there was a chance it wasn't going to get made.

Jim: Our motto could have been "Ignorance is bliss!"

Jerry: Our mascot would have been an ostrich sticking its head in the ground.

David: I always thought that odds never applied to us. Kind of like when we loaded up the U-Haul truck and moved out to L.A. What were *those* odds?!

Jim: Katzenberg assigned a guy on his staff, Tom Parry, to work with us on the rewrite. Tom was what they called a development executive; his expertise was on story and structure. Plus he always wore loafers, which was a good indication that he went to an Ivy League school.

TOM PARRY

One day, Jeffrey walks into my office and says, "Tom, I want you to work on *Airplane!*" Apparently, *Airplane!* was a picture that nobody was interested in. It was really a slate filler for distribution. And it was cheap. I was kind of the junior man on the totem pole, so I got assigned things that nobody else wanted to do! But I always liked dark-horse projects, because those are the ones that, if they have a shot at all, can deliver a big payoff. So I said, "Well, let me read the script, just to see whether it's something I think I can do before I give you an answer." I got the script, I read it, and when I finished, I thought, I don't know why anybody thinks this is funny. It didn't strike me as being funny!

David: So, around midweek, we got a call from Tom Parry, who wanted to meet with us and find out what our "vision" was.

TOM PARRY

We sat in my office, and they took me through the script, and they explained how they were going to do the jokes, and the minute they did that, I said, "That's very funny!" At the time, I was twenty-eight years old, I'd graduated from college at the age of twenty-five, my last year in college I produced the *Hasty Pudding Show*, so I knew exactly what that kind of humor was. So I took over the project.

David: Tom had a great sense of humor, and he was smart. When we explained what we wanted to do, which was basically to remake *Zero Hour!* and cast straight actors, he seemed to have an aha moment, as if the script suddenly made sense to him.

TOM PARRY

I got the *Zero Hour!* script from our library, I took a look at it, and immediately I saw what they had done. They had used the concept but gotten rid of a lot of the plot, so it was a concept without a story anymore. I said, "All you really need to think about is that the audience cares that the plane lands and that the two leads finally get together at the end."

Jim: What Tom hit on is so important in filmmaking. The audience has to care about the story and characters. We could make all the jokes we wanted, but if the story didn't work, the movie wouldn't work. In later years, when we followed this advice, we were successful, and when we didn't, we weren't.

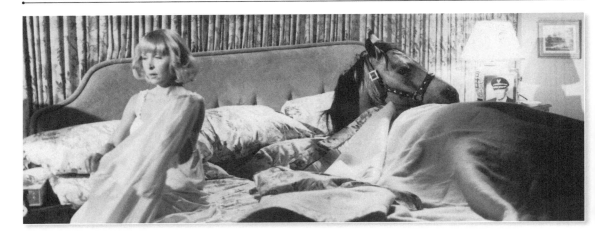

David: We were originally kind of apprehensive about doing any kind of rewrite, because at that point we had never dealt with a studio. I remember Katzenberg saying to us, "Guys, don't look at us as the big, bad studio." Still, all we could think about was a joke that John Landis had told us years before on the set of *Kentucky Fried Movie*.

JOHN LANDIS

A director, a writer, and a studio boss are driving through Death Valley. It's 115 degrees, and the car runs out of gas. They're in the middle of nowhere, so they start walking and walking. The heat is beating down, they're on their last legs, they're about to give up and die, when the writer says, "Hey! What's that? Up there! Something glinting off the sun!" So the director runs up the hill, reaches behind a rock, and brings out a can, pops it open. "My God, this is fresh, cold orange juice! Let's drink it!" And the studio boss says, "Wait! I have to piss in it first!"

JEFFREY KATZENBERG

If they had a fear of the studio wrecking their "baby," well, rightfully so. The garbage dumps of Hollywood are littered with great stuff that studios screwed up. It's not like that's an unfounded fear! There's plenty of examples of bad fingers getting into the pie and making a mess of stuff in it. Including my fingers, so I'm not innocent. I'm sure there are plenty of movies that I messed up. With the best of intentions, by the way! All you ever want is for people to win, for them to succeed, so you always come from a good place. But that doesn't mean that you actually land there.

David: No matter how much we resisted a rewrite, Katzenberg was relentless. He kept reassuring us: "We think this thing could go through the roof. This rewrite will make that possible." He was firm with us, but at the same time calming. That was also the first time I had heard the expression "go through the roof."

Jerry: And Tom Parry turned out to be an excellent choice. He helped us develop the characters and stay more on story as opposed to going on tangents just to cram in another joke. To us, he seemed like a film genius. I'm not sure if it was because he was that smart or because we were that naive. Someone would say, "You see, a movie has three acts," and we'd be like, "My God, this guy is brilliant!" Tom would always say, "Make jokes plot points and plot points jokes."

JEFFREY KATZENBERG

On the studio side, we had high confidence that it was funny and that they were funny and that they were going for something that was unique and different. The only thing that we brought a more traditional thinking to was, "That's great, but you could have the greatest, most spectacular collection of Christmas ornaments ever conceived, but if you don't have a strong tree to hang them on, you got nothing." So from an experience standpoint—and let's just be clear, at that moment in time, I probably had twelve hours more experience than they did—but with my twelve hours more experience and Michael Eisner and his enthusiasm for it, we were just looking to make sure that the Christmas tree could support all the goodies they were bringing to it.

David: Fortunately, we had Arthur Hailey's script for *Zero Hour!* At that time, we didn't know anything about structure and plot. We were coming off *Kentucky Friend Movie*, which had absolutely no plot, just twenty or so unrelated sketches.

JEFFREY KATZENBERG

Tom Parry was a really super talented development executive who I know had a very good rapport with the guys. That's always what you're looking for: how to break through and get trust. You're trying to get to where they're hearing and trusting that they're getting valuable advice, and, on the other side of it, they need to get to a place where they have confidence that, one, we understand what they're trying to do and are supportive of it, and, two, we're not trying to turn it into something it's not or maybe something that we imagined as opposed to something they imagined.

> **MATT STONE**
> The internal drama of *Airplane!* still works and still holds up. You're still rooting for them, and you're still kind of on the edge of your seat, wondering what's going to happen. Very few jokey movies also kind of work dramatically, but you're in the moment of the movie, because it's just so dramatic, the plane-drama stuff. It's just interesting that it does still work. You're still into the story.

Jerry: In *Zero Hour!*, Dana Andrews and Linda Darnell were married and had a child. It was their little boy that they brought to the cockpit to meet the pilots. In *Airplane!*, Ted Striker's romantic interest is with the stewardess. Tom helped us develop the love story through the flashbacks.

> **JEFFREY KATZENBERG**
> We weren't trying to put them in a box. We weren't trying to turn it into a sitcom or into a rom-com. We weren't trying to turn it into anything other than the best version of what they wanted to do and, at the same time, recognize that you needed a beginning, a middle, and an end. It needed a spine to it. And that's why there ended up being that love story at the center of it.

Jerry: So we tried to find one central comic idea for each flashback: their first meeting was *Saturday Night Fever*, falling in love on the beach was *From Here to Eternity*, and the first sign of trouble in the relationship was a white couple explaining Tupperware and basketball to an African tribe, and Striker's "Drinking problem."

David: I think we somehow inadvertently invented going outside of the genre of the movie that we were parodying and taking on other genres.

> **KEENEN IVORY WAYANS**
> They took what Mel Brooks did to a whole other level. They not only made fun of the genre of the main story, but within that, they made fun of ten other movies. Like, you're watching *Airplane!* and then they go into *Saturday Night Fever*, and then they come back to *Airplane!* and then they go to something else and come back.

Jim: To be truthful, I didn't realize until I read a review of the movie that the scene on the beach where they get wiped out by the waves was a spoof of a scene from *From*

Here to Eternity. I didn't know that! At the time we wrote it, I was living on the beach in Malibu, and I remember thinking, "Wouldn't it be funny if a couple was making out on a beach and got wiped out?" I don't think we had *From Here to Eternity* in mind.

Jerry: Uh, we knew that. That was a pretty famous scene, Jim. Iconic, even.

Jim: Oh, right! Now you're going to tell me that the opening scene where the airplane is cutting through the clouds like a shark is based on some other movie?

Jerry: I don't think we ever really stopped writing. We were always changing and adding. Jim used to say that the script was like an overly stuffed closet. But no matter how full it was, you could always open the door really quick and jam in one more thing—one more joke in the script.

David: At some point during the rewriting, Katzenberg called. He wanted us to add more jokes where there's misunderstanding and confusion.

The "mirror scene": *"You can't take a guess for another two hours?"*

Hays, 1980

Jerry: At least that's what we thought he wanted. So we wrote the scene in the galley where Dr. Rumack asks, "How soon can we land?" Captain Oveur tells him, "I can't tell." And Rumack says, "You can tell me, I'm a doctor." I remember we really struggled to write that, and it's one of my favorite scenes, but when we finally sent it to Jeffrey, he thought it was funny, but not what he meant.

David: But it turned out to be a great scene.

Jim: I've always felt that what we did was mostly parody. Basically, we were saying, you don't have to take these things seriously. But once in a while we'd inadvertently slip into actual satire where there's more of a political or social agenda. When Peter Graves says he can't tell how soon the plane will land and Leslie says, "You can tell me, I'm a doctor," it always got a huge laugh. But when you think about it, the line is really making a satirical joke about medical arrogance.

Jerry: We always referred to that as the mirror scene, because Leslie Nielsen and Peter Graves were two white-haired . . .

David: . . . white guys . . .

Jerry: . . . of the same age, and with that same intensity.

David: Our day-to-day, nine-to-five work on the script was with Tom Parry, but occasionally we'd get notes from the studio, and they would always come through Jeffrey.

Jim: Meanwhile, we'd get to the lot in the morning, stand in front of the gate, and still sing, "Para-mount! Para-mount! PAR-A-MOOOUUUNT!"

Jerry: We'd drive around the lot in a golf cart and see these huge sets, crews working, television shows and movies being filmed. We were working on a real studio lot! It was an exciting time.

David: And we'd run into famous people. One time, walking to the commissary, we saw Carl Reiner. I mean, we'd been watching him since the 1950s, when we were kids. We were introduced to him: "Carl, these guys are new to the lot, and are going to be doing this new movie called *Airplane!*" And Carl Reiner says, "That's great. Good luck to you." Then he thought for a second and added, "Good luck to *me!*"

Jerry: John Travolta was there shooting *Urban Cowboy*.

David: One day I liked the shirt he was wearing so I asked him, "What kind of shirt is that?" He pulled the back of his collar out and said, "I don't know. But, here, look at the label." So I made a note of the brand and bought a shirt just like it. Didn't look quite as good on me.

```
                    DR. RUMACK
Captain, how soon can we land?

                  OVEUR
I can't tell.

                    DR. RUMACK
You can tell me.  I'm a doctor!

                  OVEUR
No.  I mean I'm just not sure.

                    DR. RUMACK
Can't you take a guess?

                  OVEUR
Well... not for another two hours.

NUED:
                                    (CONTINUED)

                    DR. RUMACK
You can't take a guess for another
two hours?
```

Jim: Another time, we were having lunch in the commissary, and a waiter dropped a full tray of glasses in a loud crash. The whole room went silent as everyone turned to look. And Jerry Paris, the *Happy Days* director, says out loud, "Wait for your laugh . . ." And the entire place exploded with laughter.

David: These moments, for guys like us, were, like, "Oh, my God, we're in Hollywood! This is happening!" But if you come from places like L.A. or New York, you don't get that same rush, because half the people you know either have a bunch of friends writing a script or have a parent or a brother in the business, so it's not a big deal.

Jim: In this case, Jerry at least had a brother in the business.

Jerry: We never got used to it. We always felt like we were on the studio tour.

Jim: So we worked on the rewrite, and the script was actually getting better.

David: But all the while, they were shopping the script to other directors.

Jerry: They kept trying to talk us out of directing it. They wanted to buy it, but we refused to sell it unless it was in the contract that we were directing it.

Jim: Paramount understandably was leery. We wanted to make a comedy with no comedians, with not only one first-time director, but *three* first-time directors? Never in the history of movies had there ever been three directors on a movie. To this day we are the only threesome to direct a movie. And we were kids. And we'd only been on a movie set one time in our lives. Let's face it: they had a pretty solid case.

Jerry: I remember Katzenberg calling and throwing out some big-name comedy directors, "What if this guy directed it?" It was so obvious to them that the film would be better if it was directed by a real director. We never had illusions about being great directors. It was just that from the very beginning, our whole vision for making *Airplane!* was the idea that the actors would act like they had no idea they were in a comedy. That's what drove us, and we couldn't trust anybody else to do that. We were intractable.

David: They even shopped it to John Landis, but we felt we were ready to direct. I thought we were ready even back in the *KFT* days! I remember once doing a telethon for the L.A. public TV station. In one bit, Jim appeared blindfolded to show how easy

On the Beach: not really that romantic.

it is to shave with a Gillette razor: start tight on the face, then pull back to reveal he's shaving his armpits. But the director was starting in a wide shot, which would have given away the joke. So I walked up to him and told him it should start out tight on Jim's face. The room went silent. The guy glared at me, and I backed off. A crew member came up and whispered to me, "He directed *Laugh-In*." I was quickly ushered off the set.

Jerry: We weren't going to relent, but we weren't getting a green light either. So we just kept rewriting.

David: At one point, Katzenberg came to us with a request from the studio to identify and cut "twenty gags that couldn't happen." Things like "they're on instruments," "the shit hitting the fan," "vultures on the seats," etc.

Jerry: They wanted to make it more reality based. They were applying conventional rules of comedy to a very unconventional film.

David: We looked at each other and said, "Oh, shit!" We broke into a sweat, wondering if this was now the big, bad studio rearing its head, and how we were going to fight it.

TREY PARKER
Matt Stone and I have a big thing where we were tonally very influenced by ZAZ, but we're also really big on structure. Like, if something doesn't make sense, we won't do it, but for them, they'll just do *anything*. And, of course, they love just throwing in as many things as they can and then getting to the editing.

JEFFREY KATZENBERG
These things are like Rashomon. On their side, they may tell you how they were nervous and sweating, wondering if they got the right parking place, and all of their stuff. On the other side of the equation, I didn't feel their anxiety. In fact, just the opposite. I found them to be amazingly confident, bordering on cocky. And that, by the way, interestingly, is a very important signal that you always look for in any filmmaker coming in with their idea or their presentation, because if they don't believe unconditionally in what they're doing, why should anybody else want to buy it? So for me, over decades of doing this, I've always been looking for that conviction, that passion, the just unbridled enthusiasm, if not flat-out arrogance and cockiness. Those are actually valuable attributes, not a liability.

David: We knew they were trying to make sense out of the script, but despite "The Rules," ever since we started with Kentucky Fried Theater, we were about pure anarchy and silliness. As long as it worked, it was okay. You just couldn't start applying logic.

Jerry: I think we did apply logic. It's just that it was *our* logic. We never had a scattershot approach. If we put something in the script and shot it, there was a reason why we all thought it was going to work, as opposed to throwing in a lot of crazy stuff and waiting to see what gets a laugh.

Jim: It was scary that they would try and take the script that literally, not understanding what we were trying to do. It was another reason why we were so insistent on directing. It seemed like things were falling apart. Mind you, it was 1979, inflation was out of control, Americans were being held hostage in Iran, the most popular music was disco, and now *this*!

Jerry: And then, wouldn't you know it—all of a sudden we get a call from AVCO Embassy. They'd gotten some more funding and were still interested. They even offered us a bigger budget than Paramount.

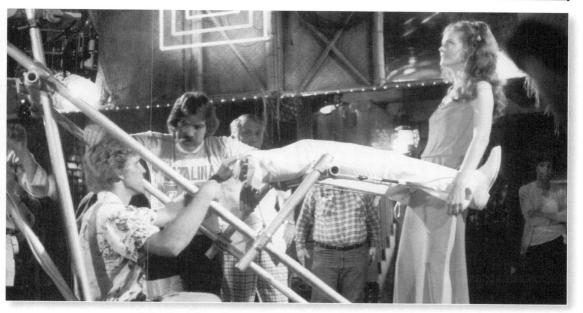

Julie holding fake legs: It's an illusion business.

David: And they said we could direct it! We didn't yet have a deal with Paramount, so we actually considered it.

Jim: We took that weekend off and sequestered ourselves away so we could make a thoughtful, balanced business decision on which company to go with.

Jerry: We even made a "pros" and "cons" list.

Jim: So after this long, heavy weekend of soul searching, we decided ultimately that the best studio would be . . . AVCO!

Jerry: So then we all started singing, "AVCO! AVCO! AVCOOOOOOO!"

David: We were convinced we had made the right decision. And we were relieved. But first, we had to call Katzenberg and tell him that we'd decided to go in a different direction, and thanks, but we're moving on.

Jim: The call lasted somewhere between three and five minutes. By the time we hung up, we were making the movie at Paramount. Three minutes is all it took for Jeffrey Katzenberg to make us realize what a mistake we were about to make.

JEFFREY KATZENBERG

There was a moment where it seemed like all was lost and I needed to reel it back in. If you had to find an attribute to label me with, "salesman" would probably be it. So my job was to make sure we didn't lose them. That was my job!

Jerry: At the time, Katzenberg was a young guy—only in his late twenties—but he was fearless and driven. You could have given Katzenberg a parachute, dropped him anywhere in the world, and within a few months, he'd be running the place.

David: So, on Monday morning, we went right back to the studio and continued the rewrite as though nothing had happened. And that, of course, turned out to be the absolute right decision. We would have been crazy to go with AVCO Embassy, because Paramount had the marketing power and the support and the ability to get the movie into theaters. In addition, there was a unique culture there that embraced our style.

Jerry: The more you play it safe with comedy, the more unfunny it becomes.

"Place the jacket over your head, and pull the cord under the left-side flap."

JEFFREY KATZENBERG

The world has changed, and what happens in the movie business today bears no resemblances to the movie business of the seventies and eighties. But back then, I would say that we were always determined to do unique and original. There was no franchise business. There was no sequel business. It was all about original ideas. And the sort of equation or the way we tended to think about this—and this came from Barry Diller—is that if you are to do things that are unique and original—which is your goal, your gold star—to do something that people have never seen before, that will surprise them, delight them. Well, unique and original equal risky. And risky means not everything will succeed. It means there will be failure.

David: We knew that doing the movie at Paramount was the right choice, but they were still resisting our demand to direct. After an exhausting week of rewriting, the three of us had a meeting with Jon Davison. We were all frustrated at the studio's non-decision about green-lighting the movie.

Jim: Davison said, "Guys, face it. It's gonna be a better movie if someone else directs it." It had been a long struggle, and I thought maybe he was right, and I said so.

David: I knew that if we didn't grab this opportunity, we may never have the chance to direct a studio film again. I mean, for most of the picture, it's people facing forward in rows of airplane seats. How hard could it be to direct? And if not now, when? Jerry looked over at me. We both shook our heads, no.

JON DAVISON

I think that not having control on *Kentucky Fried Movie* probably spurred them to approach *Airplane!* saying, "We're directing this one ourselves!"

JEFFREY KATZENBERG

Among the executives, it was a debate about letting the three of them direct the film because no one had ever done it before. And not only was that unique and a little bit confounding, in that how do you have three bosses? Two bosses—cochairs, co-CEOs, co-anything—and there's not a lot of happy endings there. So I think that certainly was a concern.

Jonathan Banks: *"He's all over the place . . . what an asshole!"*

50 years later: still a badass.

Jerry: We spent most of that weekend wondering how this was ever going to be resolved. On Sunday, David was at my apartment, helping me repaint my bedroom. The phone rang; it was Katzenberg, saying he had news for us. I took the kitchen phone, David stayed on the line in the bedroom. And then we couldn't believe what we heard. The studio had decided to let us direct!

David: After five long years, we were finally going to make *Airplane!* We were a "go" picture! We could hardly contain ourselves.

JEFFREY KATZENBERG

I think the genius of Diller as a media executive and creative executive and business executive—and he was all of those—is that he recognized that in order to be successful, from filmmaker up to studio head, failure cannot be fatal. Because if failure is fatal, that means you're not going to take risks. Or you'll do everything in your power to mitigate risk because if you fail, it's fatal. So first off is that failure cannot be fatal. And I think that was the thing Diller provided to everyone at the studio, the notion that we don't bat a thousand, that that's not the way the movie business works. There will be some failure. It has to be smart, thoughtful, economically responsible, but not everything is going to work. There will be failure; therefore we will take risks. Therefore you will do unique and original.

Jerry: It was hard to not scream into the phone from sheer excitement, but I thanked him calmly and hung up the phone, then sprinted back to the bedroom to celebrate with David. But when I flung open the door, there was David up on the ladder with his back to me, calmly paint-rolling the ceiling as if nothing had happened. He got me for a second, then we both laughed and hugged.

David: It was difficult for us then to see it from the studio's point of view, but looking back on it, somehow that particular studio at that particular time, perhaps unique among other Hollywood studios, was willing to take the risk.

Jim: So, the deal said we could direct, but there were two provisos: one, a studio producer whom they trusted named Howard W. Koch would be in charge of our production, and, two, the studio could fire us after two weeks of shooting. We were fine with being fired, but who was this Howard W. Koch?

CHAPTER 19

HOWARD

I'm working with these three young kids, and
you know, I think they've got something here,
it's really funny.

HOWARD W. KOCH

Jerry: We didn't know anything about Howard Koch. I told him how brilliant I thought his *Casablanca* script was. Wrong! That was the other Howard Koch. The one without the W.

David: Howard had been a director, producer, past president of the studio, and even president of the Motion Picture Academy. He had a production deal at Paramount, as was usual for a studio to give to past presidents.

Jerry: From our perspective, they were putting this "old guy" on our movie, even though he was probably a decade younger than any of us is today! We may have done a bit of grumbling at first, but any of that ended about a minute after we met him. We all grew to love him. In fact, Howard was another fateful stroke of great luck.

JEFFREY KATZENBERG

Howard Koch was made of gold. He didn't need to prove anything at that point in his career. All he wanted to do was be there and share his wisdom and knowledge with them. That was certainly comfort for us on our side. You will not hear anyone speak a bad word about Howard. Never. Howard was an angel.

"Would you like something to read?" "Do you have anything light?"
"How about this leaflet: Famous Jewish Sports Legends?"

David: The studio set up a meeting for us. We arrived at the appointed time, entered through a massive brass door, and were greeted by Howard's longtime assistant, Laurie Abdo. And then were led into a conference room to wait for Howard. An ashtray on the table was engraved with "To Howard, from Frank and Mia."

Jim: In Milwaukee that would've meant Frank and Mia Schlomovitz.

Jerry: Howard was a Hollywood legend. The dark-paneled walls of his office were filled with pictures of stars he'd worked with.

David: Dozens of them. It reminded me of my dry cleaner. Much later, Howard put *our* pictures up there!

Jerry: Actually, *we* did that, just to see if he'd notice. We replaced a big photo from *The Odd Couple* of Walter Matthau being kissed by two women with one of David and me kissing Jim in the same pose. About a week later, someone pointed it out to him. He had a good laugh.

Jim: He said Ava Gardner used to drive him crazy, like in a sexual way. He just thought she was the hottest, greatest thing. He would say, "Oh, those legs!"

David: That always puzzled me, a guy having thoughts like that at sixty. Ten years after I passed sixty, I realized, okay, that was possible.

Jim: The other thing about Howard was that he would always wear a sport coat and tie, and he always had an elegant look about him. That kind of added to his whole persona.

Jerry: Howard was the most charming person I've ever met. And genuine. He won people over instantly. I loved listening to him when he was on the phone, the way he talked to people. He knew everyone. He knew everyone. "Hey, Johnny baby, talk to me! How ya doin'? How are the twins? Great, great! Love to hear that!" And he meant it. He actually cared about other people. If you didn't like Howard, *you* were the problem.

David: And he drove a Mercedes coupe which had a phone in it. This was in 1979, when nobody had cell phones. He had to call an operator to get a connection, but he could talk on the phone in his car!

Jerry: He'd drive onto a studio lot, any studio lot, and know the names of the guys at the gate. He'd walk onto a set and know the names of all the crew members; he remembered them from the hundreds of films he'd worked on. And they all loved him.

ARNE SCHMIDT

Howard was an experienced filmmaker. He directed a few movies himself. He came up through the ranks, so he had a long and distinguished career, and he was really a good buffer between us and the studio. I don't remember any drama from the studio, but if they would've called him and voiced any concerns, he basically would've told 'em to relax.

Jim: Plus Howard was deeply into the ponies. So he'd take us to the Hollywood Park race track. He was a part owner. We got hooked.

David: But amid all the Hollywood stuff, he was a decent man, moral, kind of reminded us of our own dads.

Jim: He used to say, "It's not just what you do but how you do it."

Jerry: I remember he was on the phone with some agent who was just being a jerk, and I could see how much it pained him. But he still said, "Okay, okay, let's see what we can do, great to talk to you," and hung up the phone. He hated when people weren't reasonable, because to him that's what it was all about. Be smart, be kind, and leave something for somebody else. He loved win-win situations. He was also very involved in the Motion Picture Home and many other charitable organizations. Howard was the perfect mentor for three young kids from Milwaukee.

Jim: Meanwhile, it was good for Paramount, because they could relax knowing Howard was there, but for us, Howard was essential in helping us navigate the studio. We were clueless about how big studios worked, and he was the master of dodging the minefields and just knowing how to handle the studio in general. He was brilliant at managing egos and competing interests.

David: Paramount intended for him to be their man on the *Airplane!* production, but what actually happened was that Howard became our man at Paramount.

PATRICK KENNEDY (Film Editor)

There was one executive who got it—Howard Koch—and that's how they even were able to make the picture. Howard was tremendously supportive, but the studio didn't always understand it. So when they got the right guy backing it and the right audience, it worked just fine.

Our man at Paramount: on the set with Howard

Jim: Within a day of meeting him, we bonded with Howard, and realized he was totally dedicated to helping us.

Jerry: Once Howard came on board and our deal was signed, we dove into preproduction. We were already done with the rewrite, so we began making decisions about locations, sets, costumes, and, of course, casting.

David: The requests kept coming in from the studio that we had to have this or that actor in to read. Comedians like Bill Murray and Chevy Chase. Of course, we were worried.

JEFFREY KATZENBERG
Chevy Chase and Bill Murray were the biggest stars in the world at the time, so suggesting them was a vote of confidence. It was the opposite of what they thought. We were ready to go out and pay two of the biggest comedians in the world to be in their movie, because we believed in their movie, and that would help us market and promote and get people into the movie, whereas from their point of view they were probably thinking, "These idiots don't understand what we're doing!"

Jim: Howard was a big help in the casting process.

David: He would call their agents and tell them that he could send them the script, but their client wouldn't really be interested in a part like this. And that would be the end of it.

Jim: He was like a double agent. And conversely, the people that we really wanted, he would use all the leverage in his power to get them for us.

Howard leading the band.

JOEL THURM (Casting Director)
The smartest move by Paramount was to ally the boys with Howard Koch. And Howard did use his very impressive aura, if you will, to convince some of these agents or some of these B-level stars that they had to do it by saying, "Trust me on this one." Bob Stack's agent was a man named Abby Greshler, also known as the Gray Ghost because he looked about 110 years old.

David: Howard took us to meet Greshler for lunch at the Paramount commissary. I remember feeling some amount of tension that he would die before dessert.

JOEL THURM

Because of Howard's prestige, the agents just went along with it. Howard basically said, "Just listen to me and do this." And when you think about it, the worst that would've happened is that if the movie had not been a huge success, it would've quietly faded away, and nobody would've seen it. So what did these people have to lose?

Jim: A week after we found Julie, we got a call from Howard. Eisner had seen this couple who had a sketch show on Broadway.

David: In their act, they actually did an airplane skit to big laughs. Eisner honed in on that and thought they could be great for Ted and Elaine.

Jerry: The studio sent us to see the show. Although very funny onstage, they were nowhere near what we wanted for our romantic leads. But Eisner was set on bringing them out for a screen test, and of course we immediately started squawking about it. "We won't do it! This'll kill the movie!" We had no idea how to deal with a studio. But Howard did. He said, "Relax. Just do it, it's all right." I think he might have been the only person on the planet who could have calmed us down. So we brought them out to L.A., and they did a screen test, and it was again clear to us that they weren't right for Ted and Elaine. So I said, "Okay, I think we've got enough." But Howard said, "No, no, go in for close-ups." And we all looked at each other and shrugged. And shot the close-ups.

Jim: They looked worse the closer we got. They were just not movie stars. But what Howard understood was that the more we did, the more obvious it would become.

JON DAVISON

Everybody would get wildly upset when Paramount came up with whatever ridiculous casting suggestion they had. The only person who wouldn't get upset was our adult in the room, Howard, and he would say, "Well, you know, this is a studio. They'll come up with a lot of stupid ideas, but you just ignore them, and a week later I'm sure they won't remember them."

David: Screen tests are there to show you how actors look on a big screen as opposed to a photograph, video, or a live audition. It can be very different. But what we didn't realize at the time was that in our case, screen tests were also tests of us as directors. They could have pulled the plug at any time.

Jerry: Howard always knew the smart way to handle the studio. We never would have made it through the whole studio process without him. After a while, if we questioned him, he'd just say, "Have I ever steered you wrong?" And it was true. He never did.

JEFFREY KATZENBERG

Howard was a good interpreter. He could interpret them to us and, more important, having grown up as a studio producer and with decades of experience, he could interpret what we were doing to them. Otherwise, they wouldn't get out of bed every day, they'd be so scared. But he was able to say, "Ah, just ignore 'em. They don't know what they're talking about. Trust me, they'll be fine. Don't worry, I'll handle 'em." I promise you, that was every day: "Forget it, don't worry about it, I'll handle it."

JULIE HAGERTY

When Bob and I did our screen test together, I was so nervous, but Mr. Koch was so sweet. Because it was just an overnight trip. I flew in, and I had my clothes smooshed into my suitcase, so I had on jeans and a nice top. But Mr. Koch said to me, "Do you have a skirt?" I guess because that's what stewardesses wore. And I said, "Yes, sir, but the reason I wore my jeans was because my skirt got all wrinkled in my suitcase." And he said, "Well, if they're looking at your skirt, we're gonna have a lot of problems." It was a great way of saying, "I think your work speaks for itself, not what you're wearing." That was a great lesson.

David: He also had a string of really hot receptionists. My favorite story was one time Jim called Howard's office and got his receptionist on the line. He tells her he needs a certain agent's phone number. She has it, but Jim says, "Wait a minute. I can't find a pencil." And then he starts laughing. And he says, "Now, what good would that do me?" Apparently, she had said, "I have one!"

CHAPTER 20

KAREEM

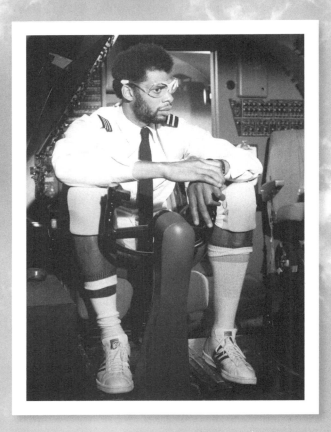

I thought that at some point I had come across the wrong way to the public. It was a great way to poke fun at my image. And just get people to laugh about a few things. I had taken my career so seriously, and was so focused on it, that people didn't think I could do anything else. So it was a great opportunity for me.

KAREEM ABDUL-JABBAR

Jim: The inspiration to use a pro athlete also came from *Zero Hour!* The guy who played the role of the pilot was a football player named Elroy "Crazy Legs" Hirsch who had been the star running back for Wisconsin and then the L.A. Rams. Evidently, after he retired from playing football he decided to test his chops at acting and was cast as the pilot in *Zero Hour!* Occasionally his performance rose to the level of wooden.

David: It was clear he'd been dropped in like some space traveler to another planet. The guy who played the copilot was even worse. It looked as if to save money, they used the production accountant.

Jim: He's really the one who inspired us to write a part for a sports figure and then call him out in the middle of the movie.

Athlete/actor Elroy "Crazy Legs" Hirsch setting the bar in *Zero Hour!*

Jerry: It's actually been pretty common over the years to put famous athletes in films—not quality films, but it can generate a lot of good publicity. O. J. Simpson was wonderfully stiff in both *Capricorn One* and *The Towering Inferno*.

David: I directed him in the *Naked Gun* movies. Although he actually improved with each film, his acting remained a lot like his murdering—he got away with it, but no one really believed him.

Jim: Didn't you guys become friends?

David: Not really. The last time I ever saw him was at the wrap party for *Naked Gun 33⅓*. We shook hands, I sold him my knife collection, and never saw him again.

Jerry: The copilot role was originally written for Pete Rose, but we were shooting during baseball season, so he wasn't available. Thank God! Nobody would have come close to Kareem—another wonderful bit of serendipity.

KAREEM ABDUL-JABBAR
I know Pete Rose, but whenever we get together, we like to talk baseball. Baseball was my first love, well before basketball, and I still follow it very closely. I'm glad he passed on the movie!

JIMMY KIMMEL
Nothing against Pete Rose, but Kareem really fit into the mold of People You Didn't Expect to Be Funny. Because he was so serious as a player, and then when you realize there's a real sense of humor underneath . . . It was fun! Kareem is great, because he's playing himself not playing himself. Like a joke on top of a joke. But I think even then I understood what that was: the O. J.–type athlete shoehorned into something he didn't necessarily belong in, just to draw attention. I loved that. And when he gets up and, after denying that he's Kareem over and over again, he's wearing his shorts!

Jerry: We sent the script with an offer of $30,000. Kareem was interested, but his manager said the offer was too low.

Jim: His manager claimed that he was keeping his client on a tight budget, and Kareem had recently told him he wanted to buy a $35,000 Oriental rug, an art piece. If we would just add $5,000, maybe he'd do it. We thought, *That's the greatest shifty manager line we've ever heard!*

Jerry: We said sure, fine, good managing. Then a couple weeks later, there was an article in *Time* magazine with a picture of Kareem standing in front of the Oriental rug that he'd just bought for $35,000! We were shocked! The manager was actually telling the truth!

                           MURDOCK
        Flight 209er, thanks a lot.
        Over and out.

Joey has been paying very close attention to Murdock
and suddenly recognizes him.

                        JOEY
        Wait a minute... Aren't you
        Pete Rose from the Cincinnati
        Reds?

                      MURDOCK
        That's right, son.

                        JOEY
                 (confused)
        Well... what are you doing here?

                      MURDOCK
        Well, a guy can't play baseball
        forever, Joey. Some guys sell
        insurance. Others go into
        broadcasting. I thought I'd
        try acting.

                      JOEY
                (unconvinced)
        Gee, that's neat.

EXT. AIRPLANE

THUNDER and lightning.

KAREEM ABDUL-JABBAR

I wasn't actively seeking an acting career, but I was exploring options that I'd seen other athletes do. I knew NFL star Jim Brown, and he'd told me that he was going to try to be an actor like some of the white athletes he knew, and that turned out pretty well for him. I had taken a few theater arts classes at UCLA and I was living in Los Angeles, so it was a natural progression. I was never intimidated by acting, but I also wasn't as passionate about it as I was about basketball, so I put most of my energy into athletics over acting.

David: Most recently, Kareem had been portrayed in a miniseries using abusive language toward the little boy who played Joey. As it happened, we were on the set, doing a cameo as ourselves! To our embarrassment, we hadn't read the script, so that scene took us by surprise.

Jim: Shame on us.

David: I immediately called Ross Harris, who played the kid, and asked if that had ever happened. He said, "Not at all. On the contrary, Kareem was always a gentleman. He was always nice to me."

KAREEM ABDUL-JABBAR

I laughed out loud when I first read *Airplane!* It was just the kind of wacky, off-kilter humor that I appreciated, so I knew I could do a good job.

KEN COLLINS

When Kareem came in, he brought a bunch of rugs with him. Someone said, "Hey, Kareem's got Persian rugs with him that are for sale!" And I was so busy at the time that I didn't really even have any interest in rugs, although over the years I've grown to love them.

FRANK ASHMORE (Victor Basta)

The Lakers had just won the championship, and Kareem was the MVP, but I had no idea he was coming on board. I don't even think I looked at the call sheet. I just walked in and there he was, standing there in his uniform. I was just, like, "Oh, my God, this is so cool! This is awesome!" Putting Kareem in the cockpit was just a hilarious sight gag to begin with. A seven-foot, two-inch man trying to duck his way into the cockpit.

ARNE SCHMIDT

My job as the first assistant director is to make sure everything runs smoothly, that there are no delays or any gaps in anything, that people are ready when they're supposed to be. So on Kareem's first day, my second AD comes to me and says, "How long 'til you think you need Kareem?" Since he was so tall, they had to readjust the cockpit seat so his head wouldn't hit the ceiling. I said, "It'll be a little while, but not too long." And he said, "Well, he wants to go and get in a workout." I said, "How long is the workout?" Now, Kareem walks up himself, and he says, "Eh, just a couple of hours." I'm looking at him, thinking about the short schedule. I said to him, "You know, I don't think so. I think it's a little too tight." He goes away, and we're shooting along, and it comes time to call for Kareem. I call for him . . . and he comes in, and he says, "I told you I could make it." He went and worked out anyway! He just decided on his own to go ahead and do it! I couldn't get mad at him because he's, well, Kareem, but that's not exactly how things are supposed to work on a movie set!

Jerry: When you cast a star athlete, you assume that acting is pretty far down on their list of mastered skills. All these athlete actors stuck out like a sore thumb, and clearly audiences were on to this. So we thought, why don't we just out one of them right in the movie?

Jim: He couldn't have been better. He wasn't supposed to be able to act. Elroy Hirsch, the pilot in *Zero Hour!*, had set the bar.

Jerry: It wasn't an easy scene to shoot. Lots of takes, again and again. Athletes aren't used to line readings, but Kareem was willing to do whatever we needed. He was very patient with the whole process.

> **KAREEM ABDUL-JABBAR**
> It was a fun take on the whole Hollywood trope of kids recognizing magical things that adults are too jaded to see. Here, the boy dismisses the entire movie to converse with his sports hero. And, of course, the sports hero turns out to be less heroic than he'd hoped. It was a bold choice for the filmmakers.

Jerry: Kareem was just terribly shy. But people often mistook that for being aloof or arrogant. The truth is, he was the opposite: kind, thoughtful, and exceedingly smart.

"Wait a minute. I know you. You're Kareem Abdul-Jabbar."

KEN COLLINS

It became clear that Kareem really couldn't play the whole scene through. He was really having trouble with his lines. So I got to be the guy who wrote all of his lines on cue cards, and I was right by the camera on everything. So if you look at the scene with him and the kid, or anything that's not shot straight on, where you see him and Peter Graves together, all of Kareem's scene work is almost, like, one line, cut, one line, cut. I still tell people, "Yeah, I fed Kareem his lines for the cockpit scenes." It's definitely a good memory for me.

"Listen, kid, I've been hearing that crap ever since I was at UCLA. I'm out there busting my buns every night. Tell your old man to drag Walton and Lanier up and down the court for forty-eight minutes!"

Jim: Even though Kareem was for four decades the leading scorer in the history of the NBA, and has a bunch of championships and MVPs, he has tons of other interests. He's an author, a columnist, an activist. He's into jazz. Today, I'm a big fan of his political blog. He's a really bright, funny, fascinating man who happens to be seven feet, two inches tall. A true Renaissance man. Basketball never defined him, ever. Not even during his heyday. In 1969, a whole decade before we even considered casting Kareem in *Airplane!*, I wrote a letter to the sports section of the *Milwaukee Sentinel*, reaming them out for their coverage of Kareem when he played for the Bucks. They were always criticizing him for his defense and saying he only tried during the playoffs!

October 26, 1969

Milwaukee Sentinel
333 West State Street
Milwaukee, Wisconsin

Attention: Sports Department

Dear Sirs:

I am a native Milwaukeean, dedicated sportsman, bred on the
Milwaukee Sentinel and Journal Sports pages. It is because of
this background that I feel compelled to share with you my thorough
disappointment with your coverage of the second bonafide super star
to play out of this city in my life. The first, of course, was
the incomparable Henry Aaron. The man around whom my disgust center
is Lew Alcindor.

Your treatment of Lew has been bush. You've made him out to be a
freak rather than a man. You've probed and dwelled on irrelevant
and insignificant aspects of the man (presumably because anything
with "Alcindor" on it will sell newspapers) and you have evidently
come up blind to the fact that in Lew Milwaukee has gained a warm,
aware, clever man who realizes that this world is not a basketball.

I've read writeups of games that sounded like Lew was the only Buck
on the floor. Well even if history proves him to be the most
proficient center of all time, Lew Alcindor is 1/5 of a basketball
team. If there were not four other highly skilled ball players
on the floor with Lew, the Bucks wouldn't win a game all year. If
we didn't have a strong bench to compliment the starting five,
Milwaukee would never be a contender.

Alcindor didn't beat Hayes. To play that up is nieve basketball
coverage. It wasn't a one-on-one back yard tilt. The Bucks beat
the Rockets. Wilt Chamberlain didn't beat Lew. Lew beat Milwaukee.
I'm not saying that personel matchups aren't fascinating and don't
deserve recognition. I'm merely making the point that the day you
stop degrading Lew Alcindor with insensitive, illogical, back woods
articles, you will be doing a great service for the man, the team
on which he plays, and the city that has the privilege of hosting
his professional career.

                         Sincerely,

                         James Abrahams

Jerry: Then years later, we had a ten-year-old boy level the same charges at him.

Jim: But in *Airplane!*, he got to tell *his* side of the story.

David: Well, it sure wasn't that difficult to *write*.

LORNA PATTERSON (Randy)
There's a scene where Kareem gets food poisoning, and I pull him down the aisle between all the passengers. And, you know, in rehearsal Jerry says, "The camera is over here, and you're pulling him down the aisle." And I pretend I'm pulling him down the aisle. And no one thought that he is enormous and I am very small. And so when it came time for us to do the scene, no one thought of the fact that of course I couldn't pull him down the aisle, it was ridiculous. So, he's lying there, dead weight, because he's supposed to be passed out. And I stick my arms under his arms, and Jerry calls action, and I literally cannot move. I have my entire body going backward, and he's not going anywhere. And Jerry says, "Go," and I'm like, "I can't go! There is no going!," and Kareem is laughing. So we had to stop everything, and they had to build a little platform with wheels on it, and even then somebody had to push him from the sides.

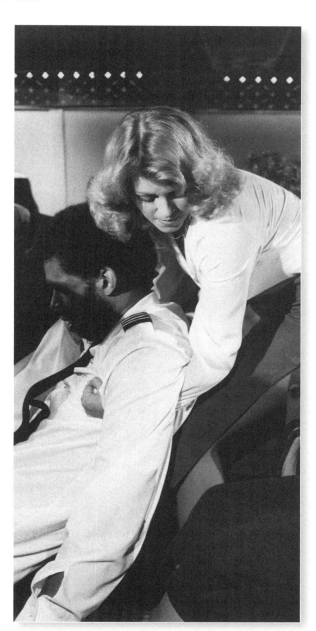

> **FRANK ASHMORE**
>
> I was the first one to succumb to the fish. When they dragged me down the aisle, I don't think I got a rug burn, but I sure was turned on by Lorna Patterson. Oh, I had a huge crush on her. There was something sexy about her dragging me down the aisle like that. So, I don't know, I may have gotten a rug burn, but I didn't notice. Y'know what I'm sayin'?

Jerry: You know, even if you're a great athlete, being that tall . . . it can separate you. I remember seeing Kareem interviewed when he was at UCLA and talking about being sensitive to people teasing him, saying things like, "Hey, Kareem, how are things up there in the clouds?," or whatever. He didn't like it.

David: And like he hadn't heard stuff like that a million times.

> **KAREEM ABDUL-JABBAR**
>
> A few years after retiring as center for the Denver Nuggets, Dan Issel comes up to me and says, "My daughter loves you." "Why?" I reply. "The Nuggets never beat us." "Not because of basketball, man," he says. "Because of *Airplane!* She loves that movie!"

Jerry: All those guys—Leslie, Peter, Lloyd, and Bob Stack—were having a laugh at their own expense, essentially making fun of the cool, tough personas they had built up over years in the business. In a slightly different way, the same thing was true of Kareem. We loved them all for their willingness to do that.

Jim: Self-effacing humor. But that's the whole point, isn't it? Parody movies don't aim particularly high. *Airplane!* had no political or social point of view. But I think when the audience laughs at some of the stuff like the "Don't call me Shirley" joke, they are in part laughing at themselves for taking that line seriously. Self-effacing. Therapeutic. Wonderful.

David: That was certainly the theory anyway.

Jerry: Forgive me for trying to find meaning in any of this, but, consciously or subconsciously, I think we *did* have a social point of view. In a way, all these tough-guy characters are just reflections of our own egos. We all take ourselves too seriously.

David: But seriously, we had never actually heard these actors say these lines out loud until the first table read, one week before shooting started. At their level, none of those guys auditioned. The reading was held on a soundstage around a big table. I'll never forget the shock I felt when Robert Stack walked in. He was wearing a tan cardigan sweater and bifocal glasses. Not exactly the badass FBI tough guy I'd expected. He was just an actor.

KEN COLLINS

I was invited to the first table read, and the Zuckers and Jim were kind of huddled up, like they always did. They were super high energy. And then the big four of the actors, Lloyd Bridges, Robert Stack, Leslie Nielsen, and Peter Graves, they're kind of standing around in their own group. They were all legends to me. I walked close enough to hear them, and they were basically all just asking each other, "Well, what do you think?" They were a little jittery about it. And Howard Koch comes over, puts his arms around them, and says something to the effect of, "Don't worry, these boys are great, it's gonna be terrific." So they sat down and began the read through. I remember one of them, I think maybe Lloyd Bridges, was the most serious of the bunch, and was, like, "So you want us to be funny?" And the boys go, "No, no, no! Just play it straight!" And that was really the key. They couldn't exactly come right out and say, "You're gonna be really funny just being yourself!" But that's basically what was going on.

David: At that time, believe it or not, Leslie hadn't quite gotten it. He was putting a bit of comedy spin on his lines and not being serious enough for us.

BOB WEISS

It's art. It's very technical. It's by design. Most people think all of that stuff was just improv. And that with Leslie, all you had to do was turn on the camera and the movie made itself. Other directors thought Leslie was this brilliant comic who was writing his own lines. No one saw how much work behind the camera went into making these actors funny.

David: So we sent him home with a video tape of *Zero Hour!* with specific instructions to watch the actor who played the doctor. Jerry said, "Just watch him." When he came in the next day, he was perfect.

CHAPTER 21

CULVER CITY STUDIOS

As a comedian, a moviegoer, or really just a human being, there's a shared timeline. It's before you've seen *Airplane!* and after you've seen it. It was the likes of something we'd never seen before and remains quite possibly the funniest thing we've seen since. The scores of comedians, screenwriters, and filmmakers it has influenced is ever apparent, but it also changed the comedic sensibilities of the general population at large. The fact that the imitators, while flattering, have never been able to top the original is a testament to its greatness. It's timeless.

THE IMPRACTICAL JOKERS: JAMES MURRAY, BRIAN QUINN, JOE GATTO, SAL VULCANO

David: So finally, after months of rewrites, casting, and rehearsals, the big day arrived, our first day of shooting. And I was late. The rehearsals had always started at nine a.m., and since I never look at call sheets, I just breezed in at nine. Unfortunately, the call time was seven a.m.

Jim: That first day was Bob (Hays), Lorna, and Leslie in the cockpit. I think Jon Davison, the producer, scheduled it there for a number of reasons. As far as being first-time directors, in that confined space, it was just people talking, and as far as "blocking," the actors literally couldn't move, the camera couldn't move. We just copied the setup from *Zero Hour!*

David: We couldn't screw it up if we tried.

"Christmas, Ted, what does it mean to you? For me, it was a living hell. Do you know what it's like to fall in the mud and get kicked? In the head? By an iron boot? Of course you don't. No one does. That never happens. Sorry, Ted. Dumb question. Strike that."

Jerry: Our style of comedy doesn't depend as much on a comedian being "on" that day. Our direction would be mostly about sticking to the kind of dramatic intensity we were mocking—trust the joke. And of course . . . timing.

Jim: Leslie wasn't *trying* to be funny but got big laughs. He made it look like anyone could do it.

Jerry: Yes, no one looks at Jim Carrey or Kevin Hart and says, "Hey! I can do that!"

Jim: As it turned out, among the deadpan lines included on that first day was, "I *am* serious, and don't call me Shirley!" The next day, Paramount watched the dailies. We were told that the room literally erupted. All the executives saw how that joke played, and in an instant they understood the concept.

Jerry: I think that's another reason why Jon scheduled that scene on the first day. He wanted to make sure the studio got what we were doing.

David: We immediately got a phone call from Katzenberg who essentially said, "Don't worry. You're not gonna get fired."

Jim: I remember David saying, "In forty-three years, when we write a book about making this movie, we've got to include that story." He was always the visionary.

David: Aw, shucks.

ROBERT HAYS

After the first day's dailies, word spread around the lot, and by midweek, not only were our dailies packed, but the studio had to add a second screening room.

BARRY DILLER

The thing I remember very specifically is watching the dailies, which was a part of our ever-endless workload. It was generally no fun at all. It was a burdensome process. It's very hard to conceptualize how a scene is actually being played. Usually, you had to be assigned to watch the dailies, because no one wanted to actually go through the work of sitting there for an hour and a half watching strips of celluloid that didn't relate to each other. But what I absolutely remember is that the projection room for *Airplane!* dailies was packed every day, because it was truly hysterically funny. Every shot made you laugh. That was a complete rarity. I would go to the dailies every day that I could. But even if you really liked things about the dailies, there's not a big majority chance that you'll end up liking the movie or that the movie will really be any good. But this movie, from the first exposure to the finished film . . . I mean, you'd have to put the audience to death to stop them from laughing.

David: All of the Paramount lot stages were taken up by other productions. So we shot at Culver City Studios. Our office was in the attic of this big old building that had been the mansion in *Gone with the Wind*.

JON DAVISON

I'd never done a studio film before *Airplane!* I'd never done a union film! I was actually used to having more control, much like the boys desired. I was in charge of production for Roger Corman for years, so when I wanted a check, I got a check five minutes later, and I didn't have to walk all over the studio lot to get people to initial the check request. So it was a little frustrating. But it was so much fun. It was, like, "Wow! This is Hollywood!" And it turned out to be incredible. I have never had an experience like it since.

JULIE HAGERTY

I remember walking on the soundstage for the first time, and I still remember that amazing smell. And then you're kind of hermetically sealed in this wonderful world until the soundstage doors would open again, and off Bob would go in his Mustang. Everybody was so kind and fun, and the boys always had barbecues and had the gang over. It was really wonderful.

KEN COLLINS

Robert Hays had a green '66 Mustang convertible, and he had a parking spot right at the stage. At the time, an orbiting satellite space station called Skylab was going to descend to Earth, and nobody knew where it was going to come down. Everyone thought for a while, Wow, Skylab might fall on my house! So one day while Bob was working inside, some crew guys got busy on Bob's car. When he came out at the end of the day, he found his car completely filled with junk, with a sign on the top that said, "Skylab." Of course, being Bob, he was a really good sport about it.

David: Bob's Mustang is the car we used for the guy who picks up Robert Stack and drives him to the airport.

ROBERT HAYS

I drove that to work one day, and Howard said, "We need your car!" I said, "Why?" He said, "We need a convertible! So we need your car!" It was a '66 Mustang convertible—her name was Sally, because she had to have a name—and I said, "Okay." So I got thirty-five dollars a day. They used her for two days. So I made my whopping twenty-five grand plus seventy bucks!

KEN COLLINS

On the stage right next to us was *Don Kirshner's Rock Concert*, a weekly TV show. One of my jobs was to go next door to the *Rock Concert* stage when they were taping to coordinate between the two shoots. I think the band Chicago was also taping at one point, so I would go over there and say, "Okay, they're rolling!" "Okay, we're about to roll!"

Jim: The coolest thing about Culver City Studios was that *Raging Bull* was filming there at the same time. So once in a while, we would walk over to their stage and watch Martin Scorsese direct Robert De Niro in boxing scenes.

David: By the time we started shooting *Airplane!*, we had already spent some time in rehearsals, so all the actors had figured out what we were looking for.

Jim: There was a big difference with Bob Hays. It wasn't until years later Bob told us his thinking was to react as though a real person in a real movie had found himself in the middle of all this nutsiness.

"Win just one for the Zipper."

When Julie and I got cast and I started in on the process of figuring out the character of Striker, I came to realize that he was the "sane" one in the show, the audience's point of view, the anchor. So when I say, "It's an entirely different kind of flying . . . altogether!" and Leslie and Lorna say in unison, "It's an entirely different kind of flying," my reaction is what the audience would have had. That was where the raised eyebrow came from. That reaction just seemed natural at the moment.

Jim: It really wasn't our direction, but it always made us laugh. And in many cases, that's why the audience laughed.

Jim and David teach dance.

ROBERT HAYS

When all the characters around me were acting so strange, I reacted to them like "that was odd," had a moment, and then went on with the scene. Never mind that I was sometimes pretty odd myself.

Jerry: Even in a parody, you need at least one character who the audience can identify with and empathize with. Bob was both part of the insanity and the logical reaction to it.

David: This was in contrast to Bridges, Stack, Nielsen, and Graves, who never acknowledged that anything was amiss.

Jerry: At some point they just threw caution to the wind and stopped trying to make sense of it.

David: Nothing made less sense than a pair of naked breasts bouncing through the frame during the panic scene.

Jim: We went through exhaustive auditions for that one.

Jerry: All these years later the performance still holds up.

TREY PARKER

I remember being ten years old in Fort Collins, Colorado, in a theater watching *Airplane!* for the first time and just thinking it was so awesome. And, of course, in the scene where they're all panicking when they first learn the plane's going down, and the woman jumps in frame with her tits shaking . . . I thought, This is the greatest movie ever!

JIMMY KIMMEL

Did that scene strike a chord with me? Well, if "strike a chord" means "did I pause on that moment ten million times?" then, yes, I think you could say it struck a chord.

David: When my son Charles was a toddler, I showed him *Airplane!* and his favorite part was "the boobies!" He loved that. Then after that, of course, we started watching soft-core porn together. But it was okay. I think he saw it as food.

> **JULIE HAGERTY**
> There was such an innocence about *Airplane!* that made it joyful and really funny. It was a real different time. And with them being the writers and directors, the naughtiness of it was quite pure. It wasn't pointed, which I find to be the best kind of humor. And even the things where you go, "Oh, geez . . ." It's not really an "Oh, geez," because it's still funny. The purity and the innocence really make it hilarious. For me, playing comedy is no different than playing drama. It's all real and all from your heart.

David: To us, it just was pure insanity. Julie blowing up the autopilot was sexual innuendo, but we got away with it because of how innocently she played her role.

> **JOHN FRAZIER**
> The shot where Julie blows up the autopilot must've lasted twenty minutes. The camera ran out of film, and here are all these stagehands—the grip, the electrician, camera people—everybody's watching Julie and trying to stifle their laughter. And then we surprised the guys by making the autopilot's head spin around!

David: The special effects guys kept coming up with stuff that not only wasn't in the script, but that we never would have thought of because we didn't know what was possible.

Jerry: Everybody wanted to add jokes, and mostly we found a polite way to say no. But the special effects guys thought differently. They just liked to think of new stuff they could rig up.

David: Frazier would come up and say things like, "You want the head to spin around?" Or, "Do you want it to bob up and down?" "How about a wink?" Those guys weren't just going about a job; they were creative and took a lot of pleasure in being able to add jokes.

Jim: Eventually, all the actors got to be very comfortable with the nonsense. We'd throw them in the water, and they'd just swim.

> **JOHN FRAZIER**
> Every day going to work was a fun day. You just knew it was going to be fun. And those guys, they gave us a chance to have fun while making a movie. These guys had been writing the movie for the better part of five years. They knew what they were doing. We were just along for the ride!

David: But Leslie told me much later of a conversation he had with Stack on set where they were just shaking their heads at one of the gags. They were convinced that the shit hitting the fan would never work, but being professionals, they never mentioned it to us.

Jerry: There were probably a lot of things they didn't mention.

> **JOHN FRAZIER**
> When we did the shit-hits-the-fan thing, Steve Stucker was sitting at a desk, and I had told the prop master the day before, "Hey, when you're out shopping, can you get me this Mamacita bean dip? I've got to use that for the shit. It's got to be that brand!" He said, "Okay, okay, I get it, I get it." Well, the next day when we're going to do the scene, he doesn't have that brand, and I said, "Oh, man . . ." So to deliver the gag, I'd made this kind of rifle thing that had an air charge behind it, a pop gun kind of thing, like a Red Ryder rifle with a cork that flies out on a string. Same thing, but only about an inch and a half in diameter. Well, I've got the barrel resting on a ladder, and Steve's looking right at me, and he says, "Stop! Stop! STOP! STOP! That shit is gonna come right on me!" And my guys said, "Relax, it's not gonna go on you. John's got this all figured out. It's not gonna go on you, it's gonna hit the fan blade, and that's gonna be it." Well, the stuff was a little bit what you'd call "loose stool." It came out of there, and it blasted Steve. Never hit a fan blade. And he . . . I mean, they should've filmed that. Or maybe they shouldn't have! But he went on a rant that must've lasted for five minutes. So then Howard Koch, of all people, goes, "You know, John, I've gotta tell you, you know a lot of things, and your reputation precedes you, but you don't know dick about making shit." And this former head of the Academy gets on his hands and knees, along with the directors and whoever else wanted to join in, and he started making this stuff. Howard's going to the craft service guy, "Get me a banana! GET ME A BANANA!" And he's got the concoction going on. "Now put that in the gun barrel there. That's what we're gonna use!" And Steve says, "I don't have too many more pieces of wardrobe here." So I fired the gun, it hit the fan blade, and it worked, and that was the end of it. But to have a video of Howard Koch and whoever else on their hands and knees making this stuff . . . It was something to see. And me and the other effects guys, we just stood back with our arms crossed, saying, "You guys have fun on the floor making the crap!" Fun times.

Jerry: We showed the production designer, Ward Preston, the stills from *Zero Hour!* A lot of the *Airplane!* sets were pretty much duplicates of the *Zero Hour!* sets. They had no relation to what a control tower looked like in 1980. Even on a jet plane, in color, we were still trying to make a 1950s B movie.

David: Paramount said it had to be in color. So, we compromised. The passenger cabin was all muted colors. Lots of blacks, whites, browns. And if you look at the *Airport* movies, that was in the height of the seventies, and, boy, that looks terrible today. The hair, overly large collars, bright, crazy, loud colors. They all look like clown suits. But because of our obsession with the black and white fifties-era *Zero Hour!* style, *Airplane!* escapes looking so dated.

Jim: By trying to make the film look like an older time, it actually became less dated. Nobody has long hair in *Airplane!*

Relaxing afterward.

David: Or at least we tried our best to tone it down. There are a few dumb slipups I remember, like the guy who stands up in the cabin inexplicably wearing a loud, checkered sport coat, but mostly we're spared from looking at *Airplane!* and saying, "Ugh, we're watching a seventies movie!"

Jim: Thank God audiences can watch now and say, "Ugh, it's an eighties movie."

David: We also worked with the studio storyboard artist, David Jonas, who sketched out various scenes to help us visualize how we would set up shots.

David Jonas's original storyboard sketches

Jim: Among my family's favorite fifties Broadway musicals was *Annie Get Your Gun*, where Ethel Merman shined as the lead. When she didn't get the part in the 1959 movie version, my sisters and I boycotted it.

David: For some reason we all seemed to have Ethel Merman on our radar. In the mid-seventies, Jerry had

How could you not love Ethel Merman?

a bookshelf in his apartment with a little cabinet built into it where, when someone opened the door, there was a little photo of Ethel Merman, and on a speaker you hear her belting out, "Everything's Coming Up Roses."

Jerry: I remember, during the negotiations, she was fine with the money we were offering for her one-day cameo, but she insisted that we had to fly out her personal hairdresser. And the funny thing is, when you look at her in the movie, you're like, "You flew someone out from New York to do *that*?!" It's such an odd hairstyle. But it was her trademark, and we were more than happy to oblige.

Jim: I think it was a dead heat whether I was more excited to meet Ethel Merman or Kareem Abdul-Jabbar.

JULIE HAGERTY

They shot the scene with me talking to Bob, who was in the hospital, and they shot each bed. So I got to watch Ethel Merman come in, and I got to watch her work, and that was amazing! You know, she came in with her group, and she was just sassy and . . . Ethel Merman! You just kind of stood there in awe and disbelief and excitement, going, "Oh, my God, that's Ethel Merman!" And then delivering that song with great joy and heart, as honest as can be, and making fun of herself!

ARNE SCHMIDT

I don't know the last time Ethel Merman was in a picture before that, but I still remembered her from watching TV when I was a kid and how she would belt out, "There's no business like show business." And, you know, those old-time actors were really lovely people on the set. Coming in for a cameo at that point in her career . . . She was really enjoying herself.

ROSS HARRIS (Joey)

I was a child actor. I did a ton of commercials and a lot of the basic TV stuff, like *Little House on the Prairie*, *CHiPs*, *Love Boat*. So *Airplane!* was just another call, like any other call. I went to Paramount Studios, read a couple of times, and got the part. That was just my life back then: trying out for basically anything. I guess the whole idea was to push the acting toward the broadest, most "gee golly whiz" acting in the world, which I was very well trained in from doing a ton of commercials for Band-Aid and Ovaltine. So it was definitely in my wheelhouse to go broad.

Jerry: We thought Ross Harris was perfect for the little boy who had to endure the creepy captain. He had this sweet, wide-eyed, all-American-boy look, and his reading was perfect.

David: That face . . . We felt like we'd seen that face in a hundred movies: the kid, heartland of America, vast fields of wheat, white bread . . .

Jim: And he was a good actor. He could really deliver a believable, "Aw, gee, really?"

Jerry: Ross Harris was great for a kid actor, but kids don't understand comic timing and pacing, and Kareem wasn't exactly a gifted actor.

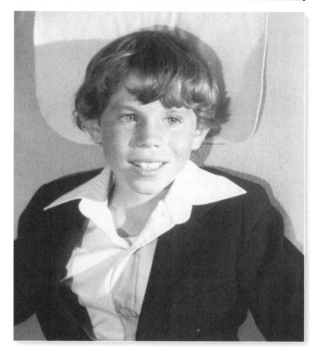

"Gee whiz!"

ROSS HARRIS

The number-one question that people ask is, "Did you have any idea about the innuendos?" And the funny thing is, I really didn't when I read the script. I thought people were just being silly. But even though it was only a year between filming and when the movie came out, something happened between nine and ten years old where, when I saw it all edited together, I was sitting there with my family, watching it, and all of a sudden I got it! And I was, like, "Oh, that's what was going on . . ."

Jim: No kidding. Fortunately, Kareem was sitting in a chair facing forward the whole time so he could read the cue cards. A couple of times you can actually see his eyes on camera reading. It was perfect for a non-actor trying to hide in a movie.

David: We hit the trifecta: a kid, a non-actor, and the need for perfect comic timing. The scene called for Kareem to really show some emotion and anger, I mean, act, and where I'm sure in real life he's had occasion to be angry, it's not his first skill to be able to deliver that at the sound of "Action!"

ROSS HARRIS

Peter Graves, of course, knew the undertones of the script, so he was very, very wary. I heard he had to be talked into doing it in the first place. Really, between scenes, he did not want any untoward contact with me, so he was a bit standoffish. I didn't really understand it at the time, but everybody else on the set was just really jovial. I didn't get it about Peter, but later on, once it all became clear, I was, like, "Oh, okay, so this is what his deal was."

Jerry: In truth, the movie *needed* three directors. Or maybe we just needed each other. In any case, if you weren't on the set to watch it, it probably seemed like a strange concept.

ROBERT HAYS

Whenever David, Jerry, and Jim do a Q&A after an *Airplane!* screening, they always get asked the question "How do three guys direct a movie?" They instantly all start talking at the same time, saying completely different things. I've been with them onstage dozens of times, and every time, it gets a huge laugh. But on set, it was actually very smooth.

"Johnny, how about some more coffee?" "No, thanks."

ARNE SCHMIDT

One of my big concerns going in was how it was going to work with three directors. And they talked that out. Jerry was kind of the point guy for speaking to the actors. There was a video feed on set, and David and Jim watched the scene from the monitor. Practically every time they were in agreement about whether it was good or not. There might be a smallish note, but nothing out of the ordinary. It went really smoothly. I wasn't sure going in. You could've had three guys who had different opinions about things, and it could bog things down. But that certainly wasn't the case. The biggest problem we had was trying not to laugh during the takes . . . myself included!

KEN COLLINS

We realized in prep that those guys were like one mind—three guys, one mind—regarding the script; they'd been living with it for so long. You could essentially ask any one of the three guys a question, and they would probably all give you the same answer. So it was really easy to work with them in that regard.

JOHN FRAZIER

The way I divided it up was that Jerry was the quarterback; Jim Abrahams, whom we called Heybroms, was the owner of the team; David brought in the plays. And that's how they made the movie. We had this big airplane that they'd built as a set, and behind that set was my special effects shop. Well, they also wanted that to be video village. So I said, "I don't know, man, that's our shop right there!" And they said, "Well, we've got no place else to go!" I said, "Okay, I'll tell you what. I'll make you a deal: I can do video village in this area, but I get to dictate who comes and goes." So they said, "Okay, that's a deal!" So I was the gatekeeper. If somebody would come in, I'd shake my head. "No, you can't go in there." And they'd be, like, "Well, who do I have to see to get in there?" "You gotta see me!" And then Jerry, David, or Jim would say, "You gotta see him. He's the gatekeeper." It was a fun time, we made this great movie. All of us, the whole crew, we just couldn't get enough.

Jim: Resolving creative differences was easy, because there were three of us—an odd number. So when two out of three agreed on something, we'd just move on. We called it Ultimate Wisdom. I'm not sure how much "wisdom" was involved. Basically it was just majority rules. I remember personally thinking, "I have no desire to be right; I only have a desire for right to prevail."

Jerry: Jim, you'll never get elected to public office with an attitude like that.

Jim: But we had an allowance for the minority, which we called "screaming and yelling."

David: *That* might get you elected to public office.

Jerry: That meant if one of us felt the need to rant on about something, the other two had to listen to him.

David: Majority rules, minority rights.

Getting the horse into bed.

Jerry: The first time I directed by myself, I'd think a lot about all the times when David and Jim caught something that I had missed, and I felt a little bit like, *Oh, God, what am I missing? Can I do this alone?*

Jim: Oh my God, don't get me started. The first time I directed alone, instead of David and Jerry, I had Bette Midler and Lily Tomlin. My back gets sore just thinking about it.

David: I think we were surprised that the DGA (Directors Guild of America) was refusing to give us a joint directing credit. Evidently the DGA rule is that there can only be one director credit for any one film.

Jerry: Yeah, that was a surprise. We didn't understand those rules, so we never imagined it would be an issue. And then we got the notice from the DGA that only one person could be listed as the director in the credits. Absolutely unfathomable to us.

David: And we thought, *What?! Can they do that?*

Jim: But there was that pretentious Frank Capra auteur theory of "one man, one film," and here we come along as a three-headed director team.

Jerry: The original reason for the rule was to prevent powerful actors or producers from sharing credit with a young director who ends up doing all the work. That's a good thing. The "one man, one film" idea is just ego. I've yet to hear anybody say, "One woman, one film." But you can appeal and make your case to the DGA board, so that's what we did.

Jim: Supposedly, we needed to prove we were a "bona fide team." And we told them we'd started in the business together, wrote together, directed the theater show together, and never done anything professionally separately.

Jerry: Foolishly, we thought this would all make sense to them. It didn't. In fact, they seemed angry. One of them held up an article in Variety where we had said that directing together is great because "three heads are thicker than one." They felt like we were mocking them. They voted against us sharing credit.

David: They had originally issued the DGA membership in Jerry's name, so we hit on a plan. Jerry drove downtown to the Los Angeles City Hall and had his name officially changed to Abrahams N. Zuckers. Then reapplied for DGA membership.

Jim: And a week later the guild's computer spat out a card with Jerry's new name.

Jerry: We figured that legally they couldn't refuse to allow me to use my new real name. Nor would they want to deal with the bad publicity if they tried to fight it. Still, we weren't thrilled about using the pseudonym, so Howard got us in for one more meeting, a final appeal. In the first meeting, we never talked about all the videos we had directed together.

Jim: By this time we were already on the set, shooting, with the clapperboard reading the new, ridiculous single director's name. Rebellion!

Jerry: So the DGA sent a representative to the set to see what was going on—a guy named Don Gold. He was super friendly, a really nice guy. We all liked him. In a fun twist, years later, my wife's brother married his daughter. So for years we celebrated all the holidays together.

Jim: A few weeks later, Howard arranged another DGA board meeting. Ostensibly because there was "new evidence."

Jerry: Once again, we presented our case. Howard said to them, "What difference does it make if there's one director or fifty directors, as long as the movie is good?" It seemed to go well, but the vote was a tie; half the board was for us, half against. In the case of a tie, the president has the deciding vote. At the time, the president of the DGA was George Schaefer, but he was out of town, so Gil Cates, the first vice president, cast the deciding vote. He voted for us to share credit. It was such a relief, and we were so grateful, especially me, because I got to change my legal name back to Jerry Zucker. I saw Gil Cates many times after that and each time I went on and on about how grateful we were. One person's kindness made a huge difference in our lives.

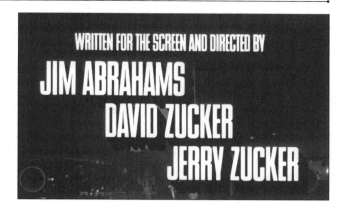

WRITTEN FOR THE SCREEN AND DIRECTED BY
JIM ABRAHAMS
DAVID ZUCKER
JERRY ZUCKER

JULIE HAGERTY
Jerry was the one who would talk to us, and then after each take they'd all three get together and either do another one or they'd all clap, and you knew we would move on. But we went at a pretty fast speed. There weren't a lot of takes. Everybody knew their job, but also there wasn't a lot of money. So, Mr. Koch kept it moving at a good pace.

ARNE SCHMIDT
It was only, I think, a thirty-nine-day shooting schedule, which is pretty short for a studio feature. In my experience, most of them have been more like in the forty-five-to sixty-day schedule range, if not longer. But they were very efficient, the three guys. They knew exactly what shots they wanted. They didn't waste time shooting things they didn't need.

HUNT LOWRY (Associate Producer)
The boys trusted the people around them, knowing they would eventually learn their way as the filming process went along—which, of course, they did to hilarious results.

Jerry: The monitor was right there on the set. It was a fairly new device at the time, and the quality wasn't great, but it was incredibly important for us to see the framing, especially when the camera was moving, or the joke was in the background. It helped avoid a lot of screaming during dallies.

David: Comedy happens within that frame. It's the only thing the audience sees. It's not like on the stage, where your eyes can wander to whatever you feel like looking at.

Jerry: Still, there were times when we'd see dailies and be shocked by something we had missed. And we'd scream, **"HOW THE HELL DID WE ALL NOT SEE THAT?!"**

David: There's one scene where Bob is rushing through the airport corridor to catch up to Julie, and you can see a grip laying cable in the shot. He's right there! I don't think we saw that until the premiere. So it may be evidence that we didn't have playback.

Jim: Or weren't paying attention. Another time, in the *Saturday Night Fever* scene, a stuntman doubling for Bob does a backward flip into a clump of people, and Bob is supposed to pop out, but you can see him crouching behind, waiting for the stunt guy to land.

STUNTMAN

BOB HAYS

ROBERT HAYS
They're like three bodies with one brain, because they think so much alike, but they're all so different, and they bring those differences and all their different flavors into the comedy.

Jerry: Although we finally got the credit issue resolved, a new obstacle appeared: Universal Studios challenged Paramount's right to use the title, *Airplane!*

David: They had their very profitable and still viable *Airport* franchise, and here we were ridiculing it, taking exact scenes, and even casting the same actors! In *Airport*, Helen Reddy plays a nun who sings a song to a little girl awaiting a heart transplant. We wanted to parody that scene and cast her in the same role, using some of the same lines. In our original script, the little girl is reading a book, and the nun comes up and asks her, "Is that a good book?" The little girl nods, "Yes, but not *the* good book." Not exactly a sidesplitter, but I did love that line.

JILL WHELAN (Lisa Davis)

Airplane! was my first film. The funny thing about kids, though, is that even though it was my first film, it wasn't overwhelming at all to me. I just looked at it as a really fun time. For my audition, I went in and they asked me to make a funny face, and the face that's in the film is the face I made. If only all auditions could go that smoothly! I don't remember getting any other direction on the face.

David: We cast Joyce Bulifant as the mom because she played the mom in *Big John, Little John*, and we had met her when we wrote an episode of the show for Lloyd Schwartz.

JOYCE BULIFANT

I was married to William Asher at the time, and when I got the script, I looked at Bill as I was reading it and said, "This is the craziest, dumbest thing I have ever read in my life. There's no way I'd do this film! They've got to be out of their minds! They have people coming down where the baggage comes down. It doesn't make any sense! I can't do this." He said, "You are an actress. You act." So on the set, we were all going around asking each other, "Do you think this is funny?" "What the hell are we doing?" Howard Koch and his wife, Ruth, came up to me, and Howard said, "This is crazy, isn't it?" I shook my head, "This film, I don't know . . ." And Ruth said, "I agree with you! It's just nuts!" So I was just doing my scenes with Jill Whelan and Lorna Patterson and getting the hell out of there. I'd get home and say to Bill, "I'm not sure I should've done it!" But at the first screening I sat next to Ruth Koch, and after the first two seconds, as people were rolling in the aisles, literally slapping their knees, bent over laughing, Ruth and I looked at each other in shock and went, "Oh well, it's really funny!" All I could think of was when they say, "Everybody assume crash positions," and they do those crazy, tortured positions!

Jerry: Since that scene with Jill Whelan and Joyce Bulifant was a parody of the exact same scene in *Airport*, Universal threatened to sue if we used the singing nun character, much less the same actor, Helen Reddy. So we had to scramble.

MAUREEN MCGOVERN

My manager, Ron Barron, saw a blurb in one of the trade papers saying that Paramount and ZAZ were looking for someone to play the role of Sister Angelina in a tongue-in-cheek disaster film. The article indicated that Helen Reddy was to play the singing nun as a send-up of her role as Sister Ruth in *Airport* but had to bow out due to contractual commitments. Recently I listened to an interview where they said that Universal threatened to sue them if they used Helen as the nun. My manager immediately called ZAZ's production office and spoke with Betty Moss, their assistant, who happened to be a big fan of mine, and she quickly set up a meeting for me on set with Howard Koch and Jerry Zucker the following day. So, thank you, Betty! The Friday meeting with Howard and "The Boys," as ZAZ were called on the lot, was quick and pleasant. Given that I'm a survivor of—and a refugee from—the Catholic school experience, I knew from nuns. Eight years of them! I also played guitar, which was required. So I was given the script and asked to learn "Respect" and "I Enjoy Being a Girl" and be ready to shoot with guitar in hand on Monday. I was thrilled. Beyond thrilled. I felt like it was a fitting and hilarious end to my "Disaster Theme Queen" decade.

David: We were able to get away with having a singing nun, and she could even have a guitar, as long as she didn't sing to the little girl. Talk about nitpicking.

Jerry: Originally, we had offered the role of McCroskey to George Kennedy, but again Universal intervened; they wouldn't let him do both, and the *Airport* franchise was a much bigger payday. Years later, we cast him in *The Naked Gun*.

Jim: Universal even objected to the title *Airplane!* because they thought we'd be trading off their title, *Airport*.

Jerry: Paramount lost two arbitrations with the MPAA (Motion Picture Association of America). But after all that, there was some TV title that Paramount owned and Universal wanted. So they traded for the right to use *Airplane!* in North America.

Jim: So the solution was that we were allowed to call the movie *Airplane!* in the United States, but around the rest of the world it had to have all these other titles.

David: *Flying High* in the UK, *The Incredible Flight of the Crazy Airplane* in Germany, and *Is There a Pilot in the Plane?* in France.

Jerry: The great irony was that when *The Concorde: Airport '79* opened, it was so ridiculous that audiences were laughing. So Universal decided to market it as a comedy with the tagline "Fasten your seatbelts! The thrills are terrific. And so are the laughs."

LORNA PATTERSON
I had gotten the part as the stewardess, and it wasn't a singing role. But they called me and asked, "Can you sing?" I said, "Yes! I can sing!" So I drove over there as quickly as I could and walked into their office; it was like a dorm room. It was frightening. But they didn't have a tape player, so we went out to the parking lot, and the three guys get in the front seat of Jerry's car, putting their faces over the front seats looking back. I get into the back seat, they put the tape in, and I sing. Of course my joke forever after that is that I auditioned for the role in *Airplane!* in the back seat of Jerry Zucker's Volvo!

CHAPTER 22

THERE ARE NO RULES

I can't begin to describe the impact that *Airplane!* had on me. It was like learning a new language. I didn't know anything could be this funny. I was one of many people who saw this movie multiple times, as it was impossible to hear all the dialogue since audiences were laughing so hard.

"WEIRD AL" YANKOVIC

David: Contrary to what people might think given the wacky feel of *Airplane!*, almost none of it was improvised. Everything was written into the script. Nothing was ad-libbed. Even Stucker's lines, which he wrote himself, were added during the writing phase. I remember we called him and gave him the questions for the press conference: "What kind of plane is this?" And without missing a beat, he answered, "Oh, it's a big, pretty white plane with red stripes, curtains in the windows, and wheels! It looks like a big Tylenol!" We did a great job writing it down.

```
                    REPORTER
          What kind of plane is it?

                    JOHNNY
          Oh, it's a big pretty white plane
          with red stripes, curtains in the
          windows, and wheels...it looks like
          a big Tylenol!

                    REPORTER
          Alright boys, let's get some
          pictures!

     The reporters immediately begin removing framed pictures from
     the walls.
```

Jim: In fact, there were very few jokes we added on set that weren't in the script.

Jerry: One of the few I remember was when the guy in the control tower says, "Should we turn on the searchlights now?" And Stack says, "No! That's just what they'll be expecting us to do!"

```
                    AIR CONTROLLER MACIAS
          Captain, maybe we ought to turn on
          the search lights now.

                    REX KRAMER
          No! That's just what they'll be
          expecting us to do...
```

Jim: I know we always bend over backward not to take personal credit, but that was David's line, and it was based on something from *The Untouchables*.

Robert Stack, *The Untouchables*, 1959: *"No. That's just what they'll be expecting us to do."*

David: I mean, we were obsessed with *The Untouchables* and everything Robert Stack. During the script writing, we actually got the idea for the Rex Kramer line "It's his ship now, his command, he's in charge, he's the boss, the top dog, the big cheese," etc., verbatim from John Byner, a comedian who we'd seen doing those same Robert Stack lines on *The Ed Sullivan Show* years before. And then as Cary Grant, interrupting, "Shut up, Bob!" And back to Stack, "Right, the lips, the mouth, the trap, shut it up, mum's the word . . ." So, we couldn't wait to do that bit, but in rehearsal, we were alarmed to hear Stack read the lines flat and normal. We looked at each other, "Oh, shit." So, as Joe Biroc lit the scene, Jerry followed Stack around the set, imitating John Byner imitating Stack doing the lines. By the time the cameras rolled, he had it. I think even at the time, we realized how truly bizarre that was.

Robert Stack, *Airplane!*, 1980: *"No. That's just what they'll be expecting us to do."*

JOHN BYNER
I wasn't aware of my *Airplane!* connection at all. I'd been doing the Robert Stack impression in my act ever since he was on *The Untouchables.* "What are you gonna do with the weed? The fix? The pot? The goodies? The stuff?" I don't think it was ever on a record, but I did do it once at a golf tournament hosted by Carl Reiner. I got up and did this Robert Stack thing, and Stack was in the audience! So Reiner turns to Stack and says, "You wanna get up there and rebut that?" And Stack gets up there, and he says, "Well, first of all, the voice is too high . . ." But he took it real well, except that I used to end the bit by saying, "Tune in next week, when *Unsolved Mysteries* tries to determine which has less expression, my voice or my face." He didn't laugh, so I told him I'd leave that out the next time I did it.

Jim: Another bit that came up on the set was the hysterical woman getting slapped. The script just called for "shaking," but Lee Bryant, who played the role of the hysterical woman, actually had the idea of getting slapped.

LEE BRYANT (Mrs. Hammen)
Lorna Patterson was going to shake me when I went into hysterics, and then she gets called away and another passenger takes over, and that was the end of the joke. But I went to the guys, and I said, "You know, in all those films like that, the hysterical person always seems to get slapped. How about that?" And they said, "Oh, gosh, you might get hurt. We could never let you do that." But I said, "No, no, we'll rehearse it, and then we'll stage it." And they said, "Oh, you've opened up such a can of worms." And the next thing you know, they've got a tire iron and brass knuckles.

David: I can't believe we would've objected to the slap on the grounds of "You might get hurt." In many subsequent movies, we learned how to fake a slap and add a sound effect. One of Howard's favorite sayings was "It's an illusion business."

MAUREEN MCGOVERN
I had never done any acting prior to *Airplane!* Because of that, I think I was afraid of hurting Lee, so I was giving a rather timid slap.

LEE BRYANT

We were following a pattern—shake-shake-slap, shake-shake-slap. But Maureen couldn't get the timing. She was so upset at the idea of accidentally slapping me.

MAUREEN MCGOVERN

Jerry took me aside and asked me to be more forceful, which I thought I did the next time, but after seeing the film . . . Sorry, guys. I should have channeled a certain grade school nun of mine. I definitely owed them a stronger slap. And yet I had no problem choking the Krishna. Go figure.

LEE BRYANT

Leslie was the only one who actually slapped me. He even threw in an extra one. I guess he was improvising.

David: Evidently, Leslie didn't get the "It's an illusion business" memo. But it's one of my favorite moments.

Jim: In the shooting script, it just says the camera pans over to "a line of people waiting to shake the woman." We saw the line of people waiting to bat her around and thought we should add to that. So we asked Steven Levine, the prop guy, and he ran out during lunch and rounded up a gun and a baseball bat, whips, and whatever else he could find, and we extended the shot.

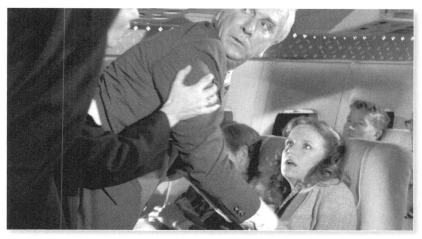

Hysterical Passenger: Leslie added an extra slap.

TIM ALLEN

Sorry to say, comedy these days has taken a step backward. There's no way we can watch a line of people punching a nun or laugh at "Ever seen a grown man naked?" God, I miss comedy.

David: It was also Bob Hays's idea to do the Russian dance during the disco bar sequence. At that point, Jerry had the brilliant insight to ask, "What else can you do?" And Bob responded, "Well, I can juggle." Within minutes, the prop guy rushed in with three balls.

ROBERT HAYS

For the choreography on that dance scene, we had Lester Wilson, who had also worked on *Saturday Night Fever*, and another guy, Tom Mahoney, who I think had done a lot of choreography for Disney. I was doing *Angie* while we were filming the dance sequence, so I get over there, and I remember that when I walked up to Julie, the camera was set up in the wrong spot. They said, "Wait a minute, we can't do it this way. How are we going to do this?" And I said, "I've got an idea. What if I come up to her, and it's like two animals stalking each other in the jungle, and I get around this side, take off my jacket and throw it, and then I strike the pose. And then the jacket comes back and hits me, and after that we start the dance." They said, "Well, let's try that!" And it worked. That was my idea! I actually came up with something!

Jim: In my mind, movie making is the ultimate collaborative, creative experience. When they roll the credits after the movie, those are the people who sat in traffic for two hours every day to make your vision come true. So, as a director, as long as you have a firm idea of what you want the final product to look, sound, and taste like, it's wonderful to take suggestions from the cast and crew. You never know whether the script supervisor or the special effects team or the prop master or, on that rare occasion, one of the other directors will have a good joke or idea.

JOHN FRAZIER

When we did the dancing scene in the bar, the guys wanted Bob Hays to do all this disco stuff. I said, "Well, why don't we put him on piano wires? And then he can do anything he wants." And they were, like, "We don't know what that means." I said, "You know, like Peter Pan!" "Oh, that's what we want! Make him Peter Pan!" So we did, and that's how he was able to do all those tricks when he was dancing in the bar.

David: During the time that we were shooting the control tower, Hunt Lowry was showing us stock footage that we could use of the cockpit view of the runway as the plane is landing. In one clip that he showed us, all the runway lights suddenly go out. So we looked at each other and came up with the idea of Stucker, having unplugged a power cord from the outlet, looking at the camera and saying, "Just kidding!"

Miniature crew preparing flight two-zero-niner for a crash landing.

ARNE SCHMIDT

There was one little thing they wanted to add at the very, very end. They were looking for some kind of topper, some final moment for Otto at the end of the movie.

Jim: So, the ending was written as, "The plane takes off, and we cut into the cockpit, and it's Otto." We asked Frazier if he could make him salute. He said, "Of course!" But still, we thought that was just clever. Not strong enough for a laugh, and especially for the end of the movie. We needed to knock down the posts.

JOHN FRAZIER
So I said, "How about if Mrs. Otto Pilot pops up at the end?"

Jerry: We loved the idea. Since they had built two autopilots for different functions, Frazier went to the paint shop and had one of them repainted to be Mrs. Otto. We thought that would do it, but Frazier had another great idea.

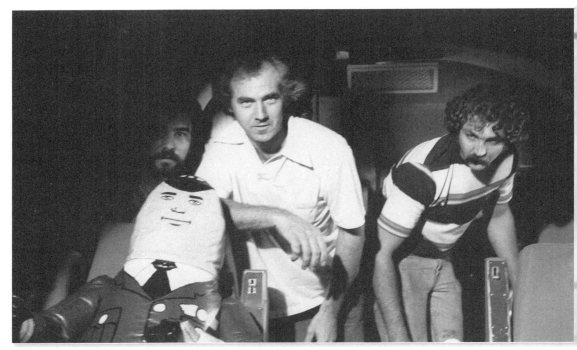

Great suggestion: special effects wizard (and future multiple Oscar winner) John Frazier and prop master Steven Levine

ARNE SCHMIDT
Frazier said, "How about Otto turns to the camera, and winks?" The guys loved that. And that's what you see in the movie.

David: It's wonderful how much people let us just get away with. For the "Stayin' Alive" sequence, we actually sped up the song. I'm not sure how many artists would have let us do that, but as it turned out the Bee Gees were thrilled about us using the song and were okay with us speeding it up.

Jerry: On the other hand, we heard Peter Yarrow was not so thrilled with the way we used *his* song.

Jim: I idolized Peter, Paul and Mary. They were probably the most popular folk group of the 1960s. My buddies and I went to a bunch of their concerts and even learned to play the guitar because of them. Paul and Mary always seemed like regular people. And of course everyone had a crush on Mary Travers. But Peter always came across as the most serious.

David: In 1974, we were on some TV show called *Razzle Dazzle Rock 'n' Roll*, along with Steve Martin, Freddie Prinze, and others. Peter Yarrow performed "River of Jordan," which he had written. It kind of stuck in our minds, because it was *so* serious and deep. "I wanted to know if life had a purpose, and what it all means in the end." We thought it would be perfect to play against the slapstick of the clumsy stewardess. On top of that, it had a long introduction that we could fill with jokes.

Jerry: I actually thought it was a great song, but yes, it was also the perfect song for the scene. So Paramount bought the rights from the music publisher. It probably seemed like a pretty good deal for Peter Yarrow, a few grand for a song he had already written. But later we read somewhere that he regretted it. His beautiful, spiritual song was being used in such a ridiculous way—people were laughing!

Singing stewardess: What if Ted Kennedy sees this?

PETER YARROW

In the seventies, I played the Snowbird ski resort in Utah on New Year's Eve. One year, the Kennedy family came to Snowbird, and because Peter, Paul and Mary not only played for JFK but were deeply connected to the family, I was invited to come over to where they were staying, and I played for the family. At the end of that, Teddy Kennedy wrote me a note saying that "River of Jordan" was his favorite song, and he was so grateful to me for having played it.

When I got the call that there was interest in licensing the use of that song for *Airplane!* to sing to the sick girl, I said, "Oh, God, I can't do this. What if Ted Kennedy sees it?" But then I read the script, and I said, "Oh, Jesus, there's no point in my worrying about that. This thing will never get off the ground!" So with an absolute assurance inside myself that it was not a problem whatsoever, because the movie was destined for failure, I went ahead and licensed the song. Then I'm out in L.A., and there I was in the hotel. I was tired, so I lay down on the bed. I turned on the TV, and what to my eyes did appear but that very section of the film. And I'm lying there, watching in horror, thinking, There's no way this isn't gonna get to Teddy Kennedy. It was the most bizarre turn of events, but it was also a reminder that you've got to watch your Ps and Qs or you're gonna get bitten in the ass.

Now, having said that, *Airplane!* was one of the funniest films I'd ever seen in my life. It's ironic, isn't it? The way it worked out, not only was the use of the song not objectionable, but I consider the film to be a hallmark of what is human, good, and fun and generous within ourselves. Some of those lines . . . I still say them! They've entered the culture in such a delightful way. It was sensational. So not only am I not mad; I give the guys my warmest regards!

David: Some of my other favorite moments are the visual jokes that play out in the background without the characters ever acknowledging them. One of my favorite examples is when we cut to Leslie in the cabin, and he looks toward the cockpit and says, "What the hell's going on up there?!" and visible in the frame is a woman's legs in stirrups and Leslie holding a speculum.

Jerry: We don't pan or cut to it; it's just there. Leslie is the focus of the shot.

Jim: Also, that joke is hidden in the drama.

David: We just let the audience find it.

"What the hell is going on up there?!"

LEE BRYANT

It's just the nature of their humor. Because they never tried to tell anybody what was funny. They just put it up there, and if you missed it, you had to see it a second time to catch it. And you have to play it straight. You have to. You could not show that you were aware of the joke. Because in their comedy, the moment the audience sees that you know what the joke is, then it's over. They're not gonna laugh.

David: Another example of this is the press conference with Johnny the air controller. All the microphones are thrust up into frame, but one of them is an ice cream cone. People may notice those kinds of jokes on the third or fourth viewing.

ARNE SCHMIDT

The scenes with the horse was tricky. I was concerned about the size of the horse and the safety of having a horse lying in a bed. How do you do that? And the wrangler said, "No, no, we're going to build a special bed, and we'll train the horse. We've got a real calm horse. It'll be fine!" So we had this stage set, just a bedroom set, it wasn't much. One side was completely open. And they said, "We'll get the horse, we'll lay the horse down in bed, and then we'll bring in the actress." They laid the horse down in the bed, they put the covers over it, the actress came in, the horse just lay there, she did her line, and the horse lifted its head. I think they put the horse's neighing in afterward, but I was still, like, "I've never seen that before!" I don't even know if they'd let you do that now. But they said it was okay!

David: It took two weeks to train the horse for that one joke.

Jerry: He was perfect. And he never let on that he was in a comedy.

BILL HADER

It just feels like every moment they were, like, "How can we maximize the amount of silliness?" And what makes it work is how straight everybody takes it. Even in the *Saturday Night Fever* flashback stuff, the thing with the two Girl Scouts battling with each other, it's, like, "What the fuck is that?!" and "Why is that even in there?" It's a real litmus test, that movie. If I watch it with someone and they're not laughing, then I'm like, "Oh, you have no sense of humor. I don't know if I can hang with you."

David: Like the incongruity of Barbara Billingsley interpreting for the Black dudes, we looked for what wouldn't belong in that rough bar. And the answer was Girl Scouts! It made perfect sense.

Jerry: Our cinematographer was Joe Biroc, this sweet old guy, always smoking a cigar. Those were the days when you could smoke on a movie set!

"Oh, it's a big, pretty, white plane with red stripes, curtains in the windows, and wheels. It looks like a big Tylenol."

David: When we were hiring crew, we leaned heavily on Jon Davison and Howard Koch. Howard recommended Joe, because he had worked with him.

Jerry: Joe was born in 1903, so he was in his seventies when we were making *Airplane!*

Jim: He would actually fall asleep on the set. He'd set the lights, retreat to his chair, and nod off until the next setup.

David: I think a good part of our early careers was spent trying to keep people awake.

Jerry: Joe had been around forever and had worked with every movie star in the business. He once told us about a time when his family was visiting him on the set, and he says, "I was shooting 16mm home movies of the wife and kids, and Cary Grant walks into the shot, and ruins the whole thing!" Joe was a character.

David: There were other connections to old Hollywood. There was an actor, I think his name was Len Mooy, who played a reporter and had the line, "Okay, boys. Let's get some pictures." He had this look that was right out of the 1940s. With his fedora, he looked like he'd been in a hundred old movies. There was another one, Ken Tobey, a very well-known character actor. He was one of the air controllers and has one of my favorite lines in the film: "Yes, birds, too."

Jim: One guy had actually worked on *The Wizard of Oz.*

Left to right: Jerry, Arne Schmidt, Jim, Hunt Lowry, Howard Koch, David, Jon Davison

KEN COLLINS

One of our key stand-ins was Ziggy, Sig Frohlich. He was one of the winged monkeys in *The Wizard of Oz!* I think he was in his fifties or sixties at that point, and he was a utility player. I think he also has a cameo early in the film when they're getting the plane ready to go. He comes up and gets the credit card from Peter Graves. It's just after Jimmie Walker has his cameo.

David: Joe had shot a lot of the old film noirs with high-contrast lighting. Movies like *The Rescue* and *Johnny Allegro*.

Jerry: I don't think Joe necessarily had an opinion one way or the other about the script, but his style fit perfectly into our vision for *Airplane!* He had done so many films that instead of trying to remember people's names on a new shoot, he'd just call them by their union number. If he wanted an electrician, he'd yell, "40!" If he needed the script supervisor he'd shout, "871!" Fortunately, we didn't have a union number, so he had to remember our names.

Jim: The other thing that I think we didn't realize, but was part of the great fortune of having Joe Biroc, was that he was quick. In our experience in comedy, it sucks to sit around for 90 percent of the day while

The camera crew: Todd Henry, Jamie Anderson, Joe Biroc, Fred Smith.

they're setting lights, because you really need to be able to do as many takes and as many variations as necessary to make it funny. If you're just sitting around while they're tweaking lights, it takes time away from telling the jokes.

TODD HENRY (Camera Assistant)

We moved pretty quick on that movie. Joe worked quickly. I worked with him on another movie, and it was one of those shows where everything seemed to be going wrong and everything was taking too long. And when it did, Joe would just go back and sit in his director's chair with his little cigar in his mouth. One day, he sees me getting annoyed at the slow pace and he calls me over. "Hey, kid!" he says to me. "Listen, kid, if they ever actually learn how to make movies, we'll all be out of a job. Just relax." And it's so true. You just have to kind of go with it and let things play out.

HUNT LOWRY

What struck me the most about working with Jerry, David, and Jim was that they were always comfortable not knowing what they did not know. *Airplane!* was their first film as directors and, of course, they also wrote the script, so they certainly put a lot of pressure on themselves. They wisely decided they were not going to get bogged down with the details of what they had to learn as filmmakers; rather they relied on what they did know . . . comedy.

David: We didn't care that Joe had little or no comedy experience. We just wanted that high-contrast B-movie look.

Jerry: For Joe, that was like saying, "Light it however you feel like lighting it!" He'd put up these cutters—black cards on a stand—in front of a light to create dramatic shadows across the actor's faces and on the wall behind them.

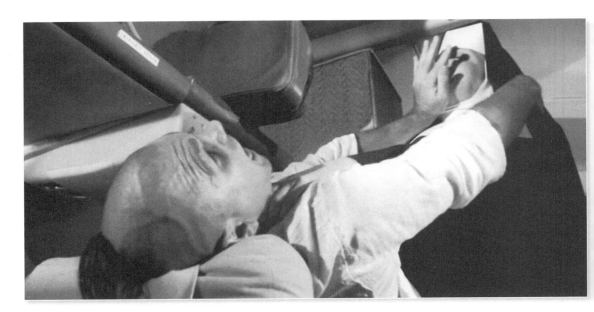

David: I probably learned more from watching Howard and Joe for seven weeks than I did in my years of film school.

Jim: Howard once told us that in his early days, they would shoot two films at once. They'd put a camera on a tripod, turn it one way, and film the scene for one movie, and then they'd turn the camera another direction and film a scene for some other movie.

David: Howard knew how to make movies efficiently and for the least amount of money. He knew in the end what would be important to spend money on and what would be a waste.

Jerry: True, but Jon Davison was the one who really knew how to wring the most out of every dollar. He knew what everything should cost, and he took it personally when he thought people were overcharging. He always found a way to get things done for a price. That was his Roger Corman training.

JOHN FRAZIER
Howard said, "On any other movie, we would put the airplane on a gimbal and rock it and everything, but you know what? I've been making movies for all these years, and we're not putting this airplane on a gimbal. If the audience doesn't get that the plane's moving, then we don't have a movie anyway." So the plane never moved. We just shook the camera. But it was that kind of movie.

Jerry: We didn't want a gimbal because they didn't use one in *Zero Hour!* or any of the old films we were parodying. Instead, Freddy Smith, the camera operator, would always be gently rocking the camera to give the feeling of motion.

David: We were intrigued by what's possible with a camera and Howard's mantra about "an illusion business." And we were curious about how far we could push the comedy visually. And that's where we first experimented with some of our own cinematic tricks, like when Robert Stack seems to walk right through a mirror.

KEN COLLINS
The scene with Robert Stack and the mirror was really complicated, because they had to build the set so that the reflection in the background was the mirror image of what he was seeing. So that one shot where he's adjusting his tie and at the end of it he goes, "Okay, let's go," and he steps through the mirror—a lot of people don't even pick it up, but it was a very meticulously planned shot so that he'd be able to step through it and you'd just go, "Wait, what? How'd he just do that?"

David: Even though it didn't get a big laugh, we loved that scene because it was so bizarre. We did a lot more of this in *Top Secret!*, but that scene was the forerunner.

ARNE SCHMIDT
The hours were really nice, and we were on a stage most of the time, so the lighting wasn't that big a deal. The interior of the airplane was lit basically once, and once that was established, it wasn't really any big deal after that. Same for the cockpit. It was heavenly. When we went over to the airport and we had people falling out of the baggage carousel instead of bags, I was worried about the airport being crowded, but they managed to put us at a baggage carousel at one end of the airport that was out of the way.

Jon Davison (left) and Hunt Lowry

David: Hunt Lowry was another one of those lucky connections we made during *Airplane!* who then became a lifelong friend.

Jim: Davison hired Hunt as a production assistant. I think the first time I ever met him, he delivered a script to my house. We wound up going fishing together the week *Airplane!* opened. I was so nervous, I needed to be out of town. But then, David and Jerry called me and said, "What are you doing? You gotta get back here."

Jerry: Hunt was great with people, very charming. And he was a doer, not afraid to take on anything. As things went on, Hunt was given more and more responsibility, and finally Jon made him an associate producer.

David: Finally, on August 8, 1979, we wrapped shooting. The final shot was the 747 crashing through the terminal. It was just the nose, mounted on a flatbed truck, which backed it through the giant glass wall. It was by far the most expensive scene we shot, but at least putting it at the end made it so we could use it as a backdrop for our cast and crew photo.

JOHN FRAZIER
That's the first time tempered glass was used in a film. At the time, our only other option was to use breakaway glass, but that wasn't going to work. I told the boys, "If you drop a piece of breakaway glass from the top of that window, it'll cut you in two. Somebody's gonna get hurt." Because on edge, it's sharp, and it doesn't even have to be that sharp to cut you real bad. It would've come down like a guillotine! So they said, "Well, what are we going to use? Because we obviously can't have that." So I said, "Well, look, we've been testing some stuff with this tempered glass. It breaks up into little pebbles." And that's what we used.

David: Howard was shocked when, a few days later, he found out how much we'd spent on that one scene. Jon Davison had handled that one, finding a way to do it cheaper than anyone else could do it, but it was still expensive, and intentionally or not, he neglected to tell the studio. That was one of the few times we saw Howard furious.

JON DAVISON

It was in the script! On the page it said something like, "The nose of the plane crashes into the terminal, scattering the waiting crowd." I'm sure Howard probably imagined a small section of wall cracking open, scaring the crap out of a few extras. But as it happened, I had the prop department build a huge, plaster, full-size model of a 747 nose and mount it on the back of a ten-ton truck. It was a pretty big deal to find a truck that was heavy enough that you could mount it on. Before you know it, we had a hundred extras, fifty stuntmen, and five cameras as the truck backed into a fifty-foot-high, all-glass terminal wall. I think we had to reinforce the stage a little bit at one point. There was no money left over for take two.

KEN COLLINS

There was a lot of coordination of all the extras in that scene, who were basically all stuntpeople. Connie Palmisano was our stunt coordinator. That was a really memorable scene for me. Later, I was the first AD on *The Dukes of Hazzard*'s second unit, and every day from sunup to sunset it would be crashing cars, flying through the air, chases, and all that. But at the time, that was the biggest stunt I'd ever been involved with!

David: We had just one shot at it, so we had like six cameras running. It was a good thing, because sure enough, the main camera malfunctioned!

Jerry: The studio would've never approved the expense.

David: But Davison was right. It ended up being worth ten times what it cost, because it was in every trailer. They could've put all that cost into the publicity budget and it would've been completely justified. And if you saw the trailer, you'd think that would be the big climactic ending to the movie, but in fact, we blew right past it in the opening credits.

Jim: In the foreground of that shot, in the waiting area, there's a woman holding a baby. As she sees the crash, she tosses the baby in the air and runs away in panic! When I see that shot, that's all I see.

CHAPTER 23

POSTPRODUCTION

My whole family—my parents and my sister and I—we watched *Airplane!* all the time. It's just one of those movies. We'd just watch *Airplane!* over and over and over again. And it was always funny. Every single time.

JIMMY KIMMEL

Jerry: Our editor was Patrick Kennedy. He was both talented and experienced, but I don't think we appreciated how difficult the process would be.

David: Editing back then took a long time, because everything had to be physically spliced together, both sound and picture separately. It wasn't all digital like it is today.

Jim: If you wanted to dissolve from one shot to the next, you had to send it to a lab, and you'd get it back a week later.

Jerry: I actually just meant how tough the editing process would be on the editor. Because he had to work with *us! Airplane!* was a very different kind of comedy, with a different set of rules, so we tended to debate with each other, not with the editor.

David: Patrick put a big mirror above him, and we'd sit behind him on a couch, so instead of having to turn around to talk to us, he would just look up into the mirror. Even with that clever setup, it was difficult for him, in that there were three of us. If there's one director and one editor, which is obviously the norm, then the two of you are talking. And even though the director makes the final decision, it comes out of a conversation. Whereas we would talk among ourselves and then say, "No, do this."

Jerry: And as usual it was two out of three.

> **PATRICK KENNEDY**
> I've heard that the boys said they felt like they may have tortured me over the course of editing *Airplane!* No, not at all. They were terrific. Even though it was three directors working with one editor, that really wasn't a problem, because ultimately what happened was that the three of them would argue it out, and then I'd get one change. So, once I saw how that worked, it wasn't anything to worry about.

Jim: The discussions we had among ourselves were frequently things like, should we keep the reaction shot to acknowledge a joke like "black like my men" when the boy reacts, or should we cut the reaction to be more subtle and let the audience figure it out, like when Bob ignores the guy who walks away from him when he says, "I had to ask the guy next to me to pinch me to see if I was dreaming."

Jerry: Over the years we had developed a shorthand about our style, and Patrick was new to this. So, understandably, his instincts were often at odds with ours. It got so occasionally he became a barometer of the opposite of what to do. Of course, we teased him about it, and he took it good-naturedly.

> **PATRICK KENNEDY**
>
> It was interesting watching them. Usually in those days, you had your director in the room, and they were all very serious and everything was all life or death, and there'd be intellectual discussions. But these guys, they were having fun. It really was like being in a college dorm. Their work method was to toss a Nerf football around while they argued among themselves about changes. I'd turn around to see Jerry wearing a red clown nose, David had a little plastic cap with a propeller on top, and I'm trying to duck Jim's football throws. I finally had to throw them out of the cutting room! But I recognize what it was: these guys were college guys together. It's what had kept them together, and that's what kept their comedy going.

Jim: Or not. Mind you, this was Patrick's forty-seventh movie and our first.

Jerry: In terms of the craft of editing, we always felt like his students. But one time, I do remember David and I were arguing about a scene. David said, "We need to cut it shorter," and I said, "No, it needs to breathe, leave it longer." We went back and forth for a while until Patrick finally said, "You know, I agree with Jerry, it's better longer." And David gave me a look like, "See? I'm right!" And I gave in!

David: That's what came to be known as "a Patrick."

Jim: The other part of the torture for Patrick was that our postproduction was nearly a year. We shot in the summer of '79, and the movie was released in the summer of '80. So it was an extended postproduction, and he had to endure us for a whole year!

> **PATRICK KENNEDY**
>
> Over the years, I've thought back on it, and these guys had everything in the world riding on this picture, and for them to pick me and trust me to edit their film . . . it was a great compliment, and they've always held a special place in my heart for that. It was a very brave move.

David: But Patrick was stoic. Unflappable. In future years, we used him as a model for the perfect editor personality. When we were interviewing a potential editor, Jim and I would be talking to the guy, and Jerry would sneak off and suddenly pop up behind him, screaming, "YAHHHH!!!!" If he didn't flinch, we knew we had our editor.

Jim: We were constantly tweaking the movie, editing the scenes down to their funniest moments. Once we started previewing it, the audience had the final decision. They were the arbiter of what was funny and what wasn't. As crazy as we might have been about a joke, if the audience didn't laugh, we couldn't get back to the editing room fast enough to cut it. In fact, the original screening time was 100 minutes and the final cut was 87.

Jerry: "I'll take it black like my men" was part of a much longer scene.

David: It was taken from a 1958 airliner-in-trouble movie called *Crash Landing*.

Jerry: A man and a woman were meeting for the first time when they were seated next to each other. So we thought it would be funny to have two ten-year-old kids using the same adult dialogue. None of it worked, except for when the guy offers her coffee, and she says, "I take it black. . . ."

Jim: As the designated typist, I just added, "Like my men." And of course, when Jerry and David read it, we all laughed.

David: We probably asked, like we often did, "Can we do that?" And the answer was, "Well, yeah!"

"I take it black. Like my men."

> **KEENEN IVORY WAYANS**
>
> I couldn't imagine anybody comprehending what they were going to do. And they were so edgy! You know, you think about "I like my coffee like my men." That shit . . . You know, from a little white girl? That was just brilliant! And they really, really kind of pushed the boundaries on everything, and they did it in a way where it wasn't offensive, it was hilarious.

> **DAVID HOLLANDER (Young Boy with Coffee)**
>
> There were some scenes that I did that were cut, where I'd go on a spiel and say, "After my wife died, I felt like a fifth wheel. I couldn't function in business, and I couldn't function socially. But I did learn one thing: you can't solve your problems in bed."

David: Our composer, Elmer Bernstein, was another great find. He had done a lot of serious scores, including *Magnificent Seven*, *The Great Escape*, *To Kill a Mockingbird*, and *The Ten Commandments*.

Jerry: We told Elmer we were looking for a really great B-movie score." He laughed. He got it.

David: He got that we wanted no silly, comedy-style music. Up to that time, comedy scores had mostly been done with a funny, quirky "wink" to them. We wanted to totally go against that.

> **TREY PARKER**
>
> It's not funny music! It's not scored like a comedy; it's scored like a *drama*. That had a huge impact on our work. That's *South Park*: we tonally take things very seriously. On *Team America* we really tried to use very serious music and very serious performances. And that's totally their thing. We learned it from them.

Jerry: Elmer was a brilliant composer, but he also had a wonderful sense of humor—and a great laugh.

Jim: When we were cutting, the music editor put on a generic temporary score so we could get a sense of the film with some music. But when we showed Elmer the movie for the first time, like most composers, he wanted to see it without a score. I remember him laughing through the whole movie.

Jerry: Elmer completely got it, the look, the cast, the whole B-movie vibe, and his score fit perfectly.

Elmer Bernstein: always our best audience.

David: In those days composers couldn't synthesize scores as they do today. So the first time we heard the score was while Elmer was conducting the orchestra. When we came to the scene where the stewardess talks to the little girl, there was no music planned and we all thought it needed some. On our lunch break, we told Elmer. To give an example, I started humming a melody that was in my head, "Da da da da, da da da da . . ." Elmer cut me off, saying, "Don't compose," and went off to sit down at the piano. I was completely embarrassed.

Jerry: Elmer composed something on the spot and played it on the piano. And it worked.

David: And I swear, it was the exact same melody I had hummed for him!

Jerry: We also got very lucky with the poster for *Airplane!*

Jim: We were in the middle of shooting when somebody walked onto the set from Paramount marketing and said, "These are some ideas for the poster." And there was the airplane tied in a knot, by an artist named Robert Grossman. We didn't know anything about marketing and didn't have a "single image" in mind to define a movie, but there it was. It was perfect!

Jerry: It was a black and white sketch, just done to convey the idea.

David: There were other ideas, of course, but when we saw that, we thought, *Well, that's it.* It was like the first time we read Julie Hagerty.

Jim: But you talk about the seas parting, that poster was brilliant. A twisted plane. Who thinks of that? And we just took it for granted, of course.

David: Yeah, we just said, "Oh, this is a great ad campaign."

Jerry: But there was one glitch. When they took the art to full color, they added a scantily clad stewardess sitting on the tail of the plane, holding a tray of drinks. It was everything the movie wasn't. The three of us went into full panic mode and called the publicity department. They told us there was nothing they could do because Barry Diller had approved it. I don't think Howard was around that day, so foolishly I picked up the phone and called Diller. Okay, here's the problem with that: I didn't fully understand who Barry Diller was. Of course, I was aware of his title . . .

David: Chairman of Paramount Pictures!

Jerry: . . . but at that moment, to me, he was just some guy who was making a big mistake and fucking up our poster. So I let him have it. He hung up on me. Later Katzenberg called and said that Barry was sorry that he'd hung up, and gently explained that in general, yelling at Barry Diller is not a particularly smart thing to do. I apologized for my stupidity, and eventually the scantily clad stewardess was removed from the poster.

Jim: You think of the poster for *Ruthless People*, which we directed a few years later, and it was exactly the opposite situation. There were a thousand different ideas, and then they finally settled on a picture of a big screw. Awful! Has there ever been a worse one-sheet?

David: Yes. *BASEketball*. I think it was by the same guy.

Good poster

Bad poster

Jim: As the years went by, our appreciation for the twisted airplane only grew.

David: After months of editing, we had over a hundred minutes of film assembled, and we felt we were ready to show the finished product to the Paramount executives.

Jerry: We all went to Eisner's house, with Howard Koch, Jon Davison, and Hunt Lowry, to show our first cut to Eisner and Katzenberg.

Jim: The movie played, and Eisner laughed hard at every gag, every beat. He loved it.

David: From the projection booth in the back, we could hear laughter. His kids and some of their friends were there. The movie ended, the lights were turned on, and I remember Eisner leaped to his feet and practically shouted, "This is great! I love it!"

Jerry: He was full of questions. "When are we releasing this? What was the budget? When will it be ready?"

David: He just was so excited, completely surprised, because all this time we had shot off the lot, and there were bigger, more important movies like *Star Trek* and *Urban Cowboy* that had occupied his attention.

Jerry: We told him we wanted to screen it right away, in front of college audiences, so we could cut the picture to the laughs.

David: Eisner said, "No, no! It's perfect! Don't touch it!" But we said, "No, we've got to. We need to hear the audience react and cut it to that." So he said, "Well, okay, but before you go out to the public, we have to screen it on the lot for the executives."

Jim: So we had to have an "executive screening." And we still didn't know what was going to work and what wasn't.

David: And instead of screening our first cut to a raucous, stoned college crowd, we had to screen it for twenty studio executives, who might sit in the audience with their arms folded, almost expecting us to fail.

Jim: We requested filling the rest of the theater with a recruited audience, who might not have read the script, might not have seen the dailies, and might be more disposed to laugh. The studio had a guy whose job it was to recruit audiences for previews, but

he was completely incompetent. The night of the preview, it was the twenty studio executives and a scattering of audience members. The "audience recruiter" didn't recruit anybody!

Jerry: We could sense disaster. And as we always did when we sensed disaster, we panicked. We rushed out to Melrose Avenue and dragged in people who were waiting in line to see the live tapings of *Happy Days* and *Laverne & Shirley*.

David: They were warm bodies, but for most of them English didn't appear to be their first language. It was at the old Paramount Theater, not a big venue anyway, but it was still only three-quarters filled.

Jerry: So *Airplane!* screened. The first half wasn't great, and the second half was pretty much silent. Not a fun night. It became painfully clear that the audience regretted missing *Laverne & Shirley*.

Jim: When the lights came up, it was obviously a bomb. We were sitting together in a row at the back of the theater, just stunned. We didn't know what hit us, why in the world they didn't laugh. Don Simpson and Craig Baumgartner walked past, and Don said, "That was, uh . . . interesting."

David: For me, it was another one of those crushing defeats like the show at Union South, the first *Airplane!* script, and the *Kentucky Fried Movie* sample reel getting rejected everywhere. I got the same knot in my stomach I had when the deals with AVCO Embassy and AIP fell through. After all this time and all we worked for and everything we had always told everyone, I had this feeling of "Shit. This isn't working?!"

JILL WHELAN
When we were making the film, my mother will tell you—because she obviously had a better perspective at the time than I did—that she felt it was either going to be a huge success or a huge flop, but there would definitely not be anything in between. There was too much of a commitment made to the comedy in *Airplane!*, and one way or the other people would feel an emotion, but it wouldn't be something in the center. But, you know, when you're making it, you don't think about it. I didn't anyway. I was just a kid, having fun on the set.

Jerry: In a way, everything we had done for the past eight years was all aimed toward this moment. And no matter how confident or headstrong you are, there comes a time when you think, *What if we've been completely wrong all this time?* This was that moment.

Jim: When we were walking out of the theater, Katzenberg said, "Guys, don't even pay attention to this, this means nothing. We'll get to work Monday morning, we're gonna recut it, and it's gonna be fine."

David: That was nice of Katzenberg to say, but we were all worried. How could they not have laughed?

Jerry: How could they not have laughed *that much*!

TOM PARRY

After the screening was over, Nancy Hardin and Maggie Wild, who were other development executives, me, Craig, Don, and Jeff all gathered in Don's office. The first words out of Don's mouth were "It's a piece of *shit!*" I said, "Well, what did everybody else think?" Maggie said, "Well, I thought it was funny, Tom." Craig said, "Well, I didn't think it worked." Jeffrey said, "Well, it *could* work. It could work." And Don said, "It's still a piece of shit!" So clearly Don did not want anything more to do with the picture.

David: The next day, I woke depressed, wishing that the previous night had been just some bad dream.

Jim: I remember driving onto the Paramount lot the next morning and seeing David hanging from the fourth-floor window of the DeMille Building.

David: I went out into my backyard and forced myself to listen to the tape of the audience reaction. The first half was passable enough. Not huge laughs, but enough good, solid laughs. When it got into the second half of the movie, I realized that there were laughs, but there was too much time between them. It just needed a lot of tightening.

Jerry: We learned our sense of pace from being onstage in Kentucky Fried Theater. We hated to be in front of an audience that wasn't laughing. And jokes always played better when they were still laughing at the one before—like spinning plates on poles: if you stop for too long, the plates are going to crash.

David: It's what I call the Flywheel Theory of comedy. I know this to be an absolute true theory, because I made it up myself.

MOLLY SHANNON

It was the first time I'd seen a movie where I missed so many jokes because the audience was laughing so hard at the previous gag. My brain had to catch up to the jokes as they came rapid-fire, nonstop. I had never seen that much comedy. If I laughed at a joke too long, I missed the next one. So at first, I watched the movie in a theater and thought to myself, I have to see this movie again—tomorrow. Nothing's come close to that EVER.

Jim: So we got back into the cutting room and started re-cutting the picture to the laughs—the same way we'd edited our live show. It was about then that Patrick developed twitches and began to speak in tongues.

Jerry: We recorded the screening, and despite the general silence there was one guy who was totally into it. He laughed all the way through the film, just by himself. So for a lot of the film, we were cutting the picture solely based on that one guy's reaction.

David: If it weren't for that one guy, the finished movie would have been 40 minutes long.

Jim: The movie would have been twelve minutes. We also realized that even though we knew what the picture was about, it might not have been clear to the audience at the beginning. They just didn't know what they were getting into. I remember Jerry saying, "Well, we need something to set the tone up-front."

Jerry: The movie originally started with the first scenes at the airport: people arriving, walking inside and out. It was the way a lot of the disaster movies we were parodying began. The scenes were funny, but it didn't tell the audience what kind of comedy they were about to watch. We needed to find a way to let people know what we were doing—how to watch the film.

David: Tonally, it was just a very different experience. Like trying shampoo for the first time.

Jim: So the airplane doing the *Jaws* thing was added after that horrible screening. It was perfect. It said, "We're doing a parody!"

Jerry: We did a lot of cutting after that screening, probably close to twenty minutes.

David: But we didn't cut many jokes out. We just trimmed and tightened all the dialogue in between.

Jim: One joke was cut was from the opening montage in the airport. We had a very attractive woman who was walking through the airport, and suddenly she turns and hocks a loogie on the wall.

David: We loved it, but no one laughed. That would've gone on the DVD.

Jim: As soon as DVDs were invented.

Jerry: Sadly, Paramount threw out all the dailies; every studio did at that time. All those reels took physical space that they needed on the lot, so they threw them out, including *Airplane!* Although I'm pretty sure they kept the outtakes from *The Godfather*.

David: There was also a joke that we had filmed where the announcer says, "Air Poland, please clear the runway." And then we cut into the cockpit, it's Jose Feliciano, Ray Charles, and Stevie Wonder. Two of the guys were look-alikes, but we actually got Jose Feliciano.

Jerry: I got a call from someone at the Jewish Anti-Defamation League. He had heard about the joke from someone at the Polish Anti-Defamation League. He explained that there were well-researched studies showing that because of Polish jokes, Polish children grow up thinking less of themselves. It was kind of a conversation stopper. Bad taste is one thing, but doing real damage to people is different. It's indefensible. We took the joke out of the film.

Jim: I remember the guy also didn't like *Famous Jewish Sports Legends*, which is one of my favorite jokes in the movie. Here we were three Jewish guys who were submediocre athletes on our best days, making fun of Jews being poor athletes. I felt it gave us permission to make fun of other stereotypes.

David: We had our first public preview at the University of California, Davis. We all flew up there, the three of us, Howard, Jon Davison, Hunt Lowry, Patrick Kennedy, and, of course, Katzenberg.

Jerry: We were nervous wrecks. After the Paramount screening, we really didn't know what would happen.

David: We all held our breaths, ready for anything.

Jim: So the lights go down, the movie starts. I grabbed Nancy's, my soon-to-be wife's, hand and squeezed it. And I guess I squeezed her hand the whole movie. It took her hours to pry her fingers apart and regain full feeling after the movie ended.

David: That was a major night. I was watching the movie but not watching the movie. I was watching the audience.

> **PATRICK KENNEDY**
> The audience started laughing right around the third frame and never stopped. It went over so well that, as a matter of fact, we cut some stuff out of the picture because the audience ran out of the ability to laugh. They were just worn out! So, to keep that going, we had to selectively trim out some material . . . so people wouldn't run out of breath!

Jerry: The first half played great. We had cut out a lot of stupid little jokes and unnecessary filler between jokes. But I was worried about the last third. At this point, the plot twists were mostly over and the audience was just waiting for the plane to land. The jokes had to work harder.

Jim: Up until the Paramount screening, the only people who'd seen it were people on the payroll. They weren't about to look at you and say, "This sucks." But then you show it to an audience full of people who don't know you or care how you feel, and the truth comes out.

Jerry: It turned out to be one of the greatest nights in all of our careers. The audience loved it! They got what we were doing. They laughed all the way through and applauded at the end. All the insults of our childhood that drove us into comedy had finally paid off!

David: It was the first real moment of success for *Airplane!* Colleges could be somewhat misleading, because those audiences were always 10 percent louder than any regular audience, but this was undeniable. It actually worked in the way we had always imagined.

Jim: There really is no cooler feeling than sitting anonymously in a screening in the midst of six hundred people who are laughing hysterically at your jokes.

Jerry: After the screening we did a Q&A, and the audience was full of questions, as enthusiastic as they were during the movie. Howard took us all out to dinner in Sacramento, and we celebrated!

Jim: After the Davis screening, we knew we had gotten it right. We still went back to the cutting room and continued to do tweaks and trims, but we knew we had it. By then Patrick was on supplemental oxygen, but at least he could see a happy ending in sight.

Floating celebration: the Delta King Hotel, Sacramento

Jerry: We continued to screen the movie at colleges across the country: Harvard, NYU, the University of Wisconsin—really fun to be back where it all started.

David: Sometimes, as a result of the reactions, we had to extend a shot to accommodate the laughs so the audience could hear the next line. When Kareem is done shoving the little boy and lets go of his shirt, we hold on Joey's shocked expression for a long time. That's because the laugh lasted that long.

Jerry: The next line after that was Peter Graves asking Joey if he likes movies about gladiators. We didn't want people to miss that.

Jim: Same thing with, "I take it black, like my men." The laughter went on forever! You can see the kid just waits.

Jerry: Of course, then you end up with a lot of long pauses that seem very odd to anyone watching the DVD.

CARLTON CUSE

At the Harvard screening, they were recording the laughter in order to time how much they got on each joke and to also decide which jokes to cut. I recall the crowd just being amazed at it. Their brand of humor was so subversive and edgy and out there. The response was total delight. Although I also sort of feel like there were a few jokes that kind of fell flat. I don't remember them specifically, but they ultimately weren't in the final cut. So it was also just kind of fascinating to see a movie in progress like that. It was the first behind-the-scenes glimpse I'd ever had of the process.

TOM PARRY

When the Harvard screening was over, the guys got up in front to answer questions, and they were smart questions, but I remember one specifically. Somebody stood up and said, "Well, I didn't think such and such was funny," and Jim Abrahams replied, "Well, geez, last night at *Princeton* they thought it was funny." And, of course, the audience ate that up.

David: Once the college screenings were over and we made all the required fixes, we were ready for the movie to open. But as it turned out, nothing in the movie business is simple. You need to strategize every step of the way. Luckily, we had another great Paramount executive, Frank Mancuso.

TOM PARRY

Frank Mancuso, head of distribution, called me and said, "I watched *Airplane!* It's a funny movie! You know, we didn't really have a slot for it, but I think we're going to use it in case our big pictures start to fall out."

David: At that time, there were a lot of big movies slated for the summer release. Frank suspected that some of them might not perform as well as expected. He shrewdly strategized to position *Airplane!* to fill what he thought might be a vacuum. We worked on the trailer with Don LaFontaine, famous for intoning in a deep voice full of gravitas, "In a world . . ."

Jim: We modeled it heavily on the trailer of *Zero Hour!*

Jerry: At first, we didn't want to give away so many of the best jokes in the trailer. We were afraid people wouldn't laugh at them when they saw the movie. Katzenberg of course knew better. He said, "Guys, there's only one thing that matters right now: asses in seats."

David: Katzenberg was right. Audiences laughed just as hard when they saw the movie.

Jim: The other unusual thing about that trailer was that it never acknowledged that the movie was supposed to be funny. The announcer never mentioned laughter or comedy. Only how gripping a drama it was. The jokes did the rest.

TOM PARRY
After the trailer was released I got a call from Frank saying, "Tom, I don't know if you know this, but we're getting phone calls from theater owners around the country where this trailer is playing, telling us that they want to book the picture because people are coming back not to see the movie that's playing, but to see the trailer again! So we're gonna start booking the picture into theaters earlier than we thought."

David: We used to go to the Bruin Theater in Westwood just to see the trailer play. Instead of standing in the back, I'd walk down the rows on the side so I could see people's faces. Not only were they laughing; arms and hands were pointing to the screen.

Jim: Later we learned that the movie opened much stronger in the theaters where they had played the trailer.

David: And just as Frank Mancuso had predicted, enough big studio pictures underperformed in the early summer weeks to give him an opening to slot in *Airplane!*

for July 2. Before we opened, there was a screening at the Directors Guild. The whole cast was there. Peter Graves was sitting right behind me with his wife and daughter. His wife was just howling, and I mean really out loud.

> **PETER GRAVES**
> In five minutes the audience is falling down and clutching their sides, and I said, "Geez, I'm funny!"

David: And Stack said later to his wife, "Never have I been so wrong about anything in my entire life." Stack was a trooper, but he had no idea the movie would work the way it did.

> **MARCY GOLDMAN (Mrs. Geline)**
> After the screening, I was standing with Jim Abrahams when Robert Stack came up. His eyes looked like Little Orphan Annie's—I mean, they were just bulging out of his head—and he said, "Jim . . . thank you! Thank you so much! I don't know what to say. That's just . . . the funniest movie I've ever seen. I can't thank you enough." I don't think any of those guys expected that it was going to turn out the way it did. I think they were just doing it as a lark, but all of a sudden, everyone in town was seeing the film, and it just reinvigorated their careers, all of those guys.

> **ROBERT HAYS**
> My folks were at that screening—my little five-foot-two mom, and my six-foot-three dad, who was a retired colonel in the Marine Corps, a fighter pilot—and here's Peter Graves, the all-American dad from *Fury* and the hero of *Mission: Impossible*, so I thought, Oh, my folks might like to meet Peter! So I said, "Peter, this is my mom and dad!" And they say "hello" and "nice to meet you." Dad was always the strong and silent type and never was a loudmouth, and my mother wasn't either, so there was one of those awkward little moments where everyone's run out of things to say. So I turned to Peter and said, "So, Peter, how've you been?" And he said, "I've been great. I've had a strange hankering for little boys, but . . ." I looked at my dad, and his face was, like, "What? What did he just say?!"

CHAPTER 24

SUCCESS AT LAST

My dad and I, over the years, have watched *Airplane!* together dozens of times. It was one of the ways we connected. In recent years, he has been battling Alzheimer's. It's gotten to the point that he no longer recognizes me, but he can still quote *Airplane!*

JAMES MURRAY

"WEIRD AL" YANKOVIC

The first time I saw *Airplane!* was in San Luis Obispo, California, during my senior year in college. The only longer movie line I had ever waited in was the one for *Star Wars* a couple of years earlier. *Airplane!* was a bona fide comedy blockbuster—the buzz on this thing was huge.

Jerry: *Airplane!* opened at the Bruin Theater in Westwood on July 2, 1980. We were about as excited as we could be, and when we arrived there was a line around the block. Minutes later, Eisner and Katzenberg arrived, just as excited as we were.

David: That night, Eisner told us the studio would make its investment back the first weekend. Just like Salah Hassanein had told us three years before, on the opening weekend of *Kentucky Fried Movie.*

Jerry: Inside the theater, I remember seeing Barry Diller walking up the aisle, watching the audience react. He had a huge smile on his face. By that time I had figured out who he was, and seeing his genuine excitement meant a lot to me.

Jim: That was an incredible night, but one of the top two or three highlights of my movie career happened a month before. In those days, the network used to tape-delay telecasts of the NBA Finals games until eleven thirty p.m. So I'm sitting alone in my apartment in the middle of the night, watching the Lakers play Philadelphia. I had no idea what was coming. Then at half time—on the national broadcast—they played the

scene where Kareem scolds Joey for telling him he didn't hustle. There I was, Mr. Nobody, alone in my apartment, in the middle of the night, watching this guy whom I'd idolized for a couple of decades, saying lines I'd been thinking of for years on national TV. I still get chills.

Jerry: The accolades were a pretty heady experience. I think our humility may have taken a leave of absence for a while there. But even in the heady times we'd mock our own hubris. We couldn't help it.

TOM PARRY

When the picture opened, it was a huge hit. The biggest hit of the summer. Not the biggest-grossing movie, but because the movie was such a super-low-budget, and the net from the theaters around the world was something like a couple of hundred million dollars—on a three million dollar investment! Up to that point, it was Paramount's most profitable picture.

David: The movie was such an instant hit that the studio couldn't hide the money fast enough. When we moved to new offices, we sent out an engraved card announcing the receipt of our first profit participation.

Jim: When we were promoting *Airplane!*, we did an interview for NBC's *The Tomorrow Show*. For the first segment, David had a fake mustache on. When they came back from the first commercial break, Jerry had the mustache on, and then for the third segment, I did. And no one ever acknowledged it. It's great when you don't have to try to be funny.

David: In one interview, we pretended that the whole purpose of doing *Airplane!* was to make enough money to own a short-order restaurant. So we did the interview at a little burger joint on Ocean Avenue in Santa Monica, answering the questions while we were flipping burgers at "our new place."

ROBERT HAYS
I've been lucky in my career, and I owe it to *Airplane!* to a huge extent. Who knows what I would've been able to do if it hadn't been for that film. I was already doing stuff—I had a series, and things were going along nicely—but I always figured that *Airplane!* was like winning the lotto. I mean, to be the star in my first feature film, and to be able to work with such incredible people—the writer-directors, the actors, everybody!

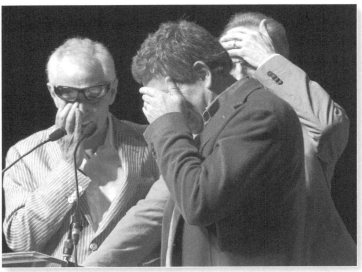

Jim: Then we were nominated for Best Comedy Screenplay by the Writers Guild, and word kind of leaked out ahead of time that we were going to win.

Jerry: They want to make sure that all the winners are there, so they'd call the studio and say, "We can't tell you who won, but make sure they show up."

Jim: So we went to the WGA theater dressed in coats and ties, but then when we were announced as winners, we took off our coats, ran up onto the stage, and revealed T-shirts that read across the three of them, "What-A-Surprise!"

David: At the Deauville Film Festival thirty-five years later, we pretended we were so overcome with emotion that we couldn't speak.

ADAM MCKAY

I was in sixth or seventh grade when I first saw *Airplane!* My friends and I went to see it. We had no idea what was coming our way. I remember laughing in a way that maybe I'd never laughed before at just how unhinged and free the movie was, and how absurd. It was just a kind of comedy that I don't think at that point I'd ever encountered. And to see it with a story and production value at the theater . . . I just never expected it. They did such a brilliant job of blending "Will the plane land safely?" with that unhinged humor. The movie actually has an architecture to it. It holds up.

David: We always wondered if Arthur Hailey, the man who wrote *Zero Hour!*, had ever seen the movie and what he would have thought of it. But then we came across this little tidbit:

Lawrence Journal-World

December 16, 2001

Hailey Still Has Nose for News; 81-Year-Old Hotel Writer Says He'll "Never Retire"

The 1980 spoof *Airplane!* was based on Hailey's serious television screenplay, *Flight into Danger*. He had no control over the movie because the rights had been sold. Nevertheless, he says, "I laughed like everybody else."

Jerry: No one enjoyed the ride more than Howard. He loved the experience. Although for him, I think it was more like "This is terrific! Okay, what's next?" He'd rather be working on a new film than wallow in the success of the last one.

David: For the time being, we were content with wallowing.

Jerry: Our friendship with Howard didn't end with *Airplane!* We all bought a racehorse together named Senior Senator (talk about throwing your money away), and I had the good fortune to work with Howard again on *Ghost*.

Day at the races: with Howard and Ruth Koch and "Senior Senator" on the present-day spot of the Rams' fifty-yard line

Jim: For the international release of *Airplane!*, we were invited to the Deauville Film Festival in France. During that week, we did what seemed like hundreds of interviews.

David: At some point, after answering the same questions dozens of times, we started to get really bored. We started to tire of it and felt that we were getting dull answering the same questions. So, we started a competition to see who could get the biggest lie in print.

Jim: A lot of the writers were interested in what the latest trends in the US were, and particularly in California, so one of us, I can't remember who, came up with "Skeet surfing, the latest California beach fad combining surfing and skeet shooting." We kind of looked at each other, thinking, *He'll never buy this.* But the guy just asked, "How do you keep the guns dry?"

David: Four years later, we used that as the opening of *Top Secret!*

Jerry: While we were in Deauville, we were invited to lunch with Charlie Bluhdorn, the chairman of Gulf and Western Industries, the conglomerate that owned Paramount Pictures. In the car on the way to the restaurant, Diller told us how scary Bluhdorn could be and how he would routinely call the heads of all his companies at any hour, once shouting at Diller, "I can make more money trading sugar in a day than you make at Paramount in a whole year!"

David: We pull up to the restaurant, a little cafe in the center of town. Eisner and Katzenberg were waiting for us.

Jim: After we were introduced, Bluhdorn says right away, "Why haven't you signed with us for your next picture?" And David points his thumb over at Diller, Eisner, and

Katzenberg and says, "We're through dealing with these middlemen. We wanted to go right to the top."

David: Fortunately, he laughed. I don't think I understood the gravity of that meeting. But I do remember being hungry.

> **JEFFREY KATZENBERG**
> Charlie Bluhdorn is one of the most epic characters of all time. Not just in my experience with him, but in the pantheon of maniacs, this guy is top ten of all time! And a genius, and a really, really incredibly smart businessman. He loved movies, he loved moviemakers, and—like the rest of us—he had a bottomless well of the need to win.

Jerry: At lunch, Bluhdorn pressed the point. He started telling us the story of a former producer and studio executive named David Begelman. Apparently, Bluhdorn had agreed to finance a picture that Begelman was producing, but when he stopped by the set, he was told that he had been cut out of the deal. It was a story about loyalty, but as he went on, Bluhdorn became more and more agitated.

David: The obvious point was "If you don't sign with us, you're being disloyal."

Jim: You have to understand that, at the beginning, Bluhdorn just came across as a personable guy in his fifties. He was pleasant and polite, even soft spoken, but as his passion escalated, he got louder and louder in his thick Austrian accent. People in the restaurant started to look over and wonder, "What's this all about?" His wife was with him, and she tried to elbow him to calm down. But he just got louder and bigger and more insane.

Jerry: I'm sure this was not a new experience for her. Suddenly, he leans forward, clenching a fist at us; veins are bulging out of his neck, his face is bright red, and his voice is quivering. "Because without loyalty . . . without loyalty, my boys"—and by this time he's literally screaming—"YOUR LIVES WILL BE AS BARREN AS THE LIBYAN DESERT!"

Che Puce Cafe, Deauville

David: The whole restaurant went silent. The three of us were plastered back against the wall.

Jerry: Eisner, Katzenberg, and Diller were just kind of avoiding eye contact, obviously having witnessed this kind of behavior before.

> **JEFFREY KATZENBERG**
> Bluhdorn wasn't going to let those guys out of that room without a deal. He was very old school, very European. "You're with us, or you're against us. You're a friend, or you're a foe. You're loyal, or you're a traitor." It was always literally black and white. There was no middle ground with him.

Jim: I don't remember how the lunch ended, but we re-signed with Paramount that day.

Jerry: Some time later, Bluhdorn came to visit the studio, something he didn't do often, and they invited us to a big luncheon in his honor. For some reason, he decided to sit at our table. It was a real treat for us. At one point, he started pitching us an idea for what he thought would make a fantastic film, *Hitler Meets Sitting Bull*. At first we thought he was joking, but we quickly realized that he was dead serious. He complained that he had pitched the idea to Eisner, and "Michael didn't like it." As soon as we heard that, we told him it was a brilliant idea and Eisner was crazy to have rejected it. He immediately turned to Eisner, who was sitting at the next table, and said, "I just told them about *Hitler Meets Sitting Bull*, and they love it! They think it'll be a huge hit!" I'll never forget the look on Eisner's face. He knew what we had done.

The sequel that never was: ZAZ's Airplane II

David: And of course, they wanted us to do an *Airplane!* sequel. At first we had no interest in that, but then we actually came up with an idea that we really liked: after Striker and Elaine fly down the plane at the end of the first movie, they want to get married, so Striker takes Elaine to meet his family, and it's the Corleones.

Jerry: We wanted to do *Airplane II: The Godfather*. The poster would be the twisted plane dangling on puppet strings, like the logo for *The Godfather*.

Jim: We thought we could use those same characters but not have to be trapped up in an airplane the whole time. And we had pretty much run out of airplane jokes.

Jerry: Eisner and Katzenberg loved the idea and thought it was really commercial. But they couldn't say yes without talking to Francis Ford Coppola. The answer was a quick no, because he might want to do a third *Godfather*. I think everyone would have been better off if he had said yes.

Jim: To this day, none of us have seen *Airplane II*.

BILL HADER

I think *Airplane!* is a benchmark in comedy movies, and I don't think you can do it again. You can just see how it's in the culture. You watch ESPN commercials, and you have the actual athletes being a version of themselves, but it's funny, and it's all played very straight. That's *Airplane!* And the kind of surrealism of it, the overall silliness of it, it's hard to replicate. I just thought—and still think—it's perfect. Many people tried to copy the winning ZAZ formula over the years, but precious few have succeeded. I often credit *Top Secret!* as being my all-time favorite film (partly because it needs the love, and partly because every single moment in it is hilarious)—but *Airplane!* is the movie that unequivocally changed the world of comedy, and possibly my DNA as well.

PATRICK KENNEDY

If you go back and look at movie comedies before *Airplane!*, you don't see any of the non sequiturs, you don't see the off-the-cuff stuff, you don't see completely fun nonsense. Now you do. Okay, maybe people overdo it sometimes, but these guys knew what they were doing.

David: People ask us if we were surprised by *Airplane!*'s success, since for five years we'd been trying to convince people to let us make it, telling them it would be a hit. When it finally was, we weren't surprised.

Jerry: But now we're surprised that it's still around.

Jim: Right. Do you think we would have put in an Anita Bryant joke if we had any idea the movie would last so long?

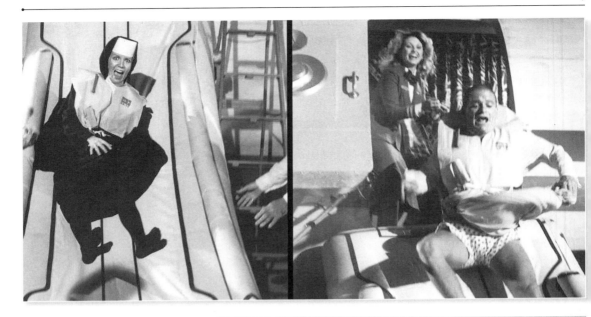

HUNT LOWRY

People continue to quote *Airplane!* New audiences are still discovering it. Many of the lines have become part of the language.

FRANK ASHMORE

You never know as an actor what's going to be a success. You show up, you do the work, you're having fun, and you experience the talent of these people firsthand, so you can see where it's going, and you kind of have a hunch that something's afoot.

JULIE HAGERTY

When the American Film Institute did its list of one hundred funniest comedies, Bob and I got back together because they wanted to do an interview with us. And we both looked at each other and said, "That's the biggest prize you could ever want to get." That it still lives and breathes and has life this many years later, it's just . . . Who knew?

PETER GRAVES

Years after the movie came out, I was once standing in a supermarket checkout line, and ahead of me is this nice lady. She's got a twelve-year-old boy with her who's looking up at me like maybe he's seen me somewhere, but he's not sure. And she casts a glance, and she's not sure either. But then she finishes paying, and the kid's still looking at me. And I just leaned down and said, "Son, do you like movies about gladiators?" She grabbed that kid and headed for the hills. No one has seen her since.

JULIE HAGERTY

Most movies don't have that kind of longevity, but generation after generation after generation has seen this film, and it's such a hoot to me to have, like, fifteen-year-olds come up to me and go, "Aren't you the lady? You know, the stewardess?" It's such a treat. Now that I'm getting older, people won't be recognizing me, but they'll go, "I've heard that voice . . ." I'll go, "Oh, God, I've gotten to the point where they recognize my voice but not me!"

PETER GRAVES

You know, one of the nice things now is that the audience that I see who really enjoys *Airplane!* the most is the airline crews. They're fabulous! Every time I get on an airplane, they say, "Good morn—"—gasp and point—"Oh! You! Hahahaha! Captain, come here! You gotta talk to the guys!"

GLEN CROW (Airline Pilot)

I flew for American for twenty-five years. All the pilots, they'd just throw out these *Airplane!*-isms. Like when we're coming in for a difficult landing, getting buffeted by cross winds and bounced around, the first officer would say, "Good luck. We're all counting on you."

KAREEM ABDUL-JABAAR

I was in Europe, flying on one of those very big planes, and the pilots came back and made me get out of my seat and come into the cockpit and take off with them, so they could say they flew with Murdock!

DAVID HOLLANDER

Even as an adult, I have been recognized by gate agents and flight attendants, and it's helped to get the random upgrade. It's one of those things that's already iconic, but then it's especially iconic for people who work in the aviation industry. It's a reference point for everyone who works in that field.

GLENN CROW

Sometimes you have an air disaster movie and it's not realistic. You're like, "God, that's hokey!" They don't hire anyone who knows how to fly an airplane to advise them on the movie! They're just terrible, and only experts realize how bad these movies are. But *Airplane!* is immune to that. Because the whole idea is just to go nuts and laugh at everything. It's ridiculous.

DAVID HOLLANDER

Ross Harris was not there on set the day I did my scene, but he was someone I knew just from acting. Many years later—after college, when I moved back to Los Angeles—Ross and I used to frequent the same record store on Melrose, and one day the store clerk told Ross, "You do know that the other kid from *Airplane!* comes in here, too, right? And he buys pretty much the same kind of stuff that you do." And that's how we reconnected. We've been friends ever since.

David: Lifelong friendships were forged on that set. To this day, Bob Hays is one of my closest friends. This doesn't happen on every picture. It's nice to see how many relationships have continued over the years.

Jim: Even the three of us are still speaking.

TREY PARKER

I showed *Airplane!* to my stepson when he was about ten, so about the same age as I was when I first saw it. I purposely didn't tell him anything about it first, and he didn't really think it was an old movie. He thought it was a parody, because of the way that it looked and the way the people looked more old-timey, but he thought it was a new movie! And he loved it. We ended up watching *Police Squad!* after that.

MATT STONE

Think about the dialogue when you watch the first *Star Wars* movie and how Howard Hawks–ian it is, which is great, but they're old movies from a long time ago! But *Airplane!* seems completely modern and contemporary.

TREY PARKER

With *Airplane!*, they invented a tone, and people like us have used pieces of it and done our own things with it, but their tone is just theirs. Usually why something doesn't hold up is because it's good, and then a ton of people copy it, and then they improve upon it, and then you go back and look at the original thing, and you're, like, "Well, that's not that great." Because it's evolved at that point. *Airplane!* has not evolved. It is still what it is. And no one's done a better version of it.

Jim: My kids tease me all the time about getting old, but nothing brings it home better than this: I was at a party about a year ago, and a young boy, maybe eight, came up to me and told me how much he liked *Airplane!* We chatted a little and then I asked him how it was that he came to see the movie. He said, "My grandfather made me watch it." Yikes.

Jerry: He's probably our age.

David: I think there was probably no greater single event than the night our parents held a screening of *Airplane!* in Milwaukee, a week before the national opening. It was the world premiere.

Jerry: They rented the Fox Bay Theater, where as kids we used to watch Three Stooges, Abbott and Costello, and all-day cartoons on Saturday.

Jim: The theater was huge, six hundred seats. Mom and the Zuckers invited only the immediate city. Everyone we knew was there. Relatives, family friends, teachers, classmates, neighbors. It was incredible.

Jerry: That's one of the great things about coming from Milwaukee. It didn't even matter if they liked the movie or not. They were proud of us.

JON DAVISON
For the guys, that Milwaukee screening was a validation of ten years of work. They were oblivious to what the odds were to come from some small town in the Midwest and make a hit movie. All they wanted to do was make people laugh. I don't think they ever took the odds against them seriously.

We just love to pose. Anywhere.

David: It was Mrs. Zubatsky's law: "Just point the hose up at the roof!"

Jerry: Ignore conventional wisdom. What's the worst that could happen?

Jim: Your house will burn down.

David: The point being, we were nothing if not headstrong.

Jerry: And too naive to know it was impossible.

Jim: We were living proof again that ignorance is bliss.

David: When I was seven years old, I had a dream that I rode up to my school on a white horse like the Lone Ranger. Premiering *Airplane!* in our hometown theater was that dream come true (unfortunately without the horse), but I don't think we realized at the time how special and amazing that night was. Reflecting after four-plus decades, what was truly incredible was the confluence of events, happenstance, fate, and strong padlocks without which we could never have had that moment.

Jim: When I think of all the serendipity that took place to get us through those ten years, it's pretty amazing—running into each other at the perfect time; getting access to video machines during a time when they were so rare; hooking up with Chudnow; getting the theater on Pico in Los Angeles; Steve Stucker; Kim Jorgensen; Pat Proft; stumbling onto *Zero Hour!*; learning how to direct from John Landis; winding up at Paramount with Davison; Bob and Julie; and then having Howard Koch as our mentor. A lifetime of good karma in just a few short years.

Jerry: I know it seemed like fate to you guys, but I arranged it all.

EPILOGUE

ZAZ continued their writing/directing partnership. Together, they created the television series *Police Squad!* (1982), so ahead of its time that it was canceled after only four episodes. They then wrote and directed the cult classic *Top Secret!* (1984), followed by *Ruthless People* (1986). In 1988, they wrote their last movie together (with Pat Proft), *The Naked Gun: From the Files of Police Squad!* As each had decided by then to pursue a separate career, David directed it solo. It became the first-ever hit movie franchise based on a failed TV series.

DAVID

After ZAZ's final directorial collaboration, *Ruthless People* (1986), I directed *The Naked Gun* (1988), *Naked Gun 2½* (1991), *BASEketball* (1998), and *Scary Movies 3 and 4* (2003, 2006). I produced *Brain Donors* (1992), *Naked Gun 33⅓* (1994), *A Walk in the Clouds* (1995), *High School High* (1996), *Phone Booth* (2002), and *Scary Movie V* (2013).

Although I found a home in L.A. and a niche in the movie business, I was still missing my native Wisconsin, but mostly the trees. After the release of *The Naked Gun*, I met Andy Lipkis, founder of a wonderful organization called TreePeople. We immediately bonded over our mutual love of trees, and I joined, participating in tree plantings every weekend. After a year, I was invited to join the board. Ever since, I have been proud to see the organization plant millions of trees, and today I've become TreePeople's longest-serving board member. I was deeply honored when Andy and Katie Lipkis chose me to be godfather to their newborn son, Henry. For his first birthday I bought him a toy chainsaw. Every summer, as a fundraiser, a talented troupe of actors performs a table read of *Airplane!* at the TreePeople amphitheater. A totally different experience from the movie, but just as fun—and even more when I'm able to attend with Bob Hays. We always get summoned to the stage for a post-show introduction and Q&A. A true labor of love.

In the early eighties, I purchased an avocado ranch in Ojai, California, and of course began planting hundreds of trees, transforming twenty acres of scrub brush and chaparral into a thriving forest. It was a great hobby, and soon the ranch became the site of the annual Davy Crockett Rifle Frolic, attracting period-dressed historians, teachers, craftspeople, and flintlock rifle enthusiasts from all over the country to a three-day camping, music and shooting event. I was always relieved when I realized as the last guest left on Sunday night, that no one had been killed.

After the L.A. riots of 1992, I decided to produce a video to be shown on PBS focusing on the importance of being good. The collection of humorous skits, cast with many celebrities I personally knew from the movie business, was titled "For Goodness Sake." Unfortunately the PBS showing was canceled since one of the celebrities I recruited to advocate goodness was O.J. Simpson.

In early 1987, some friends and I, bored with playing "Horse" on my driveway, invented our own game, combining baseball and basketball which we called BASEketball. The sport rapidly gained the interest of dozens of other friends, spawning an entire league and a championship game that was covered by the *L.A. Times* and two local TV stations. It became the basis for the movie *BASEketball*, starring *South Park*'s Trey Parker and Matt Stone. I continued my streak of never having a flop, only cult classics.

Late one night in 1994, I happened to be channel surfing and came across an Orange County cable access show featuring a former KROQ DJ and a beautiful young UCLA medical student identified only as "Dr. Danielle." She was dispensing advice on love, sex, and health. Intrigued, I decided to drive down to Orange County to get some of that advice in person. After the show, I introduced myself and two years later, we were married. Our kids, Charles and Sarah, both graduated from (where else?) the University of Wisconsin.

I've been very lucky to have had a life and career filled with a good deal of love, laughter and good friends. All I ever wanted to do was to make people laugh, and I was fortunate enough to be able to do that with Jerry and Jim. We shared in common the same outlook on life, which was to never take anything seriously. And if one of us ever did, the other two would quickly rectify it. In the process, we made each other better than we would have been individually. The whole turned out to be greater than the sum of its parts. It was a grand adventure; the three of us shared a bond that remains to this day and will never be broken.

JIM

After *Airplane!*, I married Nancy, the woman whose fingers I had nervously smooshed together while sitting through an early *Airplane!* screening, and we started a family. Joseph, Jamie, and Charlie have brought incredible pride, light, and joy—and a few sleepless nights—into my life. Once David and Jerry and I decided to work independently, I directed *Big Business* (1988), co-wrote *The Naked Gun*, directed *Welcome Home, Roxy Carmichael* (1990), and co-wrote and directed *Hot Shots!* (1991) and *Hot Shots! Part Deux* (1993). By then I had spent the first forty-nine years of my life trying to find things to laugh about.

Then in March 1993, everything changed. My one-year-old son, Charlie, had his first seizure. There's absolutely nothing funny about being the parent of a child with uncontrolled epilepsy. Nothing. After a year of daily seizures, drugs, and a brain surgery, I learned that the *cure* for Charlie's epilepsy, the ketogenic diet—a high fat, no sugar, limited protein diet—had been hiding in plain sight for, by then, over seventy years. And despite the diet's being well documented in medical texts, none of the half-dozen pediatric neurologists we had taken Charlie to see had mentioned a word about it. I found out on my own at a medical library. It was life altering—not just for Charlie and my family, but for tens of thousands like us.

Turns out there are powerful forces at work within our health care system that don't necessarily prioritize good health. For decades, physicians have barely been taught diet therapy or even nutrition in medical school. The pharmaceutical, medical device, and sugar industries make hundreds of billions every year on anti-epileptic drugs and processed foods—but not a nickel if we change what we eat. The cardiology community and American Heart Association demonize fat based on flawed science. Hospitals profit from tests and procedures, but again no money from diet therapy.

There is a world epilepsy population of over sixty million people. Most of those people begin having their seizures as children, and only a minuscule percentage ever find out about ketogenic diet therapies. When I realized that 99 percent of what had happened to Charlie and my family was unnecessary, and that there were millions of families worldwide in the same situation, I needed to try to do something.

Nancy and I began the Charlie Foundation (charliefoundation.org) in 1994 in order to facilitate research and get the word directly to those who would benefit. Among the high points were countless articles, a couple appearances of Charlie's story on *Dateline NBC*, and a movie I produced and directed about another family whose child's epilepsy had been cured by the ketogenic diet starring Meryl Streep titled *First Do No Harm* (1997). Today, of course, the diet permeates social media. When we started, there was one hospital in the world offering ketogenic diet therapy. Today, there are 250.

Equally important, word about the efficacy of the ketogenic diet for epilepsy spread within the scientific community. In 1995, we hosted the first of many scientific global symposia focused on the diet. As research into its mechanisms and applications has spiked, incredibly the professional communities have found the same metabolic pathway that is triggered by the ketogenic diet to reduce seizures has also been found to benefit Alzheimer's disease, ALS, severe psychiatric disorders, traumatic brain injury, and even some cancers.

I did dip back into the movie business co-writing and directing *Jane Austen's: Mafia* (1998) and co-writing *Scary Movie 4* (2004). Although I tried my hardest, my heart was no longer in it. I was painting by numbers. I had another passion.

There is no way I would have embraced the concept or had the ability to take on this oversight made by American medicine were it not for the confidence and skills I learned with David and Jerry during our *Airplane!* adventure. It is one more reason I will always love them—and that silly movie.

JERRY

After *Ruthless People*, our executive on *The Naked Gun*, Lindsay Doran, gave me Bruce Joel Rubin's screenplay to *Ghost* (1990). My wife, Janet, read it one night while I was sleeping. She loved it, woke me up, and told me to read it immediately. As is our tradition, I did as I was instructed, and it became my first solo film as director.

I also directed *First Knight* (1995) and *Rat Race* (2001) and produced *My Best Friend's Wedding* (1997), *A Walk in the Clouds, My Life* (1993), and *Unconditional Love* (2002). Janet and I produced *Fair Game* (2010), *Friends with Benefits* (2011), *Mental* (2012), *Dear Dumb Diary* (2013), and *1000 Miles to Freedom* (forthcoming). Amazingly, after thirty-six years we're still married, and we have two perfect children, Katie and Bob. Currently I'm working on *Intermission!*, a satirical musical comedy for the stage. We hope to mount the show in London this year . . . or maybe some other year.

In 1999, Janet and I began a very different journey. At age eleven, our daughter Katie was diagnosed with type 1 diabetes. Suddenly, the Zucker family started to appreciate the possibilities of science, and in particular, stem cell research, which at the time was under attack in Washington. It's unlikely that a real cell biologist would be able to secure a meeting with a US senator, but senators were more than happy to meet with one of the guys who'd made *Airplane!* So we went to Washington with Caltech scientist David Anderson and producers Doug Wick and Lucy Fisher, and pleaded our case. Along with Michael J. Fox, Christopher Reeve, and many others, we helped defeat a draconian bill that would have put scientists in jail for doing lifesaving research.

Seeing firsthand how our government works was both a heady experience and a frightening one. But becoming immersed in the wonders of science—despite our not understanding a lot of it—opened up a whole new world and passion for us. A few years later, we started the California stem cell initiative (Proposition 71), which passed in 2004 and raised $3 billion for stem cell research in California.

In 2008 we were approached by Ralph Cicerone, then president of the National Academy of Sciences. He was looking for a way to use the power of film and television to communicate the importance of science, both in people's lives and for the survival of the planet. Together we launched the Science and Entertainment Exchange, a way for filmmakers to engage in creative brainstorming sessions with the great minds of science. Over the years we've held hundreds of events and arranged over a thousand consults. It's been a great ride!

On June 6, 2022, David, Jim, and I celebrated the fiftieth anniversary of the day we arrived in L.A. Like this book and Green Bay Packer games, it was just another excuse for the three of us to be together. In a way, nothing has changed. We still love to make each other laugh, we still celebrate our good fortunes, and we still keep each other's egos in check. We're *all* brothers—a tight-knit family of three. We share a whole world of things that make sense only to us. I have no idea whether it was all meant to be or just random luck. It doesn't really matter. It was great to be part of it.

ACKNOWLEDGMENTS

We'd been wanting to tell this story for at least a decade, but it wasn't until we saw Will Harris's oral history of *Airplane!* in the Onion that we finally knew how to do it and who could best do the exhaustive interviews required which have formed the core of this book. Thank you to everyone who agreed to be interviewed and generously share their stories with us.

We are deeply grateful to our friend and collaborator Ellie Shoja, who has worked tirelessly and passionately since the inception of this idea. Her writing and editing skills have been indispensable in creating the style and concept of this book. More importantly, Ellie made writing a joyful experience for all of us.

Thank you to our manager, Randi Siegel, whose wise notes and guidance have been invaluable throughout the publishing process; to our agents at APA and Park & Fine, David Saunders, Steve Fisher, Kathryn Toolan, and Sarah Passick; and to our St. Martin's Press editor Marc Resnick. You have all been extraordinarily helpful in shepherding three novice writers through the process of getting an actual book published. We're grateful to Ellen Scordato, Stan Madaloni, and their talented team of designers for their inspired layouts; and to Berkeley Carter, Charles Zucker, Nicole Lemon, Tom Sylke, James Dudelson, Larry McCallister, Eric Lane, Alexandra Giffen, and the archive team at Paramount Pictures, who worked tirelessly in helping us find and license hundreds of images.

There were also countless friends and family members who read early drafts and provided much needed encouragement and helpful notes. Thank you Susan and Bill Breslau, Michael Gelbart, Rich Markey, Mahnaz Shahrestani, Mike Shah, Nancy Lahman, David Newman, Keith Merryman, Mike Robinson, Robbie Cocuzzo, Jane Butenhoff, Fred Siegel and Alice Gruenberg. Thank you also to Robert Zubatsky and Chris Dellorco for your much-needed photographic skills.

Finally, but perhaps most importantly, we'd like to thank our families—Janet, Katie, Bob, Nancy, Charlie, Jamie, Joseph, Danielle, Charles, and Sarah for their boundless love and support. And, of course, our parents, for loving us enough to have raised us in Milwaukee.

PHOTO CREDITS

MCCROSKEY
I can't take much more of this!
Johnny, how about some more coffee?

HINSHAW
Would you like half of my provolone
and roast beef?

MCCROSKEY
Looks like I picked the wrong week
to quit amphetamines.

couple pills. Fifteen REPORTERS, Cameramen,
r with Air Controller #1.

AIR CONTROLLER #!
(to McCroskey)

Steve, these reporters won't leave without
a statement.

REPORTER #1
How much longer can the sick passengers
hold out?

McCROSKEY
Half hour... maybe forty-five
minutes.

REPORTE
Who's flying the plan

oller #2 enters and ha
ling microphones are tl
McCroskey. One hand

NIGHT

KRAMER
a be a real sweat.
to mike)
et me know when y
g.

McCROSKEY
ke much more of
about some mor

HINSHAW
like half of r
beef?

McCROS
ke I picked t
amphetamines

pills. Fift
Air Controll

AIR CO
McCroskey

---

the radio
keep an ey
engine.

198A INSERT - NUMBER-THRE

A LITTLE HOT is blin

198B BACK TO INT. COCKPIT

Striker, wh
you in up t

(i
Rain.

And a little

And a little

How's it hand

Sluggish. Li

---

141   CONTINUED:

MCCROSKEY (V.O.)
Elaine! Roger, Roger! I read you. This
is Steve McCroskey at Chicago Air Control.

ELAINE
Hi, Steve!

Now listen carefully. McCROSKEY (V.O.)
Is the automatic pilot on? Over.

ELAINE
Yes. Yes, it is. Over.

OVEUR (O.S.)
Huh?

McCROSKEY (V.O.)
Very good. Now, Elaine, where
are you? Over.

ELAINE
I'm standing over Oveur. Over.

142   OMITTED

143   INT. CHICAGO DISPATCH - NITE